The Maki

For Judy,

In witchy sisterhood —

Any aunt of Liz's
is a friend of mine!

Happy Halloween,
Robin
Dec 2010

The Making of Salem

The Witch Trials in History, Fiction and Tourism

ROBIN DEROSA

McFarland & Company, Inc., Publishers

Jefferson, North Carolina, and London

LIBRARY OF CONGRESS CATALOGUING-IN-PUBLICATION DATA

DeRosa, Robin.
   The making of Salem : the witch trials in history, fiction and
tourism / Robin DeRosa.
     p.   cm.
   Includes bibliographical references and index.

   ISBN 978-0-7864-3983-6
   softcover : 50# alkaline paper

   1. Witchcraft — Massachusetts — Salem. 2. Trials
(Witchcraft) — Massachusetts — Salem. 3. Witchcraft —
Massachusetts — Salem — Historiography. 4. Trials
(Witchcraft) — Massachusetts — Salem — Historiography.
5. Salem (Mass.) — In popular culture. 6. Popular culture —
United States. I. Title.
BF1575.D47   2009
133.4' 3097445 — dc22   2009020591

British Library cataloguing data are available

Cover photograph: *center* Daniel Day-Lewis as John Proctor in
The Crucible, 1996 (20th Century-Fox/Photofest)

Manufactured in the United States of America

McFarland & Company, Inc., Publishers
  Box 611, Jefferson, North Carolina 28640
   www.mcfarlandpub.com

Table of Contents

Preface   1

Introduction   5

One: "You Seem to Act Witchcraft"
Theatricality and the Trial Transcripts   29

Two: From Shards to Meanings
Historians Make Sense of the Trials   62

Three: Fiction and the Real
Novelists Rewrite Salem   97

Four: A Dramatic Tale
Salem on Stage and Screen   126

Five: Selling the Story
From Salem Village to Witch City   152

Notes   187

Bibliography   199

Index   207

For Philip,
and for Ruby Adeline.

This was the secret law of his life —
he loved and was beloved.
— Mary Shelley's *The Last Man*

Preface

In 2004, a marketing expert hired by the city of Salem, Massachusetts, came up with a new slogan for the city: "Think you know Salem? Think again." The slogan references the fact that people today really need no introduction to Salem: it is known nationally — and even internationally — as the site of the famous seventeenth-century witch hysteria and the current epicenter for all things witch-related. Indeed, in recent years, it's hard to toss a brochure in Salem without hitting some kind of a witch; some of Salem's witches are animatronic and spooky, others are more sober mannequins accompanied by didactic panels; still others are real folks, practicing witches drawn to Salem because of the visibility of the Wiccan community there. But the witch Mecca that is today's Salem, Massachusetts, comes with a tangled relationship to the history that ultimately prescribed its destiny. City planners try to deemphasize witches to attract a new market of residents who overflow from nearby Boston; they focus on Salem's restaurants and new loft condos. Local tourist sites thrive on the millions of visitors who come to Salem every year to learn about the witch trials, but these sites conflict with each other, as "educational" venues discredit haunted houses, which, in turn, make a profit by parodying the educational sites. Historians work to correct the myths that get reified by the tourist sites, and yet these same historians don't agree with each other about what "really happened." The small city of Salem becomes a microcosm, fruitful to study in order to think about a series of questions: How do we remember — and construct — our American past? What are we really studying when we examine primary sources and original events? What are the differences — and similarities — between story-telling and history? What is the relationship between commerce and commemoration?

I first became involved in studying Salem not because of an inherent interest in the witch trials, but because of my interest in living history museums. I was struck after visiting several of these sites (among them Colonial Williamsburg in Virginia and Plimoth Plantation in Massachusetts) that what was most interesting about them was *not* how they convincingly recreated the past in meticulous detail, but how the tourists who visited the sites interacted with this recreated past. I was fascinated by the ironic celebration of authenticity that took place in these carefully constructed venues, and by the intersection of several competing aspects of the sites: the immersive performances of the actors (or "interpreters") who staffed the sites; the gift shops where the "authentic" past was mass-marketed for take-home consumption; the fetishization of the "primary sources" and "true stories" upon which the sites were developed.

As I became interested in these issues, there was a simultaneous explosion of scholarly and popular texts related to the Salem witch trials, from blockbuster films to bestselling fiction to critically acclaimed historical studies. Salem offered itself as a compelling microcosm for thinking about the historiographical and touristic issues I was curious about precisely because so many people — from scholars to sightseers — were truly entranced by the Salem narrative. This study sets itself apart from the majority of Salem scholarship because it has virtually no investment in answering Salem's most ubiquitous questions: What happened in 1692 and why? Instead, this book looks at the many representations of the witch trials narrative that have emerged through primary texts, histories, fictions, dramas, and tourist sites, and turns its attention to an analysis of how we tell the Salem story.

For their support of this project, I am indebted to many people and institutions. First, to Jesper Rosenmeier at Tufts University for his direction of the dissertation that ultimately became this book, and second, to Jim Egan of Brown University, for his feedback on the original dissertation and his mentorship over the years. In 2000, I delivered a very early version of this project as a conference paper at the Colonial Society of Massachusetts, and I am indebted to the historians there, including keynote speaker John Demos, for their provocative questions which helped guide my research. A fruitful panel that I chaired at the Northeast Modern Language Association introduced me to several colleagues, including Bridget M. Marshall, who were doing compelling and lively work on Salem. My students at Tufts and at Plymouth State University have asked wonderful questions and accompanied me on countless research trips to Salem, and I am grateful for their ideas and their company. A generous grant from Plymouth State gave me the time off from teaching that I needed to do the final revisions on the project. Finally, I am thankful to the employees of the Salem sites, from the Phillips Library to the Witch Village; I am grateful for the patient time that these staffers generously took with me despite the lines of tourists and researchers who bombard the city every day. Over the years that I have been visiting, I have come to adore Salem. I enjoy taking a quiet walk there on a winter evening, imagining that my footsteps trace the paths cut by Rebecca Nurse and Judge Hathorne so many years ago. But I also enjoy lining up with a crowd in October during Haunted Happenings, waiting hours to enter a haunted house or a shop that sells spells and potions, enjoying the way that Salem, with such dramatic flourish, brings history alive.

Introduction

Producing Origins, Performing History

> *"The simulacrum is never what hides the truth. It is truth that hides the fact that there is none. The simulacrum is true."*
> — Jean Baudrillard, *Simulacra and Simulation*

This book, like countless primary school history lessons, actually takes its point of "origin" not from Salem, but from Plimoth Plantation, which was an original Pilgrim settlement from the early seventeenth century, and is today a reproduced tourist site at a mostly arbitrary geographic location.[1] Today's Plimoth Plantation, sixty miles from Salem, recreates the year 1627, sixty-five years before the events of the witch trials occurred. A living history museum, Plimoth Plantation has much in common with many of the live-action historical sites in Salem. The first seed of inspiration for this project was generated by *Performing the Pilgrims*, Stephen Snow's critical study of ethnohistorical role-playing at Plimoth Plantation. In the mid–1980s, Snow was an "interpreter" at Plimoth Plantation; interpreters play the roles of "actual" Pilgrims, studying historical tracts, diaries, and other primary source documents to create their characters. The interpreters are often very earnest (and perhaps there is a bit of Wilde in that adjective) in their preparations, and Snow reflects a common frustration as he discusses the lack of respect he encounters in certain tourist groups: "I remember one Sunday morning when two transvestites, who were obviously either drunk or on drugs, made their way down the main street of the Pilgrim Village. The incongruity of their presence was both funny and sad. What could the experience of the 1627 village possibly mean to them, as they giggled and wriggled their way from house to house?" (164–65). Though Snow clearly means this question to be a rhetorical one (with an implied, definitive answer of "nothing, of course"), the seemingly tenuous relationship between transvestism and living history can be mined to reveal some profound ways in which they are similar.[2] Consider, for example, the way that the transgendered subject performs gender. Masculinity and femininity are generally linked to anatomy, as our culture constructs the link between behavior and biology as natural, inherent, and unchanging. Transgender, however, not only inverts the sex-gender connection, but it also denaturalizes the very connection itself. Judith Butler addresses this phenomenon in *Gender Trouble*. She argues that cross-dressing reveals the very constructed nature of *all* gender identities; when a man dresses as a woman, he not only changes his gender, but he reveals all femininity to be a kind of performance, able to be enacted by any subject regardless of sex (33). What, then, might the similarities be between a transvestite and a Pilgrim interpreter?

Just as the transvestite reveals the precisely artificial character of gender, the Pilgrim interpreter reveals the artificial character of history. This is *not* to imply that history is not *real*. No one would suggest that gender, though culturally constructed and performable, is not real, and it is the same for history. History, like gender, is generally supposed in our culture to be natural, stable, and factual. One is either a man or a woman. A historical event either happened or it didn't. The past is understood to be lurking somewhere in the shadows, and the historian's task is generally thought to be to bring it into the light. The question is, then, are the transvestites "actually" men underneath their feminine attire, or does their very performance unsettle the customary ways we understand gender itself? For some visitors to Plimoth Plantation, those who, like the transvestites, seem to Snow to be missing the point of the site, the Plimoth Plantation experience is less about finding out the truth of what happened back then than it is about baiting Pilgrims and trying to make them break character, looking for signs of modern life behind the locked doors within the Village's parameters, and purchasing kitschy items at the gift shop. The Plantation (perhaps unintentionally) encourages its visitors to notice its nether regions, encourages them to be attracted to the perverse mix of authenticity and commercialism, and encourages them to experience the site as a liminal point that exists somewhere between — or outside of—1627 and today. Even Snow himself seems to come close to seeing the parallels between his own position as interpreter and the transvestites' position in both society at large and the society of the tourist site: "In truth, [the transvestites] were putting themselves on display as much as they were touring the re-created Plimoth" (165). The "in truth" is an ironic marker of Snow's desire to cut to the core, but instead he seems dismayed to remain in a world of display, of re-creation, and of performance. It is precisely the impossibility of cutting through the performance to some internal truth that functions in both drag and in history.

Before exploring in depth the repercussions of defining history as performance and thinking about how Salem's histories reflect this definition, I would like to spend a moment or two on the anxieties that have surfaced as this definition has gained credibility in the academy. The anxiety has generally been directed at post-structuralism, which has been accused by Terry Eagleton, for example, as being responsible for the "liquidation of history" (96). Perry Anderson has similarly admonished post-structuralism for "randomizing" history (48). The fear here seems to stem from the idea that if history is connected to its methodologies and narrative structures rather than its content than that content is somehow annihilated or trivialized. Anderson in particular laments the effect that any kind of post-structuralist reading might have on chronological, historical narratives. What happens to the story of the Pilgrim settlement at Plimoth if we treat Bradford's *Of Plimoth Plantation* not as a record of events, but as a text to be interpreted? Do we suddenly lose any ability to tell the story of what happened (or to *teach* the story of what happened) if we think of the account not as "true," but as "significant"? Barbara Johnson explains this post-structuralist maneuver as a shift from asking *what* a text signifies to asking *how* it signifies, a shift from focusing on persons to focusing on personas (36). As a result of this shift away from identity and toward structures that produce identity, critics such as Eagleton and Anderson worry that we drain history of its ontology, its power, and its political value.

But post-structuralists are often as concerned as New Historicists (and Marxists, for that matter) with questions about the political effects of historical texts. In "The Discourse of History," Roland Barthes argues that history tricks us by projecting the referent into a realm supposedly outside of the chain of signification. From this exterior position, it appears to precede and determine the discourse which posits it as a referent: "The fact can only have a linguistic existence as a term in a discourse, and yet it is exactly as if this existence were merely the 'copy,' purely and simply, of another existence situated in the extra-structural domain of the 'real'" (17). What Barthes suggests is not that history is not real, but that it produces the very idea of the "real" even as it occupies a position within that term. In this sense, facts are not ontologically located before or outside of their representations; instead, the representations produce the categories of "before" and "outside" themselves. "The structure of the category of History," writes Mark Cousins, "is a little theater in which the representations of the past are assigned their part" (129). By suspending their disbelief, Eagleton and Anderson watch history's play as if it were happening spontaneously in front of them; both critics are chagrined when the mise-en-scène is exposed, wondering if the play will continue to matter once it is revealed to be art. Barthes might suggest, as do I, that instead of *representing* the thing (the historical event), the play *is* the thing. By collapsing the distinction between an original, past historical moment and the subsequent historical retellings of that moment, the theory of performing history can make concrete, real, and political the discourse of the past, while simultaneously it can explore how socio-political reality itself takes its shape from that very same discourse.

While theorists such as Lyotard define post-structuralism as an incredulity toward meta-narratives (21), the simple idea that history is not just a collection of facts is widespread, and New Historicism, which is often positioned against post-structuralism, has long been concerned with the problems inherent in any "objective" master narrative. In fact, what Alan Munslow calls the "deconstructive consciousness," the "understanding that the genuine nature of history can be understood only when it is viewed not solely and simply as an objectivised empiricist enterprise, but as the creation and ultimate imposition by historians of a particular narrative form on the past" (2), is often used by multiculturalists to advocate for inclusion of non–Western historical accounts in European and American history courses and textbooks. Munslow's own diction reflects the tension between a desire to be skeptical about metadiscursivity and a desire to replace one master narrative with another. His use of "genuine nature" implies that history itself has a core, a correct reading, which is either understood or misunderstood. Similarly, his use of "creation" and "imposition" suggest that historians develop their narratives out of thin air, and that they colonize history's pure core with their invasive readings. The goal here is not to dismiss Munslow, whose *Deconstructing History* is in many ways an excellent introduction to the complexity of post-structuralism's relationship to the past, but to note that the interesting slippage between wanting to resist a taxonomy of ontology and wanting to establish a new, solid (if polyvocal) historical methodology is a common slippage amongst politically concerned deconstructionists. If, as Hayden White famously argues, "History is as much invented as found," then we must begin to think about what we, as deconstructionists, mean by the term "invented" ("*The Historical Text*," 82). To avoid getting caught in the trap which can pitch historians and other scholars from revisionism to esoterics and back again, we must consider how it is that the category of "fact" is created, how, precisely, historical invention develops, and *how*, as Barbara Johnson would ask, history itself signifies.

As Richard Schechner writes in "Restoration of Behavior," "History is not what happened (that's its press) but what is encoded and performed" (5). Schechner argues that once any historical event is "scored and notated," even "exact replication" of the event is different from the event itself (5). Schechner's parenthetical allusion to history's press seems to me the most important of his observations. What is unique about history is not so much its distance from its own original (which is perhaps a condition of its linguistic character), but its insistence on the denial of this distance in its self-definition. This denial is part and parcel of history's own narrativizing force. Hayden White poses the relationship between history's self-colonizing narrative force and its denial of its own reliance on distance from the events that it describes as a set of questions: "What is involved ... in that finding of the 'true story,' that discovery of the 'real story' within or behind the events that come to us in the chaotic form of 'historical records'? What wish is enacted, what desire is gratified, by the fantasy that *real* events are properly represented when they can be shown to display the formal coherence of a story?" ("*The Value of Narrativity*," 23). History emerges here as a complex and invisible system that simultaneously collapses itself into its topics as it also places its topics into its own exterior organizing structure.[3] History, then, is both an object (that which *is* that which *happened)* and a subject (that which *creates* the frame to *hold* what happened).

In "Restoration of Behavior," Schechner relates a useful anecdote about Mickey Rooney. One night during a vaudevillian performance, Rooney was mistakenly de-wigged on stage. The audience roared with laughter, and at every subsequent performance, Rooney "mistakenly" lost his wig (36). History is constantly de-wigging itself, pretending to expose its own mechanisms and methodologies, while in actuality it is simply performing its part with deft dramatic skill. Revisionist history is a prime example of this Rooney-esque dexterity. Two of James Loewen's recent titles provide interesting fodder for discussion. *Lies My Teacher Told Me* and *Lies Across America* focus on historical inaccuracies in school textbooks and American monuments, respectively. His "corrective" brand of history is paradoxically aware of its own subjective position *and* critical of exclusionary or untrue historical narratives. For example, he criticizes the fact fanatics who pen many history textbooks: "[These authors] seem bent on presenting 'facts' for children to 'learn.' Such an approach keeps students ignorant of the reasoning, arguments, and weighing of evidence that go into social science" (*Lies My Teacher Told Me,* 76). Just a few pages earlier, though, he criticizes these same textbooks for getting the facts wrong. He writes, "Starting the story of America's settlement with the Pilgrims leaves out not only the Indians but also the Spanish. The very first non–Native settlers in 'the country we now know as the United States' were African slaves left in South Carolina in 1526 by Spaniards who abandoned a settlement attempt" (*Lies My Teacher Told Me,* 67). How does one make sense of these two competing impulses: on the one hand, to update and revise historical narratives based on new information, and, on the other hand, to remain critical and skeptical of a full investment in any one master narrative? Though Loewen is aware of the problematics of any fetishization of the facts, he, like Mickey Rooney, bills himself as de-wigged, as the "real" McCoy behind the historiographical bias.[4]

Is there a way to do history at all if the reliance on "fact" is completely dismissed? It's not hard to understand, with questions as revolutionary as this, why critics such as Eagleton and Anderson fear a post-structural approach to history. What would a fact-less history would look like? Certainly, Loewen demonstrates that the slippage into factualization is difficult to avoid even for historians who are skeptical about relying on the concept of a master narrative. These issues came to a head for me at a 2000 conference in Boston sponsored by the Colonial Society of Massachusetts. As a young graduate student, I was invited to present the outline of an early version of this project to this esteemed group of experienced historians. Many of the Society's members are Salem experts (indeed, the keynote speaker, whose talk immediately followed mine, was John Demos, the renowned Yale historian who wrote a critically acclaimed psychological history of the trials, *Entertaining Satan*). It was the first history conference that I, a graduate student in an English Ph.D. program, had attended, and I was stunned at the hostility which I encountered as I suggested — however timidly — that Salem's past is as much created by our current historical moment as it was by any actual seventeenth-century events. There were two kinds of scholars at the conference: those who disagreed with me that it was impossible to recreate perfectly the events of the past, and those who disagreed with me that it was politically *responsible* to *avoid* revisionist narratives which refigured, for example, the positions of Salem's slave and Indian populations[5]. In other words, to put it crudely, conservative old-school historians were convinced that there were a series of facts about Salem that were indisputable; these scholars were disputed with by revisionists who believed that they had some of their facts "wrong." I attempted to suggest that the most interesting thing about this debate was the relative agreement on both sides that something actually happened in Salem, and that if we all just argued long enough, someone could win the day.

The question of Tituba is a useful example for thinking through the different approaches taken by conservative historians, revisionist historians, and deconstructionists. In most early — and in many current — histories of the trials, Tituba, like Patient Zero, has been blamed for planting the seeds of the witch hunt in the minds of Abigail Williams and Betty Parris. Revisionist historians, who currently hold the most academic credibility in this matter, are more convinced by recent accounts which examine how both black and white magic were often used before the outbreak by Salem's white, Christian residents (the baking of the witch cake, suggested by a church member, is a fine example of this). But the question

11

of whether or not Tituba is "to blame" for the witch hunt is not a question about Tituba, as much as it is a question about *what people have said about Tituba*. In particular, what *historians* have written about her. Far from being a semantic triviality, this question of shifting emphasis from original, historical subject to historical account cuts to the very core of how we think about the field of history itself. In her discussion of King Philip's War, Jill Lepore explains the relationship of "wounds" to "words": "The injuries and their interpretation cannot be separated" (x). Lepore's brilliant study of this particular conflict presents the "facts" of King Philip's War as a series of representations, and her painstakingly well-researched book looks like many traditional studies, except that it consistently attends to the subjectivity of the sources that it interprets, and never once attempts to tell the "true" story underneath those sources. So where does all of this leave a study of 1690s Salem? If Salem's past is created, rather than revealed, through all representations of that past, then any history of Salem is, "in fact," a study of the representation of Salem. Of course, "representation" is defined broadly here. It could include, among a multitude of possibilities, court documents, archeological artifacts, recent historical studies, and current tourist productions. Now, much of this is nothing new, even to the most traditional Colonial Society scholar. Historians have always relied on archeology, on primary documents, on scholarship by their predecessors and contemporaries. What *is* new is the suggestion that no historical mode has a more direct connection to The Past than another, and that familiar scholarly modes of inquiry do not conflict with less "academic" sources of historical information.

How can the Salem Witch Museum, a stunningly kitschy recreation of the witch hunt that uses life-size department-store mannequins to reenact, in tableaux, the events of 1692, possibly offer a serious-minded scholar information about what "really happened" back in the seventeenth century? If we think of history not as an actual event, but as a complex of self-representations and self-mystifications, then tourist productions become prime examples of "history." Tourist productions are often representations of lost pasts at the same time as they attempt to mask any distance that separates themselves from those pasts. Tourism, like history, relies both on a distance from an "original" and on a self-denying mechanism which hides that distance. Consider Main Street U.S.A., Disney

World's famous center avenue that recreates the facades of small town, turn-of-the-century shops. Main Street U.S.A. is worth visiting precisely because it is a *reproduction* of such a small town and because it is a *memory* of a time past.[6] At the same time, it functions as "authentic" thanks to details like "actual reproduction" soda fountains and trolley cars. For a tourist site to be successful, it must embrace the deferral that sets it up as more interesting than its original subject, and it must embrace the immediacy that makes it seem as if it *is* its original subject.[7]

Other similarities between the structures of history and of tourism exist, as well. History is, as I discussed above, an interaction between a scholar, an original (lost) event, and a representation of that event. Tourism has a parallel structure, which is most notably delineated by Dean MacCannell.[8] He describes how all tourist productions consist of a relationship between a tourist, a site, and a marker (41). The sites, like the lost past, are virtually irrelevant to many tourist productions. The fields of Gettysburg, for example, are totally indistinguishable from any other Pennsylvania pasturelands. Would these fields be notable without the accompanying plaques? Considering that nobody visits Danvers, Massachusetts, which, as will be discussed in Chapter Five, is the main site of the original "Salem" witch hunt, and that *Salem's* gift shops and museums are overrun with millions of tourists a year, it seems evident that markers, and not sites, are what matter. The markers act much the same way that historical records act, guiding us, as tourist-historians, toward an experience that we consider "authentic." Thus, authenticity is produced, both in history and in tourism, by a referent. The irony here, or course, is that authenticity is supposedly that which is without referent. The difference between an authentic colonial artifact and an inauthentic colonial artifact is generally understood to be a question of reference: the first refers to nothing but itself, while the second refers to an original that precedes itself. "Authenticity," however, is not elemental; it is instead a part of the same touristic and historical system that produces the illusion of primacy through a complicated reference to the past. And, like history and tourism, "authenticity" is connected to narrativity, as well. Richard Handler and William Saxton assert that "historians share with other moderns the notion that an authentic life is a storied or emplotted life" (250). The relationship between reference, the illusion of primacy, and narrativity produce tourism's ability to offer up the authentic history of a culture.[9]

Referentiality (a script), illusional primacy (the suspension of disbelief), and a story (a plot or tale): all the ingredients of traditional theater. In *The Location of Culture,* Homi Bhabha discusses the theatricality of history: "The sign of history does not consist in an essence of the event itself, nor exclusively in the immediate consciousness of its agents and actors, but in its form as a spectacle, spectacle that signifies because of the distanciation and displacement between the event and those who are its spectators" (243). A historical text is obviously not a perfect replication of the event that it describes. In fact, Bhabha suggests, the closer the replication of the representation to the original, the more distinctions between the two there must obviously be: "In order to be effective, mimicry must produce its slippage, its excess, its difference" (86). In other words, if a living history performance, "primary" historical account, or scholarly historical analysis is to be considered "authentic," "true," or "real," it must in some way call attention to its own distance from its subject matter. In *Difference and Repetition,* Deleuze theorizes that the modern world is a world of simulacra. "Physical or bare representations," he writes, "find their *raison d'être* in the more profound structures of a hidden repetition in which a differential is disguised and displaced" (xx). In the case of historical tourism, this differential includes space, time, and the baggage of the discipline of history. "A scar," explains Deleuze, "is the sign not of a past wound, but of the present fact of having been wounded" (77). These present facts are precisely what are obscured by the discipline of history, but they are also precisely what gives this discipline its own perspective and parameters.

Christopher Steiner explains this phenomenon in his article, "Authenticity, Repetition, and the Aesthetics of Seriality." Steiner argues that concepts of the authentic are produced tautologically: "Tourist art effectively produce[s] its own canon of authenticity — a self-referential discourse of cultural reality that generates an internal measure of truth value.... The copy becomes associated with the true and the original with the false" (95). Steiner is particularly concerned here with the way that African maskmakers display and sell their wares to tourists, setting out hundreds of identical masks along roadsides and in shops. Steiner suggests that this is not, as others have criticized, an indication of entrepreneurial naiveté, but is instead a savvy business maneuver. As the masks repeat each other, they produce "authenticity" in much the same way that a repeated historical story gains authenticity by being retold over a number of years. The mass-marketed masks then become the authentic masks, while individual masks made for ceremonial purposes become less desirable, less recognizable, and "inauthentic" to tourist eyes.

The tourist site (in addition to the souvenir) adds another dimension to this process of authentification. In the nineteenth century, many art museums, particularly in Europe, displayed *copies* of masterpieces rather than the masterpieces themselves. The copies were often considered more valuable because they embodied an educational purpose that the originals lacked (Kirshenblatt-Gimblett 195). A copy of a Michelangelo sculpture, for example, not only offered all of the artistry of the original, it also offered a framework for thinking about the original, its qualities, and its production. Today's Plimoth Plantation functions in a similar way. Despite its rhetoric, the assumption of its basic philosophy is not that visitors will experience what it was to live in 1627, but that they will experience what it is like to be alive today while *acting as if* they lived back then. This sounds obvious and trivial, but the educational component is impossible without this distinction. School children who visit the Plantation are not supposed to assimilate into the Pilgrim culture completely; instead, they are expected to draw parallels between themselves and the Pilgrims, ask questions of the interpreters based on their own modern subject positions, and correct historical "myths" that have been taught to them throughout their educations (such as that Pilgrims wore buckled shoes and high black hats). "Authenticity," then, becomes not a pure state of past-ness, but a relationship between the past and the present that accompanies an educational component.

Dean MacCannell suggests that this is a kind of bogus authenticity, a ruse that tourists fail to penetrate; these duped tourists are in effect the quintessential fools, spoon-fed a facade while they think they are getting the whole, three-dimensional story. Erik Cohen disagrees with this characterization of the tourist. Cohen argues that tourists are aware at all times that history is "reconstructed" by these sites, but that the tourist definition of "authenticity" includes a performative aspect. In fact, Cohen asserts that things become authentic *over time,* which indicates that it is the repetition and rehearsal that create the authenticity of an object, event, or site. (379). Handler and Saxton similarly dismiss the traditional definition of authenticity, which they characterize as an isomorphism between a living history activity or event and that piece of the past it is meant to recreate (i.e., a perfect simulation). They suggest an alternative way to think about authenticity: "[It is] the privileged reality of individual experience; individuals feel themselves to be in touch both with a 'real' world and with their 'real' selves" (242). Handler and Saxton argue that everyday modern life has an "unreal" quality, and that the narrative, emplotted versions of history served up by tourist sites offer the alienated modern (and, I would add, the alienated post-modern) visitor a means to experience themselves in an integrated, cohesive narrative context. Authenticity, then, is not just about seeing what "really happened back then," but about experiencing one's own identity as authentic, meaningful, and coherent.[10] Dean MacCannell offers a useful example of the relationship of one's own identity position to the question of authenticity. A woman in California lived at the foot of a locally famous mountain for years without knowing that "her" mountain was "that" mountain. From this, MacCannell deduces that "an authentic touristic experience involves not merely connecting a marker to a site, but a participation in a collective ritual, in connecting one's own marker to a sight already marked by others" (137).

MacCannell also writes that "now it is often important to 'act out' reality and truth" (92). He gives as one example the fact that most supermarket ham is injected with chemicals to give it the pink color. Natural ham is grayish-white, but Americans think that the pink coloring makes ham more "ham-like." In this sense, authenticity is a performance constructed to make real that which in its natural state has an unreal or insignificant quality (the gray ham may be natural, but it does not easily qualify as "ham," nor does it easily signify "ham" to the supermarket consumer). Tourists, like supermarket patrons, are on a quest for the packaged version of reality, and good taste gets bizarrely attached to the ironically "authentic" yet performed object. MacCannell defines "taste" as "the knowledge needed to connect a souvenir to a referent" (150). Two actual souvenirs available in current-day Salem elucidate MacCannell's theory. In a single gift shop, a visitor can purchase both a bag of "Authentic Dirt From Gallows Hill," complete with a label that carries a graphic of a gnarled tree draped with a noose, and a sepia-toned framed photograph of the House of the Seven Gables. Most people would agree that the Gallows Hill Dirt does not reflect as good a taste as the photograph. But why? The dirt is accessible to virtually anyone, even those with no knowledge of the historical facts of the witch hunt. Anyone can see that the dirt comes from a hill where people were hanged, and that makes the dirt creepy and interesting.[11] But in order to value the photograph, consumers must be aware of the novel, *The House of the Seven Gables*, and know enough about it to connect it to Salem's witch history. To purchase the photograph at a Salem gift shop would indicate a certain literary savvy, and perhaps some historical knowledge about the relationship of Nathaniel Hawthorne to his great-great grandfather, Judge Hathorne, the hanging judge of Salem. The line between good taste and bad taste, then, is clearly delineated and defined by the knowledge of the consumer.

But how stable is this line? Are there any ways in which the dirt and the photograph function in the same way? Though I will not argue that the good taste/bad taste opposition is a false dichotomy, the system that produces the idea of "taste" does ultimately collapse many of the distinctions between what is classy and what is tacky. In fact, the photograph would be absolutely un-valuable if it weren't for the little packet of dirt. The tacky souvenirs generate the belief that "somewhere, only not here and now, perhaps just over there, there is a *genuine* society" (MacCannell 155). The only way the dirt can be recognized as a bad-taste item — as it is indeed recognized (perhaps most of all) by those who actually purchase it — is if it can be compared to a good-taste item. Similarly, the only way a souvenir can be coded as authentic or classy is if it is compared to something that is not. As Meyer Shapiro jokes, "Kitsch is chic spelled backwards" (Brown 9). This comment is wonderful not just for its catty humor, but for the perceptive way that it sets up the classy/trashy distinction as a simple opposition; the oppositional quality of the dichotomy demonstrates that one term can only exist meaningfully when it is set against its foil.

Deborah Root points out an even deeper problematic in the classy/trashy dichotomy. She writes, "Authenticity depends on a notion of the inauthentic, but this line is impossible to draw without using universalized — ie. market-driven — notions of what traditional looks like" (79).

This is reminiscent of the African masks that Steiner discussed. If authenticity is produced by mass consumer culture, then an interesting paradox emerges, since mass consumer culture, as MacCannell argued, is also the Everyman who understands the dirt and mostly fails to desire the photograph. While "knowledge" (and lack thereof) is what sets the photograph above the dirt on the classy/trashy hierarchy, it is also what popularizes the dirt, ultimately making the dirt the recognized — therefore authentic — souvenir of Salem. This paradox became abundantly clear in a course I taught at Tufts University called "Performing History: Witches, Pilgrims, and Pop Culture." The course considered many of the theoretical issues that this chapter has thus far discussed, and by the time the students took a field trip to Salem at the end of the semester, they were highly educated in both the history of the witch trials and the issues involved with historical tourism. It seemed they would be perfect candidates for "good taste" souvenirs (we had even read *The House of the Seven Gables*), and yet at the end of the day, as they showed me their loot, it was clear that there were no restrained sepia photographs in the collection. Most of them had packets of Gallows Hill dirt, and among their other treasures were Clairvoyant Witch Powder, Tarot Cards, Snow Globes, and ticket stubs from the Haunted Footsteps Ghost Tour and Boris Karloff's Witch Mansion. What was going on here? The students' knowledge of both Salem's historical past and Salem's tourist present had produced in them a desire to take home a piece of the real Salem, which to them was not about Danvers, Salem Town, or Cotton Mather, but about palm reading, wax museums, and crystals. It was the consumer market and not the primary historical texts they had studied which produced for my students a notion of what was "authentic" in Salem. Barbara Kirshenblatt-Gimblett notes that "good taste objects are just what they ought to be [while] bad taste objects are so unreal as to be immediately recognized as made" (272). What she fails to note, however, is that, like the nineteenth-century art museums that featured copies of great masterpieces, the poor taste "made" objects are often admired as "authentic," critically connected to the mass market, and essential to the duration of high art and education. This paradox — something being both tacky and authentic simultaneously — is at the core of what makes Salem function as a historical tourist site today. The dirt/photograph dichotomy fuels the entire town, not just its souvenir consumables. The two most notable tourist sites in contemporary Salem are the Salem Witch Museum and the Peabody Essex Museum. The first is the most visited museum in Salem, and it is considered by some to be a focus of "bad taste" commercialism. The Peabody Essex is a favorite among scholars and school groups, and is respected as the arbiter of "good taste" in town. The dichotomy that holds these two sites apart is also the very same system that assures their permanent dependence on each other.

In order to synthesize several of the issues raised thus far, we can pose this question: how are drag queens, Plimoth Plantation key chains, Gallows Hill dirt, and animatronic acts of torture related? "Camp" is one theoretical link that yokes many of these topics together. Susan Sontag defines "camp" as "a certain mode of aestheticism. It is one way of seeing the world as an aesthetic phenomenon. That way, the way of Camp, is not in terms of beauty, but in terms of the degree of artifice, of stylization" (277). Sontag separates camp from the authentic, the natural, and the true, and aligns it with the artificial and the theatrical. The "lens of camp," she says, "blocks out content" (281). Camp, like history and tourism, defines itself in terms of representations. But Sontag suggests that this is not the same thing as easily equating camp with bad taste: "Camp taste turns its back on the good-bad axis of ordinary aesthetic judgment. Camp doesn't reverse things. It doesn't argue that good is bad, or that bad is good. What it does is to offer art (and life) a different — a supplementary — set of standards" (286). She continues: "Camp taste is, above all, a mode of enjoyment, of appreciation — not judgment.... Camp is a tender feeling" (291–2). Though this is perhaps too much sentimentality for most of us, Sontag makes an interesting argument here: that camp, by focusing on the style and the surface, allows the content to go unmeasured. There is no room here for good and bad declarations, as camp advocates a new focus on the *experience of experiencing the performance at hand.* To experience a tourist site or a historical study or one's own identity not as an absolute, but as an entertainment, is to achieve "camp" (or just to *be* campy), according to Sontag. Of course, if this theory is applied to all historical projects, touristic or otherwise, it's questionable whether it would hold up. Are we, for example, to laugh and rollick our way through *Schindler's List*? Can there be tragedy or education in this tender, nonjudgmental, entertaining version of life?

In "Strategic Camp," David Bergman argues that camp, particularly for gay men, has been a useful way for non-dominant subjects to live within dominant society. According to Bergman, camp, rather than opposing oppressive power structures, "finess[es] the whole issue of power" (107). Instead of attacking a hostile enemy, camp sends itself up, asserting its presence and celebrating "the life of a community beset by the morbid" (107). By way of an example, Bergman describes a drag queen in an AIDS charity dunking booth, calling out to passersby, "Which of you brutes is going to make my mascara run?" (107). As the tiara-sporting drag queen, in all of her Bakhtinian, carnivalesque grotesqueness, highlights her own delicacy and brutality, she undermines the very oppositions which sustain her identity (boy-girl, classical-grotesque, delicate-brutal). The "morbid" community Bergman describes is multi-layered: a gay community besieged by homophobia, a weak community plagued by AIDS, a transgendered community in a sexually dimorphic society. But this morbidity might easily translate into the category of history. As the past passes by, the drag queen becomes a symbol for all oppositional systems that both sustain and collapse as a result of her/his presence. Camp, then, can be a strategy that, though often entertaining, can also call attention to the fundamental paradoxes at the center of any identity-conferring operation. To return to Plimoth Plantation, where this chapter first began, we can appreciate Snow's transvestites as walking symbols of how the campiness of historical tourism can be, as it seemed to be for Snow himself, pleasurable, disconcerting, morbid, and celebrational. Though Sontag fails to note this, it seems evident that camp (while focused on style, lacking in content, and truly tender) is both educational and tragic.

Embedded in these theoretical questions of performativity and authenticity, of history, and of tourism, are more specific and practical questions about how primary historical documents, subsequent narrative accounts of primary events, fiction about the past, and commercial or educational historical tourist productions can be approached and analyzed. The following chapters of this book will apply some of the concepts I have outlined thus far to the methodological and explicatory practices of academic scholars. Before we set foot in the Witch Museum or the Peabody Essex, I would like to examine in some depth the original trial documents from 1692. Chapter One, "'You Seem to Act Witchcraft': Theatricality and the Trial Transcripts," investigates the theatricality of the original Salem events. I argue that the witchcraft trials, even at their genesis, were already performative, parodic, and theatrical. This is a markedly different argument than those launched by scholars such as Charles Upham from earlier days and Bernard Rosenthal from today; my goal is not to prove that the afflicted girls were lying, acting, or conspiring. Instead, I am interested in looking at the mechanisms that surrounded the testimony. How did the court of Oyer and Terminer resemble a theater? How did testimony reflect a de-naturalizing of the organic, spontaneous physical body? What are the possible parodic elements involved with the charges and defenses? This chapter suggests that the original, core events of the Salem trials, the events which have been marketed and packaged for today's consumer economy, were, in fact, already being performed even at their inceptions.

I begin Chapter One with a brief look at several mid-twentieth-century texts on the definition of historical research. In particular, I am interested in exploring the relationship of a historian to her/his primary source. What makes a document "primary"? How do scholars evaluate the credibility of a source? How do judicial records function in the historical search for truth? By considering texts by Thomas E. Felt and Homer Carey Hockett, I summarize the traditionalists' viewpoint on how sources can be used to find answers to the age-old question of "what happened?" But in this chapter, I am most interested in the ways in which the Salem "primary sources" contradict the methodologies set forth by Felt and Hockett. As I move from an ontological approach to a more performative approach, I redefine the very notion of what it means to work with "original" source materials. Chapter One then moves to an examination of these sources themselves, as I expand my questions about the transcripts' credibility to include questions about their subject matter as well. How do they describe witchcraft? How do they separate and/or blur the definitions of "God" and "the devil"? How does confession function in the transcripts? And, relatedly, how do these questions intersect with the categories of veracity, originality, and historiography?

To examine on these multiple levels the relationship of truth and fact to history and to the trials themselves has important political, as well as theoretical, repercussions. First of all, the Salem witch trials are often condemned for their fact-finding fanaticism; indeed, people were rewarded with freedom for *confessing* to witchcraft. The *unknown* was on trial much more than was witchcraft itself. The goals of the trials were to reveal the truth about that which had always been associated with deceit, duplicity, doubling, and invisibility. People lost their lives over their refusal to codify and make explicit the demons that haunted Salem under its surface. In this sense, Salem becomes a model of what happens when the figurative or abstract (like hearsay, spectral evidence, hunches, and hallucinations) is reified by the state. Those who refused to make the so-called "underworld" real were hanged for their insolence. Thus, it becomes important for scholars of Salem to question our own methodologies as we hunt for the truth of what happened in 1692. The trials themselves demonstrate poignantly just how strong society's desire to eliminate doubt and shadow can be. In this chapter, I suggest that the trials themselves, through their performative aspect, de-stabilize the very ontology that they seek to instate, and that subsequent historical and entertainment-related tellings of the story of Salem participate in a layering effect which has, at its core, simply another script.

Chapter One also begins an examination of the subject of spectral evidence, an examination that continues throughout the book. In particular, I discuss the relationship of the physical body to the spectral body, as set forth in trial documents and surrounding texts. One of the central controversies back in 1692 concerned the question of whether or not spectral evidence should be allowed as legal and dependable proof of witchcraft. What is the relationship of the "real" Rebecca Nurse to the spectral Rebecca Nurse who flew through the air and caused mischief? Relatedly, how do the mysteriously appearing and disappearing witches' teats function to both corporealize and simultaneously metaphorize the bodies at the center of the controversies? In *Conversing By Signs*, Robert Blair St. George suggests that implication functioned as a very real language in colonial America. I agree, but I am also interested in the way in which the very "real" bodies in colonial America functioned as metaphors, linguistic signs, and figures. What I hope to establish is the way in which the signifier and the sign, arbitrarily connected as they may be, become inseparable in the landscape of the trials, and how the real and the copy get productively confused. I say "productively" because I suggest that the displacement of priority and ontology by imitative play can demonstrate both the power of the non-dominant to alter the political arena through parody, and the very thinness and porousness of the line that divides the status quo from its own undoing. Though this chapter does not deny the very real tragedy that occurred at Salem, my goal here is not to mourn, nor is it to remember fallen heroes and heroines or condemn fanaticism. Instead, I argue that performance, parody, and play were all a part of Salem, and that they, in and of themselves, refuse to read Salem as a linear tragedy. This could, if it were my project, possibly give voice to a rising resistance in Salem amongst voiceless villagers such as slaves and young girls. More importantly, though, this argument should serve to demonstrate that the natural concept of "voice," like the natural concept of "truth," tends only to silence the subtext that, by definition, accompanies every text.

Chapter Two, "From Shards to Meanings: Historians Make Sense of the Trials," deals with the most famous historical reports about the witch trials. Beginning with the first great reflection on the trials, Cotton Mather's *Wonders of the Invisible World*, and ending with the late-twentieth-century studies of Boyer and Nissenbaum, I ask questions about how Salem's narrative thread was created, revised, and sustained from 1692 to the present. *Wonders of the Invisible World* and Robert Calef's ironically titled response, *More Wonders of the Invisible World*, create a dialectic that has shaped Salem scholarship for more than three centuries. As Mather creates the picture of a Salem besieged by demonic sources from without, Calef counters that the demons exist within Salem, in the accusers rather than in the accused or in Satan. What I hope to demonstrate is that this inside-outside dialectic is actually not a choice between two competing ideological analyses of the trials, but is instead a fundamental necessity to any kind of historical scholarship. Mather's intense paranoia about Salem's tenuous battle for light in a dark continent reveals not just an externalization of his own anxieties about Salem's own piety, but also a deeper suspicion of the boundary which supposedly divides right from wrong. Similarly, Calef's response attempts to situate the evil force in the trials themselves, a familiar maneuver to modern readers of the "witch hunt." But Calef, too, by calling Mather a "liar" (and worse!), demonstrates a vehement need to contain the wrongdoing of the trials to the body of one man, one panel of judges, one legal system. The Mather-Calef section of this chapter uses both texts to outline how Salem gets constituted as an abyss that must be marked and measured through the use of historical writing and scientific "proof."

From there, I proceed to Charles Upham, whose 1867 account of the trials has influenced more historians and fiction writers than any other Salem history. Upham provides the ancestry for later novels and tourist sites that retell the witch trials story as a ghost story, for Upham treats his history like a walking dead man, a body that can be ghoulishly brought back to life — at least to a certain extent — by the Frankensteinian historian. Upham seeks to reify and stabilize the fluctuatingly dialectical historiographical model of Salem created by Mather and Calef, and he quite literally corporealizes Salem's past into a narrative corpse. More than a century later, Paul Boyer and Stephen Nissenbaum wrote a rebuttal to Upham, beginning their own *Salem Possessed* with a critique of Upham's "flawed" narrative. Boyer and Nissenbaum work to contextualize the trials, placing them squarely into a landscape fraught with sociological, political, and economic tensions. But they also double Salem's context, constantly calling attention to the ways in which it intersects with their own historical moment. They, like the Salemites they describe, enter into a bitter internal war with themselves, wanting on the one side to explain the Salem events purely with demographic facts, and wanting on the other side to offer their own impressions and analyses of what happened. As we will see with some of the fiction we will consider below, Boyer and Nissenbaum establish a kind of "crystal ball effect," which takes the events of Salem and treats them as a set of currently unfolding events — events that, though they have yet to "happen," are already foretold by the authors.

Chapter Two also explores popular yet peripheral theories set forth throughout the years about Salem, in particular Chadwick Hansen's claim that some of the witches were actually guilty of practicing witchcraft, and Linnda R. Caporael's scientific hypothesis that ergot poisoning was to blame for the behavior of the afflicted. In addition to tracing out how these varied historical readings play out, I am also interested in how and why these histories have entered into the collective imagination, how and why they have become so popular and so powerful. Chapter Three, "Fiction and the Real: Novelists Rewrite Salem," is, in many ways, proof of just how influential these historians have been. Nearly all of the fiction writers I discuss worked from the historical accounts written by the authors from Chapter Two. From Hawthorne's antagonistic personal relationship with Charles Upham to Robin Cook's obsession with Caporael's ergot hypothesis, fiction and history have more in common than not where Salem is concerned.

In Chapter Three, I examine five popular fictional accounts of the Salem events, and consider how they resuscitate Salem's past. In John Neal's *Rachel Dyer*, the first novel about the Salem events, Neal's characters struggle with the question of how to tell fact from fiction in the courtroom, just as Neal himself struggles with the question of how to blend historical accuracy with a storyteller's flair for evoking emotional authenticity. In *The House of the Seven Gables*, Nathaniel Hawthorne plays with the dividing line between the romantic and the real, as he raises ghosts that he claims don't matter, but who, in fact, end up floating off with the story. Marion L. Starkey's novel *The Visionary Girls*, like Arthur Miller's play, blends "true" events with fictitious events; as she explains "what happened," she creates the very past that she purports to "expose." This is, interestingly, the same role that Tituba plays in her novel: a fortune-teller who can predict the future, a future that unfolded long ago. Maryse Condé's *I, Tituba, Black Witch of Salem*, is more self-consciously ironic than *The Crucible*, but like Starkey, Condé explicitly aims to use fiction to get at a deeper truth than history has been able to provide. Focusing on the character of Tituba, Condé empowers the slave woman while at the same time she challenges both the apocryphal versions of Tituba's role in the trials and the notion that fiction itself should conform to the rules of history, temporality, and political correctness. Chapter Three ends with a discussion of Robin Cook's recent bestseller *Acceptable Risk*, which, in a tour de force of over-the-top emplotment, links the use of primary source documents to the production of re-engineered ergot mold, a mold that functions in the novel as a kind of Prozac-gone-dead-wrong. Cook tries to celebrate the uses of history and science, but his novel keeps churning up horror. The library, the lab, the museum: all become spaces where mysteries solved are grotesque disasters.

Chapter Four, "A Dramatic Tale: Salem on Stage and Screen," extends the fiction discussion into a more self-consciously performative arena. The performativity that inhered even in the trial transcripts becomes more deliberate in the plays, films, and television shows that treat the Salem story. To begin, Henry Wadsworth Longfellow's play about Giles Corey being pressed to death mixes concrete political critique with angry, testifying specters; like Hawthorne, Longfellow focuses on the realm of the "real," but the play's definition of the "real" — that it can be stabbed with a stick! — falls short of its own mark again and again. Arthur Miller's popular play *The Crucible* uses a "non-fiction" running commentary to situate the play's events in history, but Miller continually uses the commentary to establish "fictional truths," things that never happened in 1692, but which become "real" in Miller's new definition of the term. Miller uses confession and nakedness to indicate purity and veracity, but over and over again, the play suggests that no confession can ever really be un-ironic. Two earlier films from Hollywood's golden age, 1937's *Maid of Salem* and 1942's *I Married a Witch*, focus on the relationship between patriarchy and witchcraft, and how female power gets contained and deployed through charges and acts of witchcraft. As Abigail Williams does in Miller's play, the figure of the "real" witch gets productively confused, as female sexuality and failed female domesticity challenge the status quo. Finally, the chapter examines two recent television shows where characters participate in recreated versions of the witch trials. In both *Bewitched* and in *Sabrina, The Teen-Aged Witch*, the real witches escape persecution, but must speak up to defend their loved ones who are wrongfully accused. The two episodes under analysis here reveal how the mock trial functions to define — ironically — the category of a "real" witch.

From Sabrina and Samantha, it is a short jump to Chapter Five, "Selling the Story: From Salem Village to Witch City," which focuses on the twentieth-century tourist market that surrounds Salem. After a brief history of Salem's economic shifts from a port-mercantile Massachusetts capital to a New England tourist highlight, I consider in depth the difference between "high" and "low" tourist productions. What are the differences in economic and educational motivation between the Peabody Essex Museum and the Witch Dungeons? How do Boris Karloff's Witch Mansion and the Witch Museum work in relationship to the memorial and graveyard sites? Drawing on scholarship by Dean MacCannell, Erik Cohen, Barbara Kirshenblatt-Gimblett, and others, I deconstruct the ideologies involved with Salem's tourist market, and consider the (false) dichotomy that separates education from entertainment. The first section focuses on "low" tourist sites (Wax Museum/Witch Village, Witch Museum, Dracula's Castle, Dungeons, shops), and the second on "high" sites (Peabody Essex Museum, monuments, Tercentenary events). I consider the specific criteria for categorizing sites as "low" or "high," and deconstruct the division between the tacky and the tasteful. The goal here is not to celebrate the authenticity of Dracula's Castle, nor to condemn the Peabody Essex for its sensationalism; instead, I aim to consider practically the theory I have outlined above about how authenticity gets produced against a definition of the "inauthentic," and how the performative permeates even the most patently "true" Salem productions. This chapter deals with specific tourist sites, and the way that camp, kitsch, commercialism, and entertainment function with and against education, commemoration, and moral lessons.

In addition, this chapter investigates how *packaging* impacts the tourist's understanding of American history, and how such packaging changes the very definition of history itself. Are there any problems associated with the selling of Gallows Hill dirt, for example? Are there any real ways that this "dirt-as-past" corrupts society, or is the "corruption" always already a part of any historical inquiry? How does "dirt-as-past" function in relation to the Peabody Essex Museum, and its cases of primary source documents? In one documentary film about Salem, Arthur Miller's reaction when he is shown the package of Gallows Hill dirt was a sad shake of his head.[12] What does it mean for the author of the fictitious play that has so defined popular understandings of the trials to judge so harshly the commercialized work of the Witch Museum? What, precisely, are the differences between these cultural productions, and how are they all related to American mythology, authenticity, and 1692? This chapter addresses these questions, emphasizing the way that performance connects apparently disparate tourist/art forms.

It is a somewhat hypocritical maneuver to turn now to the "primary sources." Why begin with the actual trial transcripts if I have just claimed that chronology is highly suspect, that primacy is an illusion created through repetition? One reason I would like to begin this project's explications with the "original" documents is to inquire whether or not they, on their own, have any "original" qualities. If an origin can only exist after it has been passed — and thereby self-produced by the ironic loss of itself— then what will we find in original documents if we examine them without reference to what followed them? It is, of course, an impossible practicality to abandon our own modern minds as we investigate the past; but if we begin with the "primary sources," we can see just what Salem had to say about itself before it became "original."

ONE

"You Seem to Act Witchcraft"
Theatricality and the
Trial Transcripts

In a book about Salem witchcraft, it seems imperative that somewhere the reader get an outline of the basic narrative of events of 1692. Though the trials have certainly passed into the general American consciousness, disciplinary protocol assumes that readers need not trust their own potentially flawed knowledge about the historical moment under discussion in this text. But in a project such as this, which argues that history is always already *re-presented*, even when it is relayed by primary sources such as trial transcripts, how can a thumbnail account of "the facts" be provided? To explore this question further, consider three texts that attempt to answer it.

Researching, Writing, and Publishing Local History is a how-to manual for people who wish to study original manuscript documents from the past. The author, Thomas E. Felt, was the Senior Historian in the New York State Education Department in the late 1970s when the book was first published. He offers three criteria for evaluating the credibility of any historical text or manuscript:

1. *Closeness.* The source closest to the event in time and space, if not an actual observer or participant.
2. *Competence.* The source most capable of understanding and describing a situation.
3. *Impartiality.* The source with the least to gain from distortion of the record [7].

If these criteria are applied to the trial transcripts,[1] a series of problems quickly emerges. First of all, "the event" referred to in the first criterion is

29

difficult to determine as far as the trials are concerned. Is "the event" the moment of affliction? The articulation of the testimony? The recording of the testimony? Most of the trial records refer to a past crime: a pinching, a broom-moving, a hole-removal, etc. And most of the records are oral testimonies offered by one party but recorded by another. So which "event" is "the" event? The recorders of the testimony are aware of the fact that they are at a remove from some (phantom) original event. Simon Willard signs his record of the examination of Jane Lilly this way: "I und'r written: being appinted by Authority to take the within examination doe testifie upon oath taken in Court: that this is a true Coppy of the Substance of it: to the best of my knowledge" (Boyer and Nissenbaum, *Papers*, 541). Willard, who records the examination that is executed by the judges, uses the interesting phrase "true copy" to describe his transcript. He implies that the actual examination is the original, and that the written document is a copy of it, and this highlights history's inability to produce any "actual" events. The representation that Willard provides is still considered "true," but only "to the best of [his] knowledge." The transcripts continually call attention to their distance from the events that they aim to present, even as they claim to function as "true" documents with "substance." It is this fluctuation, between the true/substantial and the copied/unsubstantial (or unsubstantiated), which characterizes the transcripts' position on their own authority.

This fluctuation appears not only in the signatures of the recorders, but also when multiple accounts of the same testimony are placed side by side. Consider, for example, the examination of William Barker Sr., which is recorded in two unsigned versions. There are no substantive differences between the two accounts, but the words used to describe Barker's crimes and confession are certainly dissimilar in places. What is even odder than the slight dissimilarities (such as the date of the examination, which is recorded in one account as September 16, 1692, and in the other as September 5, 1692) are the many exact replications between the two accounts, as if one had been copied from the other. How can we account for the multiple records, so much the same and yet not exact replicas of each other? On the one hand, this suggests that the two accounts are produced much like a game of "Telephone"; instead of being copied from a single original source — i.e., the actual examination — it seems likely that one account was copied from another account. This likelihood is increased when we compare certain testimonies that have an uncanny resemblance to each other. In the case against Abigail Hobbs, afflicted girls Mercy Lewis, Mary Walcott, Ann Putnam, and Elizabeth Hubbard offer testimony of being afflicted that is so similar in diction, it precludes coincidence (Boyer and Nissenbaum, *Papers*, 415–17). Did the girls just repeat verbatim what their friend before them said? Or did the recorder of the testimony simply copy his previous record for ease of reference? Whatever the reason for the similarities, it is evident that the transcripts are not always (not ever?) a direct record of a participant's spontaneous testimony; instead, the transcripts are a representation, a copy, of some lost or unknowable original. Felt's search for "closeness" then, is a self-consciously Sisyphusian endeavor, for the trials demonstrate through their recorders and their repetitions that originality is, like a mathematical limit, only an illusion of proximity.

"Competence" and "impartiality" are, of course, related fallacies. Felt describes "competent" as "capable of understanding and describing a situation." But, he cautions, "The banker is an unlikely authority on how to cook chitlins" (8). According to Felt, people have expertise in particular areas, and should be trusted only when they discourse on their specializations. But where does this leave the category of "experience"? Who is an expert on "what happened": the person to whom it happened (the afflicted) or the person who was on trial (the accused); the person who can legally characterize such happenings (the magistrate); the person who has knowledge about the demonic (the reverend)? At their core, the Salem trials were always controversial for the very reason that nobody knew where the authority to judge lay.

On impartiality, Felt offers this advice: "There is a way to get candid snapshots of past events and personalities, and in principle it is simple: read a document for information it was not intended to give. You use it to yield answers to your own questions rather than those it was created to answer" (9). This advice, which I do follow in this project to a certain extent, is patently ridiculous. Felt implies that the only way to eliminate the effects of bias in a manuscript is to replace that bias with one's own (biased) agenda. What Felt demonstrates is the futility of actually finding a transparent record of events, and he also explains — unintentionally —

how historians' own scholarship replicates this futility even as it works to overcome it. The Salem witchcraft trials thematize this dilemma by constantly calling attention to a core of central questions, questions that are particular to both the witchcraft trials *and* historiography itself. Where is the original event described in the testimony? Who best understands that event? How does the recorded version of that event differ from the event itself and from other accounts of the event? Felt would be dismayed at what the trial transcripts do to "closeness," "competence," and "impartiality," but it is the trials' inability to resolve issues of originality that make this historical "event" so appealing to generation after generation of historical scholars.

Decades ago, the field of history had solidified into an objective discipline, one in which irresolvability could be eliminated by hard work and good science. For example, in his 1955 book, *The Critical Method in Historical Research and Writing*, Professor Homer Carey Hockett outlines the pitfalls that await historians who are working with copies of original manuscripts. One by one, Hockett explains how to overcome each dilemma one might face: how to determine if a document has been forged, ghost-written, plagiarized or "corrupted"; how to tell the difference between the "literal" meaning and the "real" meaning of a text; how to discredit gossip, rumor, slander, lies, and impartiality (24–64). After listing all of the possible textual corruptions that can plague the historian, Hockett writes, "By this time the student may be tempted to conclude that it is useless to try to distinguish the true from the false sufficiently to make the historian's efforts worth while." But he continues, "That myths and errors have found their way into much written history must be admitted; but the purpose and justification of these pages lie in the effort to show that proper criticism may both establish facts and purge history of erroneous statements" (63–64). Obviously, historiography has come quite a distance from Hockett's platform, but his corrective approach to history is still a useful model, as it demonstrates history's desire to strip off the ornamentation of duplicity in order to arrive at naked, unadorned truth.

What Hockett also suggests — perhaps unintentionally — is that historical errors are not all caused by historians. Sometimes "original" authors themselves are responsible for "corruption." He cites the example of James Madison, whose journals were collected and edited by John Quincy Adams.

Upon reading the edited version, Madison noticed many discrepancies between his original journal notes and the published version. What did he do? He went back and changed his *diary notes*, because it seemed to him that the published version "was correct and his notes wrong" (Hockett 32). Hockett also describes the history of the publishing of Ben Franklin's *Autobiography*, which I would like to quote at some length:

> The late Max Farrand attempted to restore the original reading of [the *Autobiography.*] The original is known to have been composed of four parts written respectively in 1771, 1784, 1788, and 1790. Franklin himself revised the first three parts and made two copies, both of which have been lost. However, a French translation, never printed, was made from one of these copies by Le Veillard, and the manuscript of this translation is now in the Library of Congress. Franklin's grandson, Temple Franklin, published an English version in 1818, which Dr. Farrand believes was based on the copy used in Le Veillard's translation. In 1868 Joseph Bigelow edited Le Viellard's copy and thought he had corrected errors made by Temple Franklin. Dr. Farrand concluded that the Temple Franklin version did not reproduce Le Veillard's exactly yet is the "best obtainable" form of the *Autobiography* [34].

Hockett, in his anecdotes about the Madison journals and the Franklin autobiography, demonstrates how "originality" is almost always provisional: that it is a contract agreed upon by historical agents and historians alike, and that it is therefore contractual rather than ontological. Hockett, for all of his antiquity, is an excellent example of how fact-finding historicism collapses into a rhetoric of representationalism, even as it aggressively insists on "originality."

Judicial records are doubly vexed by this tendency to seek the "truth." The very proceedings at Salem were enacted to "determine" ("terminer") the facts about the girls' strange behavior. In her study of sixteenth-century French pardon tales (confessions and letters of remission), Natalie Zemon Davis counters the myth that legal archival records are somehow more objective than other kinds of historical manuscripts. "As the sixteenth-century rhetorician Daniel d'Auge observed, drawing on Aristotle," Davis writes, "judicial speech is one of three kinds of oratory — deliberative, demonstrative, and legal; it needs 'artifice' just like the others. The verb *feindre* itself was used in the literary exchange of that time to mean 'create,' rather than merely to dissemble; its fruit was 'fiction'" (4). She continues:

To be sure, fictive creation had its most appropriate expression in poetry or a story, not in history, which was increasingly praised (though not always practiced) as a truth, which was "bare" and "unadorned." But the artifice of fiction did not always lend falsity to an account; it might well bring verisimilitude or a moral truth. Nor did the shaping or embellishing of a history mean forgery; where that line was to be drawn was one of the creative controversies of the day [4].

Though sixteenth-century France and seventeenth-century New England were certainly two different places, in a Puritan culture which relied heavily on the persuasive powers of its sermons to legislate behavior and belief, we can see how figurative language, narrative momentum, and other literary techniques would be popular ways to strengthen "Truth," whether biblical, legal, or historical. What Davis suggests is that historians should not be as concerned with eliminating fictional interference in the texts we consider as much as we should pause and study the most fictional moments in the records, since fiction may well be a useful path to historical understanding. In my study of the transcripts, I focus not on sorting through the "forgeries," but laying the fictions side by side in order to consider why the testimony emerged as it did.

So, because this chapter on the abundant primary source material that survives about the witchcraft trials cannot offer an encapsulated version of "what happened," it will take as its narrative jumping-off point an account of how I have come to these trial documents. First of all, while summary records of the witchcraft trials before the Superior Court of Judication held from January to May 1693 do survive, virtually no records exist today from the 1692 court of Oyer and Terminer. Most of what I will be discussing in this chapter are documents from the preliminary hearings held before the convening of Oyer and Terminer. Also, original depositions — pre-recorded testimonies — that were used in Oyer and Terminer do survive, along with the formulaic papers such as warrants and arrest records.[2] For most of the surviving transcripts and documents (hereafter referred to as the "transcripts"), I have relied on Paul Boyer and Stephen Nissenbaum's *The Salem Witchcraft Papers: Verbatim Transcripts of the Salem Witchcraft Outbreak of 1692*. But Boyer and Nissenbaum's formidable collection is not a direct xerox of original documents. To understand how the collection was produced, one needs to return to the late 1930s, when

Roosevelt's Works Progress Administration, a New Deal work relief agency, provided funding for a new, extensive compilation of Salem witchcraft materials. Under the supervision of Archie N. Frost, multiple archives were searched and the records were transcribed. Forty years later, in 1977, with Boyer and Nissenbaum as editors, these transcriptions were published by Da Capo Press. Already, it is clear that the materials with which I am working are not in any sense "original." Despite the subtitle's ambitious diction ("verbatim transcripts"), Boyer and Nissenbaum are themselves aware of the slippage that has occurred between the original events and their own published collection. They refer to "mis-label[ings]," "inclu[sions] under the wrong cases," "obvious errors," "illegible" and "illiterate" testimony, and "mis-readings," mostly perpetrated by the WPA (*Papers*, 32). Though they claim most of these mistakes have been "corrected" in their version, they admit that "a few perhaps remain" (*Papers*, 32).[3] The question I had to ask myself at the outset was if I should use the easily accessible Boyer and Nissenbaum collection, if I should use the 1938 WPA transcriptions, or if I should spend a year or two assembling my own "original" collection by visiting the multiple archives that Frost visited so long ago. Though there is something to be said for a dusty archive, particularly in terms of sensory enjoyment, I am interested in the ways that the copied and recopied versions function in the academy and in popular understanding as "primary sources." What I hope to suggest is not that there is no reason to work with original documents, but that the category of "original" is always vexed when it comes to historical scholarship. Primary sources seem to become more primary as they are copied, published, disseminated, transcribed — in short, as they proliferate into multiple copies and versions.

Because the "original" transcripts — the parchments from the 1690s — were themselves copies of previously given and previously recorded testimony, and because they were almost always edited copies of oral testimony, any sense of spontaneity or true originality is already lost. Direct transcripts of the actual Oyer and Terminer hearings have not survived, and since stenography did not exist at the time, one can only wonder how readable direct transcripts would be to us anyway. The Boyer and Nissenbaum records are mainly *not* direct recordings as much as they are prepared statements to be used during the proceedings and deliberations or recollections by various participants on how the testimony unfolded. I use the Boyer and Nissenbaum collection not because it has corrected Frost's errors, but because Boyer and Nissenbaum are the most widely studied transcriptions of the trials — interesting given the critical distance between the parchment and *The Salem Witchcraft Papers*.[4]

This emphasis on copies, evident in the methodological choices I have made in assembling my "primary" sources, is precisely what characterizes my reading of the trial testimony. Nearly every incident of bewitchment that occurs during the trials is preceded by a verbal description of what is about to happen. In some instances, the verbal description functions like a prediction: "Some of the afflicted cried, there is Procter going to take up Mrs. Pope's feet. — And her feet were immediately taken up" (Boyer and Nissenbaum, *Papers*, 660). The afflicted girls' declaration works like a stage direction, describing what action is to be taken in the scene; then, as if scripted, the action transpires according to the direction: "Abigail Williams cried out again, there is Goodman Procter going to hurt Goody Bibber; and immediately Goody Bibber fell into a fit" (Boyer and Nissenbaum, *Papers*, 660.) Sometimes, as when the girls see demonic birds flying from beam to beam in the meetinghouse, a directive utterance produces not a physical incarnation of the Devil's presence (such as Mrs. Pope's elevated feet or Goody Bibber's fit), but an afflicted group reaction to the presence. As the birds flutter past, the girls point, look, and scream. The trial transcripts, then, read as a play, not just because of their dramatic tension or their dialogic form, but because inherent in their very texts is a scripted quality which writes the drama before it is enacted. But there is an interesting distinction between the transcripts and *The Crucible* (to take one play as an example). The transcripts include within their pages the performance as well as the script. While Arthur Miller pens the words that the actor playing Abigail must then enact on stage, at a moment removed from the moment in the script, the transcripts include both the directive words from an "author" and the performance by an "actor." The transcripts are script and performance in one. This relates directly to the question of the primary source, suggesting that even if one locates the "original" document at issue, the Salem events are always already scripted.

"You seem to act witchcraft before us," says Judge Hathorne to Bridget Bishop at her examination, "by the motion of your body, which seems to have influence upon the afflicted" (Boyer and Nissenbaum, *Papers*, 84). This phrase, "to *act* witchcraft" appears several times in the transcripts, and I think it worth examining in some detail. The theatrical sense of the term, which to the Puritans would have suggested a blasphemous tendency towards ornamentation, duplicity, and inconstancy,[5] highlights the performative nature of witchcraft's manifestation during testimony. The "influence" to which Hathorne refers is a parodic display that occurs throughout the trials. "Then [Bishop] turned up her eyes," writes Hathorne in his record of the examination, "[and] the eyes of the afflicted were turned up" (Boyer and Nissenbaum, *Papers*, 84). Witchcraft, then, often demands two events in order to gain its definition; first, the accused must act, and then the afflicted must copy that action. As with the levitated feet and the reaction to the bird on the beam, Bishop's turned-up eyes become another script in the play of the trial testimony.

The other sense of "act," to take action, is also significant here, as it implies an exterior physical repercussion for an interior condition of the soul. Consider Hannah Bromage's response when she was asked in what shape the devil appeared to her: she answered that "she believed the devil was in her heart" (Boyer and Nissenbaum, *Papers*, 143). Though there is no question that the Salem Puritans believed that the devil was a real, concrete being with tangible bodily characteristics, many confessed witches feared that they had somehow taken the devil into their bodies and souls. But witchcraft, as distinguished from the state of being a witch, occurs when the interior condition of being possessed by the devil reaches out of the witch to touch an innocent person; after all, most accusations centered on the way that witches "afflicted" the people around them.[6] In this sense of the word "act," witchcraft is a byproduct or a result of some interior state of being. Though, on the one hand, this seems to bolster an antitheatrical concept of witchcraft as a natural condition of the true soul of a sinner, in actuality it serves to reiterate witchcraft's inherently projective, performative quality. First, the devil must invade the witch, then the newly invaded interior soul must reach outside of said witch. If witchcraft has as its locus a position of interiority, such interiority can only be defined when exterior action is taken. If the devil is in Hannah Bromage's heart, it hardly seems to matter until Bromage afflicts Mary Walcott and Ann Putnam. Like a script, demonic interiority functions as a

textual road map for the action of witchcraft that is performed throughout the trials.

The trial afflictions are, of course, just one aspect of the witchcraft
that emerges in Salem in 1692. The making of "poppets" also reiterates
the scripted quality of witchcraft during the outbreak. Mary Lacey, Sr.,
explains during her testimony how poppets work: "If she doe take a ragg,
clout or any such thing and Roll it up together And Imagine it to represent such and such a persone; Then whatsoever she doth to the Ragg or
clout so rouled up, The persone represented thereby will be in lyke manner afflicted" (Boyer and Nissenbaum, *Papers*, 514). Here, the poppet not
only resembles in general shape the person that it represents, it also acts
as a stand-in for the targeted person. Like a play or puppet show, the
witchcraft is enacted in miniature with the doll; unlike a play, however,
"real" effects are supposedly felt by the "real" person represented by the
poppet. On one level, this is interesting for the way it continues the theatrical paradigm that runs through the transcripts. On another level,
though, this complicates the paradigm by suggesting a direct connection
between that which is enacted and that which is real. The poppets posit
a definition of the theatrical that would have sounded perfectly rational
to Puritan anti-theatricalists, even if to a modern sensibility it might seem
far-fetched. Anti-theatricalism was fueled by a fear that the performed
could become real, that the stage and the world shared an uncomfortably
fluid relationship.[7] The poppets feed into this, serving as they do as a conduit between the play and the thing.

The poppets themselves in their physical construction bear out this
metaphorical link between play and reality. Elizabeth Johnson, Jr., brings
out several poppets during her confession. They were "made of rags or
stripes of clothe too of them ... one poppet: had: four pieces or stripes of
cloth rapt one upon another which she s'd was to afflict four persons"
(Boyer and Nissenbaum, *Papers*, 504). The dolls are not stuffed with anything but are instead a series of layers of cloth. If each poppet acts a representation of a singular person, this is compelling for the way that it
destabilizes the notion of an interior identity; there is nothing but exterior to these dolls. Johnson's multi-layered poppet is used to torment four
innocent people: one person for each layer of cloth. Here, identity is tied
not to the singular body (which here houses four identities), nor to inte-

riority, but to a cloaking or wrapping process where one's identity is created by over-wrapping and thus slightly shifting a different identity beneath it. In this sense, the poppets enact a complex of performative qualities. They replace interiority with exteriority, replace singular identity with a process of layering, and replace a focus on the body with a focus on the body's accoutrements. While this focus on outside, on copies, on ornamentation is distinctly theatrical, the poppets terrorize the Puritans by implying that this theatricality is reaching off of the stage and into the homes of the innocent.

But, if witchcraft is a performative act, does that mean that to live a Christian, pious life is to reject theatricality? In her own defense, accused witch Mary Bradbury has this to say about her Christian faith: I "have endeavo'red to frame my life; & conversation according to the rules of his holy word, & in that faith & practise resolve by the help and assistance of god to continue to my lifes end" (Boyer and Nissenbaum, *Papers*, 117).[8] A close explication of the words used here reveals that despite the anti-theatrical platform of many Puritans, Christian piety has its own performative characteristics. Bradbury "frames" her life, using the "rules" of God's "holy word" to structure her world. This frame, like a stage, works to denaturalize Bradbury's existence, which is not an existence of impulse and inclination, but an existence that follows previously outlined rules for living. The "holy word" becomes a script, and Bradbury's "conversation" a bit of stage dialogue written by the Almighty. If there is a "faith" which springs from a natural well of belief, here it is yoked irrevocably to "practise," the repeated acting-out of the framed code. This is not to say that there is an intentional theatricalizing of Christianity at play in the Salem witch trials, but instead of simply being a dialectic between natural piety and calculated witchcraft, the trials reveal a widespread anxiety that there is little anywhere that can be taken on faith.

Though some scholars have previously argued that there is testimony in the trials that seems to parody, mock, and/or critique Christianity,[9] this has generally been discounted by mainstream critics who counter that such blatant attacks against Puritan ideals would have been quickly punished and/or suppressed by magistrates and religious leaders. But such parodies *did* exist, though they were not so much aggressively critical as they were unintentionally subversive. It is less important to question whether these parodies were launched intentionally than it is to explore precisely how they were launched. Again, as Barbara Johnson might argue, it is crucial not to determine *what* these parodies signify, but to explore *how* they signify. Not only that there are repeated instances of Satan being dressed up like God throughout the trials, but also that the line between good and evil is porous and flexible, and that this line is itself produced by a theatrical mechanism that is neither natural nor divine. In the individual testimonies given throughout the trials, this mechanism functions through the category of representation, as the accused, the afflicted, and the judgmental battle to define and deflect the devil himself.

Sarah Bridges describes how she sold her soul to the devil: "The Divel Came to her like a man ... & told His name Was Jesus & that She must Serve & worship him" (Boyer and Nissenbaum, *Papers*, 139). In plain terms, Bridges demonstrates the slippage between God and Satan. If Christ *was* a man, the devil is just *like* a man, and if Jesus *is* Jesus, the devil just has his name. Jesus is set up as a real original, while the devil gets constructed as an imposter, a copycat, and a false God. But what is most fascinating about Bridges' testimony is not that the devil can masquerade as holy (we've known this since the Bible), but that accused witches repeatedly cite this confusion of good and evil as reason for their sins. I don't mean to imply that confessed witches were, like Eve, tricked by a devil in disguise, but that the Lord and the devil operate so similarly throughout their narratives that it becomes difficult to understand the difference between the two powers. Mary Bridges, Jr., for example, is one of many confessors who claim to have been "baptized" by the devil (Boyer and Nissenbaum, *Papers*, 135). The devil is repeatedly described as "a black man"; when Martha Carrier is examined, she defends herself by claiming that she "saw no black man but your own presence" (Boyer and Nissenbaum, *Papers*, 185). Though Carrier was probably referring to one of the Salem judges (though Samuel Parris was also known to examine the accused on occasion), she alludes to the fact that *clothing* and not skin color is what most of the trial participants were referring to when they talked about the "black man." The black man, then, is an obvious metaphor for both the authority of the courts, and, more significantly, the rules of the church. The black man is devil, magistrate, and minister simultaneously.

The devil-minister appears most poignantly during George Bur-roughs' trial. Ann Putnam's testimony is recorded as follows: "At evening she saw the Apperishtion of a Minister at which she was grievously affrighted and cried out oh dreadfull: dreadfull here is a minister come: what are Ministers wicthes to: ... [I] tould him that it was a dreadfull thing: that he which was a Minister that should teach children to feare God should com to perswad poor creatures to give their souls to the divill" (Boyer and Nissenbaum, *Papers*, 164). The most obvious significance of this passage is how it highlights the supposed distance between a minis-ter and a witch; when the minister and the devil are collapsed into one, the result is a dreadful irony. The irony is produced because the very definition of a "minister" clashes with the very definition of a "devil." "Minister," as a term, gathers its meaning only from its enforcement of the distance between itself and its opposite ("devil"). So what is a minis-ter if he is also a devil? Or, to rephrase the question, "what are Ministers wicthes to?" The grammatical ambiguity of this question leads to several possible responses. The obvious answer — that ministers are enemies to witches — does not apply in this scenario. Perhaps another response, how-ever, is that ministers are witches to Ann Putman ... and to those who believe that she is afflicted.

William Barker, Sr., confessed that "he was at a meeting of witches at Salem Village ... that the meeting was upon a green peece of ground neare the ministers house, He said they mett there to destroy that place by reason of the peoples being divided & theire differing with their min-isters" (Boyer and Nissenbaum, *Papers*, 66). Few scholars dispute that the rivalry between Parris and his detractors was to blame at least in part for the witch hunt in Salem, but Barker makes the link between this rivalry and the witch outbreak concrete. For Barker, it was not that the minis-ter's land was holy land that stood in opposition to the devil's designs, but that the minister's land was tense land, a breeding ground for the sinful divisions tearing Salem apart, and fertile ground for the devil to begin his development. Relatedly, Mary Warren testifies that Henry Salter "used his witchcraft by the Key & bible & sometimes by the seive & seissors" (Boyer and Nissenbaum, *Papers*, 723). The use by Puritans of certain commonly owned items such as sieves for fortune-telling purposes is well docu-mented.[10] And the random picking out of biblical verses to predict the future and offer advice was also not uncommon, but despite the previous tacit acceptance by most Puritans of such superstitions, here Salter is accused of witchcraft for believing in and using them. Particular intriguing here is the "witchcraft by bible" accusation, which suggests that the "holy word," once used as a "frame" for living the pious life, can here be an instrument of witchcraft. A similar use of the bible emerges during Mary Toothaker's examination. "The Devil is so subtel," William Murray writes in his report of her testimony, "that when she would confess he stops her and deludes also by scripture and being asked what scripture he made inser of to her she mentioned that in Psalmes where it is said Let my enemies be confounded" (Boyer and Nissenbaum, *Papers*, 768). This passage is remarkable for a number of reasons. First, the devil uses the scripture to trick Toothaker into thinking that he is "God her creator." By adopting the appearance of God and the holy word of God, the devil is able to fool Toothaker into signing on with him. Yet again, the scriptures become the link between a Puritan and the devil. More interesting here is the particular passage which the devil chooses to quote in order to prove his existence as God: "Let my enemies be confounded." Though "to confound" does of course mean to foil, it also means to confuse, baffle, or perplex. The devil not only confuses the enemy (the innocent, pre-possessed Mary Toothaker), but he also confuses the *definition* of an enemy, since by looking and talking *exactly like* God, the devil has collapsed the distance between himself and the Lord.

The dividing line between God and the devil blurs many times in the transcripts. Petitioners for John and Elizabeth Proctor have this to say about the relationship of God to the devil: "It may be A Method w'thin the Seveerer But Just Transaction of the Infinite Majestie of God: that he some times may p'rmitt Sathan to p'rsonate, Dissemble, & thereby abuse Inocents, & such as Do in the fear of God Defie the Devill and all his works" (Boyer and Nissenbaum, *Papers*, 681). Citing Job and other examples from the Bible, the petitioners suggest that God might allow for Satan's dirty deeds in order to teach mankind "Adoration, Trmbling, & Dependanc" (Boyer and Nissenbaum, *Papers*, 682). In this model, God's power is actually strengthened by witchcraft. The petitioners imply that God's omnipotence includes control over Satan and his temptations. By aligning God and Satan, they make their friends' guilt irrelevant, as the Proctors become like Job, innocent — and specially chosen — examples used to highlight God's overwhelming power.

Of course, it is left somewhat mysterious how exactly this equation works; the petitioners leave off before their argument is fully realized. Consider the final part of their explanation about this Satanic God: "[It] may be arg'd Besides the unsearcheable foot stepps of Gods Judgments that are brought to Light Every Morning that Astonish o'r weaker Reasons, To teach us Adoration, Trmbling, & Dependanc, &ca but — We must not Trouble y'r Honr's by Being Tedious" (Boyer and Nissenbaum, *Papers*, 682). Though it is always a challenge to draw conclusions about grammar from the period, as there was little uniformity to the rules of writing at the time, it is worth noting several issues in this passage's construction. First of all, the passage is a self-conscious fragment. Though "it may be argued" is, in fact, an independent clause, the implied "that" which should follow the clause makes it dependent, and the prepositional phrase ("besides...") does not complete the announced argument. Instead of a concrete argument explaining why God occasionally permits evil, the sentence drifts into a dependent clause about God's awe-inspiring effect on people, and then breaks off abruptly with "&ca but —." This sets up God's actions as unexplainable, as non-linear, and as unutterable. Instead of being explained, God simply provokes adoration, trembling, and dependence. His rationale is represented only by a dash (—). What is compelling about God's unrepresentable motives is the way that he is seemingly lifted outside of and above the chain of linguistic signification. Repetition and copies appear so frequently in the transcripts, and here the petitioners suggest that God is, like an ultimate signified, free from meaning anything other than what he is.[11] The unavoidable distance that language necessarily injects between itself and its subject makes words (and the written word in particular) useless in discussing God. The tedium of language's constant signification is abandoned, and God is left unexplained, all-powerful, and silent.

Mary Easty, who was hanged as a witch on September 22, 1692, seems desperate to free herself from the repetitive cycles that characterize the trial testimony. "Confess if you be guilty," Judges Corwin and Hathorne implore her. She responds: "I will say it, if it was my last time, I am clear of this sin" (Boyer and Nissenbaum, *Papers*, 289). As if she is struggling to stop an endless chain of signification, Easty tries to finalize her statement of innocence. Easty hopes to locate herself, like God, outside of the realm of language's symbolism. By calling herself "clear," she aligns herself with the transparent, hoping that she, like God, will ultimately just be accepted, not interpreted. But of course Easty is on trial, and the express purpose of her "examination" is that she be "examined." Her attempts at transparency and finality are foiled over and over again. First of all, within her very declaration of innocence, she lapses into performative discourse. "If it was my last time" is in fact preceded by an implied "as." By acting "as if," Easty creates a slippage between her "real" self (who is not speaking for the last time) and her performed self (who is). This slippage ironically produces the very performance that the statement itself tries in vain to obliterate. In addition, her statement of clear innocence is followed by an almost ridiculous series of repetitions.

When asked if she is sure that Mary Easty was the woman who bewitched her, Ann Putnam "said that was the woman, it was like her, & she told me her name" (Boyer and Nissenbaum, *Papers*, 289). Easty's guilt rests on her being "like" the woman who bewitched Putnam and her sharing a "name" with the guilty witch. Suddenly, her clear innocence is retracted by an accusation based on association. Next, it is reported that Easty's "hands were clincht together, & then the hands of Mercy Lewis was clincht" (Boyer and Nissenbaum, *Papers*, 289). The judges then exclaim, "Look now you hands are open, her hands are open" (Boyer and Nissenbaum, *Papers,* 289). The copy-catted actions are seen as additional proof of Easty's consort with the devil. Despite her attempts to make her words transparent, Easty finds that there is no way for her to escape the associative and performative traps that continually remove her from purity, from godliness, and from innocence.

"What do you say to this?" Easty is asked at the conclusion of her examination. "Why God will know," she responds, trying, once more, to locate a final determination — even if it be in heaven — which would end the doubt about her piety. But as if to mock her attempts at this finality, the examiner retorts: "Nay God knows now" (Boyer and Nissenbaum, *Papers*, 289). The retort suggests that God's ultimate and transparent pardon is a fallacy, that instead God's determination is manifested through the examination itself. God, then, is yanked by the judge out of the realm of the singular, and into the realm of the repetitive. Even the repetitive sound of the two statements ("Why God will know"/"Nay God knows now") reinforces the idea that for the Salem magistrates, the only godly determination that can yield from the examinations is solidly part of language's earthly play. But of course, there is an end to the doubt about Easty's innocence; it comes not with her pardon but with her execution. Only in death can she achieve the finality that she struggled for during the trials. Does death at last make her transparent? I would argue that it both does and does not. On the one hand, her hanging frees her from the copy-catting, from the associative accusations, from the drama of the trial. But on the other hand, her death, ordered by the court of Oyer and Terminer, does not determine her guilt as much as it does determine *that she could not determine her innocence.* Her failure to stand — like God — outside of the accusations that circled around her in the end led to her death. She hanged as a symbol for her failure to be transparent, for her failure to be anything but a *symbol.*

Repetition appears in numerous other examinations. Consider this exchange between Tituba and Judge Hathorne:

"Titibe what evil spirit have you familiarity with"
"none"
"why do you hurt these children"
"I do not hurt them ... 4 women sometimes hurt the children...."
"what did they say to you"
"they said hurt the children"
"and did you hurt them"
"no ... they tell me if I will not hurt the children they will hurt me"
"but did you not hurt them"
"yes, but I will hurt them no more" [Boyer and Nissenbaum, *Papers,*748].

Here, the repeated asking of whether or not she hurt the children produces different responses each time. Tituba reverses her answer, saying at first that she did not hurt them, and then changing her answer and saying that she did. On its own, this might seem like a simple case of bullying on the part of the intimidating Judge Hathorne, but the patterns in her testimony suggest that repetition is more than just a tactic to elicit confessions. An interesting phenomenon develops throughout her examination, as Tituba repeatedly claims to see what her accusers say they saw. "Did you not see Sarah good upon elisabeth Hubbar last Saturday?" she is asked. Tituba replies, "I did see her set a wolfe upon her to afflict her[.] the persons with this maid did say that shee did complain of a wolf[.] she furder said that shee saw a cat with good at another time" (Boyer and Nissenbaum, *Papers*, 749). Tituba confesses not so much what it is that she herself saw, but what she heard the accusers and their friends saw. The final sentence above ("she furder said...") is attributed in the transcripts to Tituba, but it seems more likely that this is not actually what Tituba herself said, but the description of what she said offered by the reporter, Ezekiel Cheever. The uncertainty readers must have about who owns these words mirrors the general uncertainty in the testimony about where the confession originates: with Tituba or with her accusers.

While Tituba confessed her guilt through repetition, others of the accused asserted their innocence in similar ways. Sarah Good, we are told, answers her charges "in a very wicked, spitfull manner reflecting and retorting aganst the authority with base and abusive words and many lies" (Boyer and Nissenbaum, *Papers*, 357). Her "reflecting and retorting" suggest that she takes her cues on what to say from that which is said to her. And the emphasis that the reporter (once again Ezekiel Cheever) places on her "lies" (though no lies are clearly revealed in the transcript) suggests that there is a core truth — presumably a confession — that Good refuses to reveal. While Tituba manufactured her confession out of the accusations against her, Sarah Good apparently uses the accusations to manufacture her plea for innocence. Though the "reflecting and retorting" is not recorded,[12] we get a sense of how this might have worked from the early parts of Good's examination. Here, Hathorne questions the accused witch about her "muttering":

"What is it that you say when you goe muttering away from persons houses"
"if I must tell I will tell"
"doe tell us then"
"if I must tell I will tell, it is the commandments I may say my commandments I hope"
"what commandment is it"
"if I must tell you I will tell, it is a psalm" [Boyer and Nissenbaum, *Papers*, 357].

The repetition of "if I must tell I will tell" acts as a refrain, which Good invokes over and over again. The refrain draws attention to the idea that

Good's responses are produced by the questions that elicit them. In effect, Good suggests that what she says is not so much the truth as it is *what is required by the court*. This idea is reinforced when she switches her answer from "commandment" to "psalm"; she knows that telling the truth about what she muttered is not half as important as finding an answer that the court considers credible and pious. Finally, by claiming that her mutterings are prayerful, Good not only absolves herself of witchcraft, but also uses the very religion she is accused of abandoning as her alibi. If the project of the court of Oyer and Terminer is to hear and to *determine*, Good foils this by suggesting that all determinations are based not on truthful testimony, but on a cat-and-mouse game of playful rhetoric. The "reflection" that occurs here is not that of a woman looking inward to acknowledge the true state of her soul, but that of a woman mirroring the desires of her examiners, and in doing so, foiling those examiners' attempts to determine whether or not she is "truly" guilty.

But of course, Sarah Good, like Mary Easty, was ultimately hanged for witchcraft. The deaths of these witches, though convicted, is not so much about conviction as it is about the need to alleviate lingering doubts about their guilt. This brings us to one of the more curious and infamous characteristics of the Salem witch trials: that most confessed witches were spared, while most of the hanged maintained their innocence until their executions. In 1692 Salem, confession functioned as a validation for both the court and Puritan faith. Confession meant that examiners were effectively eliciting the truth and that Satan was being exposed. In an unsuccessful attempt to elicit confession from Nehemiah Abbott Jr., Judges Hathorne and Corwin tell him, "If you will confess the truth, we desire nothing else that you may not hide your guilt, if you are guilty, and therefore confess it so" (Boyer and Nissenbaum, *Papers*, 49). In many ways, this was the literal truth. Oyer and Terminer desired little else than confession. Even repentance is rarely mentioned in the transcripts. Once an accused witch confessed, it was almost automatically presumed that s/he would thereafter be free from the devil's grasp. After Tituba's confession, her accusers claim that they are no longer tormented. "As soon as she began to confess," testifies Elizabeth Hubbard, "she left ofe hurting me" (Boyer and Nissenbaum, *Papers*, 756). Ann Putnam similarly claims, "Senc she confessed she has hurt me but little" (Boyer and Nissenbaum, *Papers*,

756). Even Samuel Parris notes the effectiveness of confession at ending Satanic affliction: "The aboves'd afflicted persons were grievously distressed until the said Indian began to confess & then they were immediately all quiet the rest of the said Indian womans examination" (Boyer and Nissenbaum, *Papers*, 756–67).

A December 1692 Bill "against Conjuration, Witchcraft and Dealing with Evil and Wicked Spirits" suggests that confession was appropriate enough punishment for consorting with the devil. The Bill calls for convicted witches to "stand openly upon the pillory by the space of Six houres, and there shall openly confess his or her Error and offence, which said offence shall be written in Capitall Letters & placed upon the breast of said offender" (Mass. Archives, Vol. 135, No. 68–69; reproduced in Boyer and Nissenbaum, *Papers*, 886). Here, the confession functions as the punishment for the crime, and like Hester Prynne's scarlet letter, the confessor's badge of shame marks the witch as guilty. This marker serves to make visible that which was previously invisible; confession is chiefly about articulating a crime which can only be committed by those in hiding. As Tituba's confession proved, once witchcraft was named, affliction ceased. The witch's confession and badge are simultaneously punishment for the witch, validation for the court, and weaponry against Satan. What this suggests is that fear of affliction was not the greatest terror that existed for Salemites during the witch hunt. Instead, Salem was frightened of the unknown, the unnamed, and the doubtful. Instead of killing confessed, convicted witches to release themselves from the threat of affliction, Salem chose to kill those who maintained their innocence in the face of accusations against them. Those who could not be marked, who refused to stand upon the pillory (or in the meetinghouse) and confess openly, were seen as the real threat to Salem's security.

But if confession was meant to clarify and expose, its purpose was often subverted by those who made confessions. For example, Samuel Braybrook testified that Sarah Good told him that "shee would not owne her selfe to be a wicth unless she is provd one" (Boyer and Nissenbaum, *Papers*, 372). Though Good's decision not to confess unless she is proven guilty first may be a common legal strategy, in this situation it is a bit complicated. On the one hand, her hesitation to confess could be explained by the very real fear that Puritans would have felt at lying or aligning themselves with the devil; both might have drastic repercussions after death. But Sarah Good, according to all accounts, was not the kind of woman who took her piety seriously. Good demonstrates the way in which trial testimony produced confessions. Viewers of current-day television police dramas are familiar with the pattern in which cops solicit confessions — voluntary or coerced, true or false — from a weekly bevy of thugs and unfortunates. Just as these cop shows point out the active role of the officers in producing the confessions they acquire, Sarah Good suggests that the court of Oyer and Terminer plays a hand in producing the confessions of Salem witches.

In a petition for several accused and confessed witches, a group of concerned Salem citizens makes this suggestion: "It is probable, the fear of what the event might be, and the encouragement that it is said was suggested to them, that confessing was the only way to obtain favour, might be too powerful a temptation for timorous women to withstand" (Boyer and Nissenbaum, *Papers*, 619). There is much noteworthy ambiguity in this statement. "The event" could be either execution or demonic association. In other words, women might confess because they feared they would be killed if they did not *or* women might confess because they had genuine fear of their own associations with Satan.[13] Sarah Wilson, Sr., for example, testifies that "the afflicted persons crying out of her as afflicting them made her fearful of herself" (Boyer and Nissenbaum, *Papers*, 855). Did "timorous" women confess out of fear of death or fear of their own potentially demonic natures? Perhaps it was a little bit of both. As women tried to save their lives by confessing, they also may have been truly exposing their own fears about their sinfulness. This suggests that a confession might simultaneously be both a lie fabricated to elude death and a truth told to relieve their soul's guilt. Confession, we are told, is the only way to "obtain favour"; I think it too simplistic to reduce such "favour" to life. In many ways, confessors were rewarded by Salem's religious and legal communities. They were allowed to live; they were considered pious (after all, they chose to do the right thing when asked); they validated the court's power to persuade and keep the peace and the church's teachings about heaven and hell. Perhaps women were not only fighting for their lives by confessing, but were also fighting to gain the kind of favor that women were often denied in seventeenth-century New England: the favor that allowed them to be part of the rule-making structure, part of the religious order, part of Salem's status quo. And in Puritan culture, where belonging to the community was of paramount importance, confessing women, even if they faced embarrassment or even excommunication, were ultimately able to stay within the bounds of the community from which they took their solace, their safety, and their identities.

In this way, women who confessed had a particularly complicated relationship to Salem's power structure. They were guilty witches and pious goodwives. They were saving their lives by confessing to a crime punishable by death. They were validating the structures that persecuted them even as they freed themselves from persecution. Were confessed female witches "timorous," or were they savvy in the way in which they subverted the goals of Oyer and Terminer? By confessing, women used the witch hunt's aggression against itself, and managed to satiate the court and the church by using the examiners' questions and coercions as a road map to freedom. This confessional character becomes even more complex when confessed witches begin confessing *that their confessions were lies.* In a letter from prison, confessed witch Margaret Jacobs writes this to her father:

> The reason of my Confinement is this, I having, through the Magistrates Threatening, and my own Vile and Wretched Heart, confessed several things contrary to my Conscience and Knowledg.... But blessed be the Lord, he would not let me go on in my Sins, but in mercy I hope so my Soul would not suffer me to keep it in any longer, but I was forced to confess the truth of all before the Magistrates, who would not believe me [Boyer and Nissenbaum, *Papers*, 490].

Jacobs' confession is doubled, as she first confesses her guilt and then her innocence. Interestingly, both confessions are characterized as being produced from within Jacobs' interior soul. Though she passingly accuses the magistrates of coercing her confession, Jacobs calls her own "vile and wretched heart" the site of origination for her false confession; somehow, her heart produces testimony that contradicts her conscience and her knowledge. Then, in yet another reversal, she retracts her confession (and confesses the *real* story) when her internal voice can no longer be contained. What is stunning here is the number of times that Jacobs links her many confessions to an interior landscape, which she variably terms "knowledge," "conscience," "heart," and the "in[ner] truth." In Salem, confession was considered a triumph of the truth over a performance, but Jacobs' confessional gymnastics suggest that the natural, interior state of the soul is as changeable as any costume. Because "confession" refers both to Jacobs' initial testimony and her subsequent retraction, and because both "confessions" are said to stem from the *real, underlying* state of her own soul, it becomes impossible to delineate a true confession from a performed or falsified confession (and this does not presume that "performed" and "falsified" are the same).

In addition to these reversed confessions — when a confession of guilt turns to a confession of innocence — there are also several retracted confessions when a confession of guilt is explained away as an error. Several accused witches who were imprisoned with her testified that Mary Warren, an afflicted girl who became an accused witch, told them this: "When [she] was Aflicted [she] thought [she] saw the Apparission of A hundred persons: for Shee said hir Head was Distempered that Shee Could not tell what Shee Said, And the Said Mary told us that when Shee was well Againe Shee Could not Say that Shee saw any of Apparissons at the time Aforesaid" (Boyer and Nissenbaum, *Papers*, 803). When the affliction strikes, Warren cannot tell what she herself *says*, and when the affliction passes, she cannot say what she *saw*. This suggests that affliction causes a lack of control of speech, as if the affliction is not happening *to* the afflicted, but *within* her. Because she is internally altered, her perceptions are altered as well; this produces the effect of distrust of one's own experience of the external, ontological world. Warren's retraction (if it was actually made), which effectively deflates her previous testimony, suggests that affliction itself, which was by far the most pervasive manifestation of witchcraft in Salem, is a tautology: at the same time as it launches accusations, it also produces an afflicted person who cannot be trusted. Warren's retraction has less to do with her individual unreliability than it does with the quality of affliction itself as internalized and self-reflexive.[14]

Confession thus often collapses on itself, either by inverting and becoming a confession of innocence or by retracting and becoming a tautology. Even while invoking the rhetoric of truth, depth, soul, and reality, confession consistently retreats back into a play of surfaces. And surfaces are, of course, of central importance to the trial testimony. Much of the evidence offered up during the hearings relies on appearance. Though I will deal with "spectral evidence" in depth later in this chapter, "appearance," and the question of how outward looks are related to inner (if phantom) reality, is consistently debated throughout the trials. While implicating Sarah Wilds in her own occult excursions, Deliverance Hobbs is asked about the nature of her companion's participation. "Was it Goody Wild in body, or appearance?" ask the judges. "In appearance," responds Hobbs (Boyer and Nissenbaum, *Papers*, 422). What, we are provoked to ask, is the difference between "in body" and "in appearance"? Throughout the trials, doubt surfaces about whether or not one can reliably insist that a specific person's physical appearance is consistently the same as the person him/herself. Consider, for example, the arrest warrants, which are almost always worded like this one, for John Alden: "In their Maj'ties King William & Queen Maryes name [I] Authorize & Comand you forwith to Apprehend the body of the said John Alden" (Boyer and Nissenbaum, *Papers*, 51). Whatever does the afflicting, it is certain that it will be *bodies*, and not appearances, which stand trial in Salem. These two examples suggest that bodies are associated with a person's real identity, and that appearances are associated with a bewitched — or spectral — form, which may or may not be related to the real identity it impersonates.

But of course, much confusion ensues as trial participants try to sort out the bodies from the appearances. Ann Putnam testifies against Mary Bradbury, "I have seen mist. Bradbery or hir Apperance most grievously afflicting Timothy Swan and I beleve that Mis Bradbery is a most dreadfull wicth for sence she has been in prison she or hir Apperance has com to me and most greviously affected me" (Boyer and Nissenbaum, *Papers*, 121–22). Unless Putnam thinks that Bradbury has escaped from prison and then voluntarily returned there — on multiple occasions — it seems likely that Putnam is simply attempting to add credibility to her statement by testifying only to what she saw, and not to what significance her visions might have. In other words, she can claim to see what looks like Mary Bradbury without actually saying that Bradbury herself was present; this not only releases Putnam from charges of perjury should Bradbury be acquitted, but it also suggests that she is building a testimony based only on what can be factually determined. It may not be a fact that Bradbury was present in body, but it is certainly true (it could be argued) that Bradbury's appearance was there. This has the interesting effect of producing a hyper-attentiveness to fact while simultaneously reifying a distinction between appearance and reality. If there is a disjunction between what is real and what appears to be real (but isn't), then Putnam's insistence on precision in language seems to be an attempt to close this gap in her own testimony. By trying to make her words singular in meaning, Putnam works to align the signifiers she employs with the signifieds they represent, which is, of course, exactly what she raises doubts about as the issue relates to Bradbury. Over and over again in the trial testimony, participants struggle to tell the truth, to be clear, to follow the letter of the law, and yet over and over again, the very content of the testimony raises questions about the relationship of a sign to that which it intends to mark.

As a result of these questions and doubts, the denotative language of the trials, which strives hard to eliminate contradiction, often unintentionally lapses into a language of connotation. Consider this excerpt from the examination of Nehemiah Abbott, Jr., which is worth quoting at some length:

> This is the man say some [of the afflicted], and some say he is very like him. How did you know his name? He did not tell me himself, but other witches told me. Ann Putnam said, it is the same man, and then she was taken with a fit. Mary Walcot, is this the man? He is like him, I cannot say it is he. Mercy Lewis said it is not the man. They all agreed, the man had a bunch on his eyes. Ann Putnam, in a fit, said, be you the man? Ay, do you say you be the man? [Boyer and Nissenbaum, *Papers*, 49].

There are three key points worth making about this passage. First, the repetitive drone of "is this the man" calls attention both to the insurmountable doubt that exists over whether Abbott or his appearance is to blame *and* the desperate hunt for clarification and a final answer. The repetition suggests that the question cannot be suitably answered, but the content of the question works against this displacement, as it indicates that there is a simple yes or no answer lurking just after the question mark. Second, the attention in the passage to Abbott's name is intriguing; his name is raised as a potential way to lay to rest the doubts about whether or not Abbott is culpable. But, of course, the name issue just raises more doubt. Ann Putnam gets Abbott's name secondhand, as if to reinforce the idea that a name is always somewhat removed — even if only by the process of language itself— from the thing which it names. Not only might the secondhand information be flat-out wrong, but it also calls attention to how naming, like all attempts to reify or stabilize the ultimately ungraspable, fails to produce the certainty it desires. Third, Mary Warren's assertion that Abbott is *like* "the man" demonstrates how literal evidence in these trials often changes into simile. The juxtaposition of "like" with the definite article "the" shows the slippage between a referential, metaphorical, connotative language, and a precise, transparent, denotative language. Throughout the trials, the second kind of language is repeatedly revealed to be closer to the first kind than many of the participants might have hoped.

If there is a dubious relationship between the body and the appearance, there is also a question of how clothing and other bodily adornments relate to the bare naked truth. Clothes are used to implicate several of the alleged witches. Bridget Bishop is named by Samuel Gray as the woman who tormented a young child. He recognizes her when she returns to the scene of her crime: "Some tyme after within a weeke or less he did see the same Woman in the same Garb and Cloaths, that appeared to him as aforesaid, and althow he knew not her, nor her name before, Yett both by her Countenance and garb doth testifie that it was the same Woman that thay now Call Bridget Bishop Alias Oliver" (Boyer and Nissenbaum, *Papers*, 95). Here, the consistency of Bishop's clothing is nearly enough to cement her guilt. Richard Coman similarly recognizes Bishop for a witch: "S'd Bishop came in her Red paragon Bodys and the rest of her cloathing that she then did usually ware, and I knowing of her well also the garb she did use to goe in.did clearley and plainely know her" (Boyer and Nissenbaum, *Papers*, 102). Here, the accusers suggest that Bishop can be proven guilty based on her clothing. More specifically, what they need to prove is that she is the same woman who committed acts of witchcraft at an earlier time. Thus, the clothing is not so much an indicator of witchcraft as it is a sign of a stable, consistent identity. Outward appearance, then, is one of the main ways during the trials that identity was "identified."

Accused witch Martha Corey tries to use this to her advantage, but it backfires in an interesting way. Ann Putnam, her accuser, is asked to testify as to what Corey was wearing during her tormenting escapades. Putnam is unable to tell, claiming that Corey blinded her during the torment so that Putnam would be unable to provide proof. When Edward Putnam and Ezekiel Cheever visit Corey to investigate, Corey immediately asks them if Ann Putnam had been able to provide concrete testimony about what Corey had worn during the crimes: "We made her no answer to this at first," report Misters Cheever and Putnam, "Where upon shee asked us again with very great eagernes but does she tell you what cloathes I have on at which questions with that eagernes of mind. with which shee did aske made us to thinke of what An Putnam had told us before wee went to her" (Boyer and Nissenbaum, *Papers*, 261). In this rather confusing exchange, Corey's insistence that Ann Putnam should provide concrete proof of what Corey had been wearing is used against her as proof that she had intentionally prevented her clothing from being noted by her accuser. Here, clothing is both the defining crucible that could unequivocally condemn Corey *and* the phantom proof that cannot be obtained. This is very much how clothing functions throughout the trials: as both an indication of fixed identity — and therefore guilt — and as a mark of that proof, that certainty, which is always hidden, elusive, or unknowable.

Of course, the quintessential example of how appearance during the trials functions as both concrete, stable, and true *and* intangible, fluctuating, and duplicitous is in the question of whether or not the devil can appear in the shape of an innocent person. Accused witches, many of whom probably believed that the afflicted were telling the truth, often suggested that the devil might take their shapes to wreak havoc on Salem and its inhabitants. Rebecca Nurse, at a loss as to how to explain why so many young girls accuse her, testifies, "I cannot help it, the Devil may appear in my shape" (Boyer and Nissenbaum, *Papers*, 587). Though they tried to resist, some of the accused were simply appropriated in body by Satan. Elizabeth Johnson testifies, "[The Devil] awaked me & S'd he would goe and afflict in my Shape but I never Sett my hand to his book" (Boyer and Nissenbaum, *Papers*, 500). The accused raise the possibility that their shapes are duplicatable, copied by the devil for his own use. This again suggests that identity, which might seem to be attached to outward appearance, cannot reliably be determined by observation. Like clothing, all properties of appearance — even countenance — can be replicated by the devil. Again, appearance becomes both the standard of proof and the red herring. This paradoxical quality of appearance parallels the paradoxical nature of the testimonies given by the accused. While some, such as Nurse and Johnson, are unequivocal in asserting their innocence and their utter befuddlement about Satan's use of their personas, others of the accused seem to play with the liminal state which they inhabit, a space between knowing agent of the devil and victim of identity theft. William Barker, Sr., confesses to witchcraft, saying, "I being at Cart a Saturday last, all the day, of Hay and English Corn, the Devil brought my Shape to Salem, and did afflict M[artha] S[prague] ... by clitching my hand; and a Sabbath day my Shape afflicted A[bigail] M[artin]" (Boyer and Nissenbaum, *Papers*, 69). This confession, reminiscent of the doubled confessions discussed above, attempts to accept guilt even as it exonerates Barker because he was more a dupe of the devil than an active agent of Satan.

Abigail Hobbs offers up a similarly paradoxical testimony. After admitting that she "pinch't" Mercy Lewis and Ann Putnam, Hobbs is questioned by the judges:

> "How did you pinch them, do you goe in your own person to them?"
> "No."
> "Doth the Devil go for you?"
> "Yes."
> "And what doth he take, your spirit with them?"
> "No. I am as well as at other times: but the Devil has my consent, and goes and hurts them" [Boyer and Nissenbaum, *Papers*, 407].

Here, Hobbs explains how the devil's soul-appropriation works. Even as he co-opts Hobbs' body and will, she remains fully herself. Hobbs effectively makes it impossible to decipher where her "real" identity rests: with the devil or in her original body. As she doubles both her body and her will, she redefines "self." "She" is no longer a stable, singular person, but a montage of appearance and will which can be replicated and deployed like a performance in a play. Just as a character on stage is both fully the actor and fully *not* the actor,[15] Hobbs' devilish incarnation is both Abigail Hobbs herself and *not Abigail Hobbs at all*.

This performative identity, associated with the devil and ambiguously connected to the "original" persona that it copies, is termed "spectral" during the hearings. Whether or not "spectral evidence" could be used to condemn an accused witch was one of the central controversies of the Salem witch trials. Because there were so many questions about whether or not the accused were guilty of conspiring with the devil or whether they were, like the afflicted, just innocent victims, magistrates and accusers often tried to establish a direct link between spectral evidence and physical proof. Even before spectral evidence came under direct attack, one can see the attempts being made to turn the spectral into the concrete. During the examination of Bridget Bishop, the following testimony is recorded: "Mary Walcot said that her brother Jonathan stroke [Bishop's] appearance & she saw that he had tore her coat in striking, & she heard it tare. Upon some search in the Court, a rent that seems to answere what was alledged was found" (Boyer and Nissenbaum, *Papers*, 83). There is a concerted effort here to reify the spectral into the physical, as Bishop's "appearance" is proven to exist by the tear in the coat of the actual Bridget Bishop. Of course, the evidence complicates matters more than it does simplify them. Does the torn coat prove that an appearance and a real body are indistinguishable? The language of the testimony ("seems," "alledged") suggests instead that doubts linger, or possibly that the tear *seems* to *answer* the accusations, but that in *reality,* this is just coincidence. Also, the fact that the "rent" exists in a coat reminds us of all of the attention to clothing and superficial disguise throughout the trials. Though the coat is offered up as evidence to Bishop's stable identity (i.e., that she is a witch all the time), its status as a covering and the language of the report strengthen the suggestion, raised throughout the examinations, that there might be a difference between the real Bridget Bishop and a performed and costumed Witch Bishop.

But as much as this difference constantly injects itself into the magistrates' efforts to condemn the accused, there is also another implication raised by the spectral-physical debate. Though doubts often surface about whether an accused witch's appearance is the same as her real physical body, doubts also surface about whether these accused witches even have real physical bodies at all. Perhaps more than our modern minds can truly conceive, that there was a very deep fear on the part of seventeenth-century Salemites that physical reality was becoming harder to define. Consider, for example, one of the main complaints about many of the accused: that they tormented the afflicted and then removed — as if by magic — the physical evidence of that torment. The transcript of William Stacy's testimony against Bishop reads: "Being gone about 6 Rod from her the said Bishop; with a small Load in his Cart: suddenly the off Wheels Slumped or Sunk downe into a hole upon Plain ground, that this Depon't was forced to gett one to help him gett the wheel out afterwards this Depon't went Back to look for said hole where his wheel sunk in but could not find any hole" (Boyer and Nissenbaum, *Papers*, 93). This passage is interesting both for the way Bishop allegedly makes physical evidence disappear *and* for the fact that the physical evidence is itself a "hole." Metaphorically, Bishop's "hole" represents the absence of ontology that repeatedly appears (or fails to appear) throughout the transcripts.

Ontology implies a relationship between what *is* and what is *articulated*. That is, what I perceive and simultaneously name (to myself or to others) aligns with what others have perceived and named. Without the articulation through language (the sign) of the signified "thing," ontology becomes, at the least, irrelevant (and at the most non-existent). Ontology depends upon a script, since reality is produced through a series of associative processes which link signifieds to commonly understood signs. Ontology is related to linearity and logic in the sense that all three functions depend upon a pre-conceived — or scripted — notion of what "comes next."[16] But just as ontology — the connection between signifieds and the signifiers that stand for them — gets collapsed throughout the trials, so, too, do logic, linearity, and narrativity get collapsed. Over and over again, the alleged witches are accused of particular "crimes" that make absolutely no sense at all. One example arises during the case of Sarah Good. She is accused by Susannah Sheldon and two men who rescued Sheldon of tying up the afflicted woman and biting her. This alone makes some sense. But the accusations continue: "We furder testifie that in this time there was a broome carried a way out of the house in visibble to us and put in a apple tree two times and a shirt once and a milke tube once was carried out of the house three poles from the house into the woods" (Boyer and Nissenbaum, *Papers*, 371). This testimony is striking for the way that it takes ordinary household objects and inserts them into inappropriate or unexpected contexts. In fact, the objects mentioned — a broom, a shirt, and a milk tube — could not be any more mundane or domestic. And the apple tree and the woods are both familiar, common settings. But the placement of the broom in the tree and the milk tube and shirt in the woods detaches the items from the household, which is the expected context for each. This scenario, and many others like it which arise during the trials, illustrates how spectral evidence fails to conform to normal standards of context. Context is so crucial since it, like the signifier in the signifier/signified connection, is what lends meaning to the items it contains. By taking familiar objects out of context, witches once again seem to collapse the very fabric of Salem's reality. The fact that these events are offered up in testimony immediately following the (literal) biting accusations shows that in Salem, it is considered a crime akin to assault to destabilize the mechanisms through which the world can be decoded and explained.[17]

A final example of spectral evidence being reified into physical proof concerns the relationship of the flesh to the spirit. Accused witches were often given physical examinations to determine if their bodies betrayed any signs of demonic possession. A team of physical examiners makes this report: "The first three, Namely: Bishop: Nurse: procter, by dilligent search have discovered apreternathurall Excresence of flesh between the pudendum and Anus much like to Tetts & not usuall in women." Of more concern to the team is the fact that "upon a second search about 3 or 4 houres distance, did find the said Brigett Bishop alias Oliver, in a clear & free state from any p'eternaturall Excresence, as formerly seen by us alsoe Rebecah Nurse in stead of that Excresence w'thin Mnetioned it appears only as a dry skin without sense, & and as for Elizabeth procter which Excresence like a tett red & fresh, not any thing appears" (Boyer and Nissenbaum, *Papers*, 107–8). Extra "teats" were considered to be places where the devil could take suck, and finding one did not bode well for the accused. But here, the teats appear and then disappear. Like the hole that Bishop allegedly made disappear (can a *hole* disappear?), the witches' teats function as an indication that facts and evidence cannot be relied upon. The body, which was once set up as the opposite to an unstable spectral identity, is now revealed to be changeable even in its most naked state.

But if physical examinations sometimes foiled the court's attempts to mark the bodies of witches, trial testimony often attempted to provide physical proof that bodies could indicate and reveal who is a witch. Joseph and Mary Herrick provide this testimony against Sarah Good:

Elizabeth Hubbard one of the Afflected parsons Complaned that Sarah Good came and afflected hir ... and Samuell Sibley that was one that was attending of Eliza Hubbard stroke good on the Arme as Elizabeth Hubbard said.... I took notis of Sarah Good in the morning and one of hir Armes was Blooddy from a little below the Elbow to the wrist: and I also took notis of her armes on the night before and then there was no signe of blood on them [Boyer and Nissenbaum, *Papers,* 370].

This account suggests both that witches do *not* bleed like normal women, *and* that witches bleed *when they are* normal women. In other words, Good, the passage claims, does not bleed when Sibley strikes her. It is not until the next morning, when she is no longer afflicting Hubbard as a specter but is instead back to her "normal" self, that the blood appears on her arm. Perhaps the witches are immune from physical fallibility when they are specters, but when they return to their own physical bodies, they resume their bodies' mortal properties. This paradoxically suggests that specters and bodies are distinct (each one responds differently to a cut) and that they are indistinct (if you cut one, the other will bleed). This is perhaps the closest one can get to delineating the connection between the spectral and the physical during the trials: like two sides of a single coin, they are not one and they are one.

The trial transcripts wrestle over and over again with these questions: What are the facts of the events at hand? What constitutes hard evidence? Who produces an affliction? What is the relationship between God and the devil? What constitutes a pure confession? What connection does a "body" have to a "specter?" Interestingly, these questions are also intimately tied to the methodological questions that accompany any historical inquiry. The primary source documents from 1692 suggest that repetition and copies, theatricality and performance, and ambiguity and parody complicate the legal task of deciphering witchcraft. Similarly, the very nature of the primary source evidence in this case — duplicated, biased, and fraught with fiction as it is — should compel researchers to wrestle with the deferrals and distance that separates any historian from the past. In this examination of the transcripts, I have rejected objective methodological standards of the kind advocated by Felt and Hockett in favor of a more interpretive process of the kind supported by, for example, Natalie Zemon Davis, and my attention to performativity in the trial texts themselves is consistent with my attention to the performative nature of my own investigative project. The Salem transcripts reveal an unstable, fluctuating definition of "witchcraft," of "God," of the "self." And in a larger sense, they question the efficacy of any hunt for "truth." Of course, many people in 1692 Salem were put to death for witchcraft; the hunt for "truth" was, at least in some legal sense of the time, successful. But the transcripts reveal that this quest was a fantasy: a fantasy of wholeness that could unite body and specter, deed and desire. Within the primary texts, the fantasy gets played out as powerful, seductive, *and* often ineffectual. As the fantasy is revealed time and time again — through confessions and testimonial theatrics — to be a performance, it loses credibility but gains an anxious momentum. Like most historical projects, the Salem transcripts reveal through the course of their quest that the end point is just another beginning. As categories of analysis are established and explored, they are continually challenged and redefined. Even if the witch gets hanged and the historian explains what happened, the "truth," embedded in its "primary source," remains hopefully unstable. Throughout the years since 1692, even the most traditional of historians have realized that Salem's story remains open to interpretation. The next chapter will examine the ways in which historians have rediscovered and/or rewritten Salem's past, and how the fantasy of wholeness and the instability of truth have conflicted in Salem historiography over the past three centuries.

TWO

From Shards to Meanings
Historians Make Sense
of the Trials

The time, 1692. The place, Salem Village, Massachusetts. The role of historian and the role of the playwright both begin with the establishment of setting. As historians have written their texts on Salem, they have, in effect, created sets, scripts, characters. They have asked readers to suspend their disbelief and enter with them into a past that, however recent, is, in reality, irretrievably lost. In the accounts I will discuss below, historians have chosen different ways to bring the past to light. Some have used rhetoric, while some have used science. There has been sleight of hand and remorseful honesty. In addition to examining the content — what do these writers have to say about *what happened* in Salem? — this chapter is as much examining the methodologies employed in these accounts. Within the series of arguments made by multiple historians about the events of Salem's past, a shifting notion of what it means to look back at all begins to take shape. Ultimately, even in their vast disagreements over the particulars, these writers seem to be interested in the same dramatic quest: to seek out and define not only an era, but also a historical process. As they collide with each other and with the ultimate unknowability that haunts them all, they invent sometimes playful, sometimes horrifying, always creative methods to collapse the distance that separates them from the truth they seek. These methods, which — unlike truth itself — are representations, are what comprise Salem's history, and what, more than witches and ministers, keep the Salem story alive.

Cotton Mather and Robert Calef: A Foundational Dialectic

Cotton Mather's *The Wonders of the Invisible World* was one of the first major written historical accounts of the Salem witch trials. Mather, who is known by most current-day scholars as the great defender of the trials, was pressured into writing his account by the turning tide in Salem, a tide that was flowing towards an embarrassed, even horrified, reconsideration of the recent executions, and a tide that threatened to emasculate Mather's own potency and credibility as a religious leader with a direct line to God.[1] From the beginning, Mather's *Wonders* was less a monologue produced from the origin of raw conviction than it was a dialogue, a response to charges leveled by a changing political landscape. *Wonders* was first published in Boston in 1693, and though it has served — perhaps appropriately — as the document that cemented Mather's historical reputation as a rabid witch hunter and a defender of the Salem court, as Bernard Rosenthal puts it, "That characterization misses his complexity.... There is more than one way to misconstrue what Mather was about in his defense of the trials" (147). While Rosenthal argues passionately for Mather's well-intentioned and earnest religious fervor, it may be more productive to consider the multiple ways that Mather can be *construed*, rather than just "correcting" perceived historical errors. Though Mather may have been both well intentioned and sorely misguided, what is most interesting about *Wonders* is the way that Mather wrestles with the complexities and paradoxes of some central theoretical questions from the trials: What is the nature of truth? How does the devil relate to God? And what are the connections between witches and historians? Unlike Rosenthal, this chapter is less interested in redeeming Mather's reputation than in exploring the ways in which his text complicates the central issues involved in the trials.

Even though Mather's stance has generally been understood to be uncomplicated and overly zealous,[2] his part in establishing the "origins" of Salem historiography reveals a deeper level of complexity in his position. The Salem histories emerged from a central schism between apologists and critics of the trials, and both "sides" of the debate reflect this divisionist beginning. Mather's *Wonders* begins with an "Author's Defence," which sets Mather up as an opponent. The question is who or what does Mather oppose (and who or what opposes him)? Mather opens:

> This, as I remember, the learned Scribonius, who reports, that One of his Aquaintance, devoutly making his Prayers on the behalf of a Person molested by Evil Spirits, received from those Evil Spirits an horrible Blow over the Face: And I may my self expect not few or small Buffetings from Evil Spirits, for the Endeavours wherewith I am now going to encounter them [v].

On the one hand, it is clear that Mather sets himself up in opposition to the Devil himself. "I countermine the whole plot of the Devil," he writes (vi). But Mather also conflates the evil of the Devil with the evil of those who had begun speaking out against the trials. "I am far from Insensible," he writes, " that at this extraordinary time of the Devils coming down in great Wrath upon us, there are too many Tongues and Hearts thereby set on fire of Hell; that the various Opinions about the Witchcrafts which of later Time have troubled *us*, are maintained by some with such Fury, as if *they* could never be sufficiently stated, unless written in the Liquor wherewith Witches use to write their Covenants" (v, emphasis mine). Here, Mather sets up the trials as a dichotomy between good and evil; this was a self-evident dichotomy to seventeenth-century Puritans who each Sunday (and often more than that) heard sermons about their duty to counter Salem's attacks with piety, religious conviction, and moral righteousness. But Mather also sets up the trials' *histories* as a dichotomy between "us" and "them," between good supporters of Mather and those evil townspeople who oppose him. For Mather, the unfolding debate is not just between God and the devil, but between *representations* of good and evil, representations that can be consciously deployed and rebutted by Salem's earthly inhabitants.

Robert Calef, Mather's counterpart in establishing this initial historical dialectic, underscores this dichotomized way of framing the Salem histories from the very first word of his major account of the trials, published in response to Mather in 1700. Indeed, his title, *More Wonders of the Invisible World*, comes — sarcastically — from Mather's own text; Calef's book is a collection of essays, letters, and testimony, much of which is not written by Calef, but by Mather and others who support the trials. Calef critiques the trials by presenting a dialogue between himself and his opponents, and by explicating — often line by line — the faulty logic employed by the Matherites. In one of *More Wonder*'s letters (here, to Thomas Brattle), Calef writes this about Mather: "I have sent him letters of quotations out of those Books, to know how much of them he will abide by, for I thought it hard to affix their Natural consequences till he had opportunity to explain them" (30–31). These letters, many of which appear in *More Wonders*, use Mather's own words to weaken the case for the trials' credibility. While Calef subscribes to the same notion as Mather of a dichotomized debate, he is more interested than Mather in discrediting his opponent's argument from the inside out. But both authors include within their own positions a sense that the issue on the table has more than one side, more than a single representable perspective.

Though this paradigm seems not overly complex, it gets complicated by the association of dichotomy and instability with witches and the devil. Mather quotes William Perkins' criteria for discovering witches, one of which reads as follows: "If the party examined be Unconstant, or contrary to himself, in his deliberate Answers, it argueth a Guilty Conscience" (Mather 15). On the one hand, this maxim simply suggests that someone caught lying on the stand should be looked upon with suspicion. But more broadly, it alludes to the anxiety about instability that lurks below the surface of the spectral evidence issues raised during the testimony. Can witches shape-shift? Can they become invisible? Can their bodies be one place while their spirits are another? This kind of "unconstancy," when the self is literally "contrary to [it]self," was, as was discussed in Chapter One, one of the major fears that Puritans had about the devil and his minions. Spectral inconstancy and the dichotomized early historical accounts of Salem's witch hunt have much in common. While both Mather and Calef seem to uphold an "inconstant" historiography, one that fluctuates across a dialogic axis, both also seem highly anxious about such an unsettled history. Several times, Mather alludes to his discomfort with the debate-like form that the Salem history takes; he mentions over and over again his distaste for the word "sides" to describe the two poles of the historical accounts. He writes, "On the other side (if I must again use the word *Side*, which yet I hope to live to blot out) there are very worthy Men, who are not a little dissatisfied at the Proceedings in the Prosecution of this Witchcraft" (12). Even as he affirms the credibility of his opposition, Mather highlights his desire to quell such opposition, and to shift the Salem history from a debate to a monologue.

Calef similarly reveals his own anxiety about the history's dichotomized framework. Unlike Mather, who hopes to use the persuasiveness of his own arguments to eclipse the arguments of his detractors, Calef works to deconstruct Mather's arguments to show their limitations. Most notably, Calef is concerned with Mather's failure to cite specific scripture to back up his claims about the characteristics of witches and their relationship to the devil: "The not bringing Scripture to prove these [arguments], is a sufficient demonstration there is none" (Calef 32). This grammatically challenging declaration suggests on one level that Mather's failure to cite scripture — in this case to prove that witches can commission the devil to kill for them — means that no appropriate scripture exists on this topic. On another level, though, the grammatical ambiguity can also suggest that there is not only no scripture ("none"), but no *argument* ("none"). Calef considers the Bible to be the literal word of God, and he continually asserts that if the Bible does not provide proof for a certain argument, then that argument is null and void. And by "null and void," I *do* mean, literally, non-existent. Even more compellingly, Calef uses the lack of scripture to make his *own* words as stable and authoritative as those of the Bible. On March 18, 1695, Calef sent a letter to a group of local ministers asking them to provide scriptural evidence in support of the trials' use of spectral evidence. In a subsequent letter to minister Samuel Willard, Calef writes that he sent the letter "praying them if I erred to shew it me by Scripture, I have as yet had no Answer to, either by word or writing, which makes me gather that they are approved of as Orthodox, or at least that they have such Foundations, as that none are willing to manifest any opposition to them" (Calef 38). Here, the lack of scripture acts as evidence of Calef's own orthodoxy. He establishes himself as original, and casts his opponents as derivative and, thus, erased. Just as the Bible is a work cast in stone, a book whose words are original, incontrovertible, and literal, Calef's words are presented as the first and the only authority on the trials. Mather's and Calef's discomfort with the polarized debate is interesting, as both were educated men who would have been familiar with public oratory, debate, and rhetoric as fields of study.[3] Their efforts to "win" their respective arguments might appear to be just an extension of their training in theological and philosophical disputations, but their desire to stress *not* their positional superiority, but their utter *lack* of credible opposition, demonstrates that where witchcraft was concerned, debate did not provide the access to certainty that was needed to quell the growing uneasiness about the place of God and truth in Salem.

But Mather and Calef cannot quell the emerging paradox. Even as the first two major witch trial historians work to establish their own historical accounts as factual and uncontestable, they both also end up reifying the debate's ultimate dichotomy and revealing an intense anxiety about the instability inherent in their quest to present the definitive history of what happened. This anxiety is manifested not only in Mather's attempts to eradicate the "other side" and Calef's attempts to turn his history into a commandment-like stone tablet, but also in both authors' attention to the question of the "original." The trial testimony that we have already examined clearly illustrates the problems inherent in locating an original or seminal point in the Salem story, and Mather and Calef similarly reveal a fear that corruption has infiltrated Salem, supplanting what once was a pure and fundamental utopia. "New England was a true Utopia," writes Mather, "But, alas, the Children and Servants of those old Planters must needs afford many degenerate Plants" (6). Mather asserts that as New England generations pass the torch down, the colony corrupts, spiraling away from its "true" core and "degenerating" into copies, offspring, or mutations of the original. Mather spends much time contemplating this corruption, and trying to determine just what has caused the degeneration of the society that he once respected. He wavers between blaming the devil and blaming the people of Salem themselves. "An Army of Devils is horribly broke in upon the place which is the Center," writes Mather, "and, after a sort, the First-born of our English Settlements" (7). Here, it is the devil who has polluted Salem, which is figured as a center, a core, of foundational (or "first-born") English values. Even though, as a colony, Salem is in some ways already copied from — already the offspring of— England, Mather makes it clear that before the devil's encroachment, Salem had claim to some kind of elemental purity that removed it from the charges of degeneration. But is Mather so convinced that it is only the devil who is to blame for Salem's unlucky corruption?

"Were it not for what is IN us," writes Mather, "for my part, I should not fear a thousand Legions of Devils" (11). The devil, he explains, "fetches up the Dirt which before lay still at the bottom of our sinful Hearts" (10). Mather suggests, perhaps unintentionally, that the corruption of Salem is due, at least in part, to corruption which was always already present ... even in the hearts of those perfect founders of the town, the "old Planters." The utopian vision of the original Salem, a vision that pitted a holy settler against a howling heathen, begins to falter. "It is a vexing Eye-sore to the Devil," writes Mather, "that our Lord Christ should be known, and own'd and preached in this howling Wilderness" (37). What was once a pure (if oxymoronic) English colony has now been recast as a "wilderness," and the originally cultivated plantation becomes a land devoid of civilization. Christ has become not the fundamental genesis, not the mark of the unmarked, pure Salem colony, but the over-written or represented mark upon a once demonic landscape, a landscape that, howling and wild, preceded Christ and the Christians. "Such is the descent of the Devil at this day upon our selves," laments Mather, "that I may truly tell you, The Walls of the whole World are broken down!" (40). Mather seems to imply that the borders that once held the devil out are now porous and impotent; in addition, these borders no longer support a world view that separates the corrupt from the pure. In this new world, the devil is not outside, not apart: he is within.

While Mather mourns the loss of a pure Salem utopia and clings to a hope that the devil can be cast out and corruption can be eradicated, he simultaneously suggests that utopia's unspoiled holiness is a fallacy or an always-lost fantasy. Calef, like Mather, tries in vain to reinstate a lost, original, uncorrupted Salem. He writes to Brattle, "The Flames we have seen threatning the utter extirpation of the Country, must own their Original to these dangerous Errors (if not heresies) which if they remain Unextinguished, may and most likely will be acted over again" (33). If the flames of evil that threaten Salem derive from the errors that Mather makes by drifting away from the word of God, then Mather is set up as the cause of the corruption. The emphasis on "acted over again" demonstrates the performative quality of these corruptions; unlike the word of God, Mather's diatribes on witchcraft are unoriginal, multiplicitous, and unauthoritative: more script than scripture. Calef goes so far as to say that "lying wonders" are the "principle cause of the delusions," punning on

Mather's (and unwittingly on his own) part in fanning the flames (4). But the diction Calef uses suggests a subtle tension between the pure country and the repetitive burning heresies. The heresies are at once derivative (they are perversions of the right word of God) and original (they are the fundamental source for the corruption). Salem is threatened with "utter extirpation" (a complete annihilation) and with unending performance (over and over again). What this suggests is not that a pure, holy Salem stands in stark opposition to a corrupted, demonic Salem, but that the original and the performed are difficult to separate. For Mather and for Calef, originality functions as a fantasy, an overwhelming desire that is ultimately always deferred or lost. Both men seek a finite, monologic, uncorrupted solution to Salem's devilish problems. Both men seek to use their own historical accounts to shore up this solution. And both men ultimately reveal the multiplicitous, dialogic, and derivative nature of both Salem's ties to the devil and its ties to its own history.

But Mather and Calef do differ substantially in the way that they characterize the devil himself. Mather wants to be sure that his readers know that he believes in the almighty power of God. He consistently makes reference to the idea that the devil is not outside of God's law. "The devil cannot come at us, except in some sence according to Law," he writes (Mather 8). According to Mather, the devil appears in court before God and pleads to be allowed to torment and kill the living; if he can convince God that the human subject in question is "hypocritical" or "disobedi-ent," God might allow the devil to come down as a destroyer (9). Already we can begin to see the problems here. Do people somehow already hold the devil's corruptions inside of them, even before they are afflicted or co-opted? And in this relationship between God and the devil, is the devil autonomous, or does he act out God's will?

Mather tries hard to keep the devil on God's leash. "[The] Mighty Hand of ... God ... indeed has the Devil in a Chain," he writes, "but has horribly lengthened on the Chain!" (44). In fact, Mather's metaphorical chain has lengthened so much that it begins to look as if the devil has bro-ken free altogether. "Where will the Devil show most Malice," he asks rhetorically, "but where he is hated, and hated most?" (5). So much for due process, and for God's wise decisions to punish the already corrupt. Mather, at the same time as he tries to assert the devil's obedience to God, simultaneously demonstrates a palpable fear that the devil has gone out of control. But the devil's malicious and uncontrollable behavior has an even more disturbing characteristic: it seems to spring from duplicity and imitation, which makes it all the more difficult to oppose. The devil, Mather claims, "do's ordinarily use more Fraud than Force, in his assaulting of us" (51). And the fraud, according to Mather, is especially disturbing for the way that it utilizes God in its unholy deceits. He makes this prediction about Judgment Day:

> When our Lord is going to set up His Kingdom, in the most sensible and visible manner, that ever was, and in a manner answering the Transfiguration in the Mount, it is a Thousand to One, but the Devil will in sundry parts of the world, assay the like for Himself, with a most Apish Imitation [15].

This passage establishes several themes in Mather's understanding of the devil. First, the Lord's plan is "sensible" and "visible," which contrasts with the devil's (and witches') irrational and invisible behaviors during the witch crisis. Second, the devil "apishly imitates" God, setting up a copied kingdom for himself. And third, the use of "a thousand to one," even if it is only used as a figure of speech, still reinforces the idea that God — the one and only — stands in contrast to a multiplicitous devil. These ideas — that the devil is irrational, invisible, imitative, and multiplicitous — reappear throughout Mather's writing. The devil is accused of using instruments of torture "cloaked by invisibility," of using scripture "falsely," of being a "God" to the unregenerate, and of coming "in multitudes" to afflict a single person (Mather 41, 92, 53, 5). As much as some of Mather's diction tries to contain the devil's threat, much of his language shows his anxiety that the devil is not so much controlled by the Lord as he is *performing the role of Lord*. Like a performer, the devil's "real" self is hidden behind a facade. His empty words and multiplied personas are, like a script and costumes, just props in a stage play that seeks to overthrow the solid, monolithic truth of God.

Calef's critique of Mather's characterization of the devil is not, as historical myth often has it, that he finds Mather too swept up by religious fervor to see clearly the horror of the witch hunt. Actually, Calef accuses Mather of failing to adhere strictly enough to religious law. Just as Calef criticized Mather for his lack of scriptural proof, he also criticizes him for letting the devil usurp God's just place at the top of the Chain of Being.

Calef recognizes Mather's intense — if subliminal — fear that the devil is overstepping his bounds, and Calef believes this to be proof of Mather's own blasphemy. Calef writes:

> These [are] my belief: That the devils bounds are sett, that he cant pass; That the devils are so full of Malice, that it cant be added to by Mankind; That where he hath power he neither can nor will omit executing it; That 'tis only the Almighty that sets bounds to his rage, and that only can Commissionate him to hurt or destroy [34].

Calef addresses one by one the hidden anxieties in Mather's text. Calef, like Mather, works to reify God as an all-powerful and singular God who controls the devil. Calef is obviously uncomfortable with Mather's implication that the devil imitates the Lord, possibly supplanting or equaling his power. "What were all this," he writes to Mather about Mather's imitation theory, "but to Rob God of his Glory in the highest manner, and giving it to a Devil and a Witch" (29).

But even though Calef seems to agree with Mather's surface claim that God controls the devil and his deeds, Calef points out the frustrating tautology that emerges from such a claim. He writes:

> [The] answer is so far an owning the Doctrine, that the Devil has in his nature a power to do all these things, and can exert this power, except when he is restrained, which is in effect to say that God has made Nature to fight against itself. That he has made a Creature, who has it in the power of his Nature to overthrow Nature, and to act above and against it. Which he that can believe may as well believe the greatest contradiction [49].

Calef wrestles with a fundamental catch-22: either God controls the devil and thus the devil acts against God as a function of God, which seems an impossibility to Calef, or the devil has escaped God's control, which seems an impossibility to Calef, who takes his scripture literally. What Calef does is effectively eliminate the existence of the devil as an agent in the Salem incidents, since there is no reasonable way to argue that he exists in a world ruled by God. Without going so far as to disclaim in language the reality of Satan, Calef demonstrates how Mather's arguments contradict each other and the Bible. But if Calef highlights the tautological and paradoxical nature of Mather's claims, Mather might just have the final word in the debate about the function of the devil in Salem. "That there is a Devil," Mather writes, "is a thing Doubted by none but such as are under the Influence of the Devil" (5). For both Mather and Calef, the devil occupies a space just outside the reaches of logical argument, in a realm of contradiction, tautology, and instability.

The history that Mather and Calef create together is by definition dialogic, and their concern about corrupting the original and defining an indefinable devil combine to create an account of Salem that is less history than it is historiography. Indeed, Mather and Calef spend significant time theorizing just what their own roles as historians are, and these roles are solidly connected to the questions of truth, originality, and definition that surround the witchcraft debate. Halfway through his text, just as he is about to begin recounting the "facts" of the trial testimony, Mather makes a surprising revelation about the trials: "For my own part, I was not present at any of them" (55). While this might seem to detract from the credibility of an author about to offer verbatim testimony from the testifiers, Mather cites his absence from the proceedings as a positive: "Nor ever had I any Personal prejudice at the Persons thus brought upon the Stage.... I can do no other than shortly relate the chief Matters of Fact, which occur'd in the Tryals of some that were executed, in an Abridgement Collected out of the Court-Papers.... You are to take the Truth, just as it was; and the Truth will hurt no good man" (55). Mather sets up a paradigm in which the historian is better equipped to write history if he is removed from the actual historical event. For Mather, his use of trial transcripts, which are themselves copies of oral testimony, is proof positive of both his impartiality and his attention to primary sources. The "truth, just as it was" is, for Mather, twice removed from the original witchcraft.

In addition, Mather is quite comfortable admitting that he has altered, abridged, excised, and erred in his retelling of the Salem story. "There might have been more of these," he says about the testimonials he includes in *Wonders*, "if my Book would not thereby have swollen too big" (55). While here he justifies his own editorial cuts, in other places he seems to lament gently the incompleteness of his account: "I am forced to omit several passages, in this, as well as in all the succeeding Tryals, because the Scribes who took notice of them, have not supplied me" (64). And his desire to prove the reliability of his account while still giving credit to his own originality competes at several moments in the text. For example, he writes, "I shall Report nothing but with Good Authority, and what I would invite all my Readers to examine, while 'tis yet Fresh and New, that if there be found any mistake, it may be as willingly Retracted, as it was unwillingly Committed" (43). On the one hand, Mather refers here to the "fresh and new" character of *Wonders*, recently published and still open for revision. But Mather also alludes to the conflicting nature of his particular history. It is both copied from a reliable source — sure proof of its reflection of original events — and *copied*, that is, not an exact representation, from a copied, incomplete, possibly erroneous source. Mather claims to be a "historian" rather than an "advocate," but for him, the unbiased, objective role of the historian — historian as impartial outside observer — rests next to the role of historian as *outsider*, an author who can never quite gain access to the full story he wishes to reveal.

Calef, too, articulates a historical method that values his own authorial intrusion even as it acknowledges that this intrusion necessitates a certain distance from the historical events he describes. He does seem to be making a confession when he says that if he made any omissions in his history, it "was past any Power of mine to remedy, having given a faithful account of all that came to my knowledge" (16). Calef admits that his history is less a product of fact than it is a product of subjective, selective perception. His narrative is, he says, "as near as Memory could bear away" (25). But Calef is aggressive in his conviction that "truth" is not necessarily only fact-based. In response to an anonymous letter that challenged him to admit that "truth is truth regardless of men and devils," Calef responds, "The great question is what is Truth?" (66, 78). Over and over again, Calef resists the idea that the Salem story should be told with objectivity. In fact, he sees it as a moral imperative to "expose the actors" in the witchcraft drama and to assure that no further executions take place (7). Unlike Mather, Calef believes that the role of the historian is to advocate: "I thought it my duty to be no longer an Idle Spectator" (30). Though Calef tirelessly pursued Mather for his lack of scriptural evidence for proving witchcraft in Salem, he also demonstrates his own doubts about just how powerful and transparent the Word actually is. He writes:

> It is a known Truth, that some unwary expressions of the primative Fathers, were afterwards improved for the Introducing and establishing of Error.... For were they to be understood Litterally and as they are spoken, it must

73

seem as if the Authors were Introducing among Christians very dangerous Doctrines [29].

The "primative Fathers," who in this context are the Church Fathers, need to be corrected and revised by more recent authorities — in this case, Calef himself. What once stood as the law of the Fathers is now revealed to be just a metaphor open to multiple interpretations. In fact, taking the Fathers literally can lead to "danger." Calef's revision of the primitive fathers is a model for his own historical methodology. He believes that the role of the historian is corrective, interpretive, and progressive.

There is no doubt about the animosity that exists between Mather and Calef. Mather calls Calef a "gross" teller of lies, and Calef claims that his duty is "not to imitate the like of" Mather (Mather 21, Calef 35). Calef critiques Mather's tendency to make up words, and Mather says that "nothing" in Calef's account is true or fair (Calef 32, Mather 20). And certainly Mather defends the Salem witch trials while Calef finds them tragic and disgusting. But in many ways, these two historians align on many theoretical questions relating to the understanding of the events of 1692. Both Mather and Calef wrestle with the question of where demonic corruption originates: with the devil? With God? With mankind? Both find it impossible fully to define the devil as anything other than a tautology, and both similarly envision their own roles in the Salem story as trustworthy *and* highly partial. This complex of contradictions ultimately suggests a kinship between the devil and the historian. Neither is fixed or singular in the way that God is. Mather says that the devil "makes a whip for his own back" when he drives humans to prayer (52). If the devil is both independently evil and "whipped" by God, the historian is both impartially removed and helplessly underinformed. The devil and the historian occupy a paradoxical, madly fluctuating, unstable space at both ends of a pole; God and the historical event sit high above, unchanging, alone, and utterly apart. While Mather tries hard to cement himself first to one side and then to the other side of his pole, Calef seems more content to acknowledge the instability of his own position. This small distinction aside, these two authors, positioned in history as archetypal enemies and the framers of the two sides of the Salem debate, actually work together to present one — dialectical — witchcraft history.

Charles Upham: History and the Corpse

Charles Upham published his voluminous history of Salem and the witch trials in 1867. He served his community as a congressman, mayor, and minister, and it was his account that, according to one scholar, "became the standard interpretation, repeated for generations in textbooks on American history" (Mappen 36). If Mather and Calef present a dialectical and unstable historical foundation, Upham works hard to stabilize it. Nearly two hundred years after the trials, Upham wrestles with both his dissatisfaction with the lack of an authoritative history on Salem and his doubts about his own ability to embody such an authority, removed as he is from the events in question by the passage of so many years. In order to reify the past into a constant collection of statistics and anecdotes, Upham must resuscitate that past and then pin it down like a butterfly under glass. This tension — between the resolution of the story and his own removal from the past — is one that characterizes not only his history, but the many derivative histories that follow his, that take his text as a model and a road map for studying Salem's past.

Upham begins his prolific work by lamenting the incompleteness and inaccuracies of the histories — Mather's and Calef's among them — that have come before his. "It constantly became more and more apparent," he writes, "that much injury was resulting from the want of a complete and correct view of a transaction so often referred to, and universally misunderstood" (Vol. I, viii). Already, Upham establishes his goal: to tell the real story — in its entirety — of what happened in Salem. For Upham, history is a hidden secret waiting to be discovered by the diligent researcher. Celebrating the recent settling of America, Upham writes, "Our first age will not be shrouded in darkness and consigned to fable, but, in all of its detail, brought within the realm of knowledge" (Vol. I, ix). This quotation is telling for several reasons. First, it demonstrates Upham's commitment to historical research, and his belief that to reveal history is to do benevolent work for the nation as a whole. But the diction of the quotation goes beyond this self-evident revelation. In speaking of the "shroud" of darkness, Upham sets the foundation for a metaphor that will persist throughout his text. Over and over again he associates history with a corpse, a body wrapped in winding sheets and even buried until it can be resuscitated by the life-giving breath of the historian. This section will explore Upham's use of this historical corpse, and examine how the corporealization of the historical event works in his text both to save history from unknowability and to relegate it forever to the realm of the symbolic, a realm that makes it both legible and irrevocably unoriginal.

"The public life of the past is but the outline," writes Upham, "or, more strictly speaking, the mere skeleton of humanity. To fill up the outline, to clothe the skeleton with elastic nerves and warm flesh, and quicken it with a vital circulation, we must get at the domestic, social, familiar, and ordinary experience of individuals and private persons.... In this way only can history fulfil its office in making the past present" (Vol. I, 200). Upham quite literally raises the dead by writing the history of Salem. His emphasis on the private, familiar, and domestic mirrors his conviction that history itself is a process of going inside, of seeking out the "interior of society" (Vol. I, 110).[4] By corporealizing these private acts, by making history visible as a living, breathing body, Upham hopes to transcend the divisions of time and transport his historical subjects forward into the present. He makes a pun that summarizes this corporealizing effect. "We must understand their characters," he writes of the seventeenth-century Salemites, "Enter into their life, see with their eyes, feel with their hearts, and be enveloped, as it were, with their associations, sentiments, beliefs, and principles of actions. In this way only *can we bring the past into our presence*" (Vol. I, 321, my emphasis). Upham's goal is twofold: to bring history into the present time, and to bring history into our very presence, so that readers can experience the actual identities and perspectives of the people about whom they read. Historians — and museums, which I shall discuss later — often talk about bringing history alive, and for Upham, this metaphor is salient and powerful. Historical research is the process of bringing the dead to life, of sitting down with them and having a chat, of peeking inside their heads and hearts with the intimate access that only a historian can have.

In explaining how this raising of the dead occurs, Upham extols the benefits of primary sources. I would like to quote at some length Upham's discussion of one of Deodat Lawson's sermons given during the trials, a sermon which Upham includes in his text just before he writes the following:

76

No description of a person looking back from our point of view, not having experienced the delusions of that age, no matter who might attempt the task, could adequately paint the scene ... [Lawson's sermon] bring[s] before us directly, without the intervention of any secondary agency, the thoughts, associations, sentiments, of that generation, in breathing reality. They carry us back to the hour and the spot. Deodat Lawson rises from his unknown grave, comes forth from the impenetrable cloud which enveloped the closing scenes of his mortal career, and we listen to his voice, as it spoke to the mul- titudes that gathered in and around the meeting-house in Salem Village, on Lecture-day, March 24, 1692. He lays bare his whole mind to our immediate inspection. In and through him, we behold the mind and heart, the forms of language and thought, the feelings and passions, of the people of that day [Vol. II, 88].

In praising the directness of the primary source, Upham implies that the historical writer is always at a remove from what he describes. Here, the "impenetrable cloud" that Upham delineates is not only the cloud of the death that removed Lawson from the realm of the living, but also the cloud of temporal distance that hid him from our view. Again Upham implies that if history wishes to be accurate and complete, it must breathe life into a corpse, rescuing the historical subject from both death and obscurity. But as "people looking back from our point of view," we are in need of divine help to raise the dead. Like Christ, the primary source functions to resuscitate the deceased and save us all from our own frightening posi- tions as isolated, obscure, and mortal historical subjects. A paradox emerges in Upham's taxonomy. On the one hand, history is that which saves, revives, and unites. But on the other hand, history demands "a wisdom greater than ours" to function (Vol. II, 156). Upham seems to desire a kind of divine one-ness that transcends temporality and identity borders, and yet, at the same time, he mourns his own earthly limits to enact such tran- scendence without the aid of the primary source. The primary source, then, is the symbol of both the historian's embodiment of the original his- torical subject *and* the historian's own insurmountable distance from the very subject he can sometimes become. In this sense, the corpse is a deadly serious and simultaneously parodic symbol: a symbol of the historian/his- torical figure corporealized into a living person and a symbol of the his- torian/historical figure trapped forever in the body of a dead man.

In talking about the relationship between spirituality and science, Upham delivers a commentary on this paradoxical connection between the historian and the history he wishes to encounter so directly. Again, I will quote at some length, so as to let Upham's language build its own metaphors between the spirit and the actual history, the science and the historian:

> It admits of much question, whether human science can ever find a solid foundation in what relates to the world of spirits. The only instrument of knowledge we can here employ is language. Careful thinkers long ago came to the conclusion, that it is impossible to frame a language precisely and exclusively adapted to convey abstract and spiritual ideas, even if it is possible, as some philosophers have denied, for the mind, in its present state, to have such ideas. All attempts to construct such a language, though made by the most ingenious men, have failed. Language is based upon imagery, and associations drawn from so much of the world as the senses disclose to us.... We are here confined, as it were, within narrow walls. We can catch only glimpses of what is above and around us, outside of those walls [Vol. II, 424].

Though he is literally discussing the human being's inability fully to explain or understand divine and/or demonic actions (and thus, bolstering his critiques against the use of spectral evidence in the Salem court), Upham also makes a point here — intentionally or not — about the relationship of a historian to his historical subject. Like a specter, the historical subject has a body, appears real, can tickle and pinch the historian in ways that feel, indeed that *are,* physical. But like a specter, the historical subject is distinctly not of the historian's own linguistic realm, what might now be called the symbolic order. Thus, as the historian approaches the specter of history armed with the language of his or her discipline, the specter flees. The "glimpses" that historians catch of the past, which come to them through texts such as Lawson's, keep them jumping to see over the wall, a wall that they will never be able to climb. Upham continues, "Such glimpses may be vouchsafed, from time to time, to rescue us from sinking into materialism, and to keep alive our faith in scenes of existence remaining to be revealed when the barriers of our imprisonment shall be taken down, and what we call death lift us to a clearer and broader vision of universal being" (Vol. II, 424). For Upham, history, like religion, promises more than it can deliver in the moment, and it is only faith that can assure us that one day — just not today — historians will be able to understand and articulate the purpose of our existence.

And Upham's faith is strong. Despite his ardent wish to know the truth about Salem, he seems comfortable with the hope — a combination of desire and deferral — that Salem's mysteries will one day be revealed. He certainly sees his own text as one that approaches (perhaps like a mathematical limit) a reifying, corrective, true account of what happened. All of these threads come together in Upham's discussion of the role of monuments in historical research. Just as Upham's commentary on the spiritual world proved an apt metaphor for his treatment of history, his discussion of the monuments erected to "superstition" proves an apt metaphor for his treatment of the monument to Salem's history. In describing the yielding of the age of superstition to the age of science, Upham has this to say: "As the hour of [superstition's] dissolution was at hand, and [it] was doomed to vanish before the light of science and education, to pass from the realm of supposed reality into that of acknowledged fiction, it seems to have been ordered that [it] should leave monuments behind [it], from which [its] character, elements, and features, and [its] terrible influence, might be read and studied in all subsequent ages" (Vol. I, 467). Upham's "monuments" are — literally speaking — the many plays and epics, Shakespeare's and Milton's among them, which "crystallize" the "forms" of these superstitions, recording them forever in the pages of the texts (Vol. I, 467). Again, we can see connections between the spectral/superstitious and the historical. For Upham, monuments are intimately connected to the role of history. Just as the corpse gathers the threads of a historical subject and weaves them into a revived human form, the monument reifies the past and transports it into the present, textualizing it along the way. This textualization, like the corporealization of the corpse, serves both to open the monument for interpretation and remove it from the realm of the "real." In other words, the monument is a living, breathing testimonial that is, despite its appearance, always already a fiction.

Upham carries this idea of the monument into a more specific discussion of the history of 1692 Salem. "Witch Hill," sometimes called "Gallows Hill," is the location in Salem where accused witches were hanged and subsequently — and haphazardly — buried. Upham begins his comments on this site this way: "There is no contemporaneous nor immediately subsequent record, that the executions took place on the spot assigned by tradition" (Vol. II, 376–77). Indeed, no physical or textual proof has ever been discovered which can once and for all guarantee the location of the executions and burials. But despite this, Upham proceeds with a proposal:

> When, in some coming day, a sense of justice, ... a discriminating discernment of what is really worthy of commemoration among men, a rectified taste, a generous public spirit, and gratitude for the light that surrounds and protects us against error, folly, and fanaticism, shall demand the rearing of a suitable monument to the memory of those who in 1692 preferred death to a falsehood, the pedestal for the lofty column will be found ready, reared by the Creator on a foundation that can never be shaken while the globe endures, or worn away by the elements, man, or time — the brow of Witch Hill [Vol. II, 379–80].

Upham's monument is, like his definition of history, a sort of living corpse. Though it would reify a history that is still in flux, the monument, located as it would be on a site that may or may not be "original," would also be a symbol of the death of the historical event, its inability to survive and communicate with the now living. Upham extols the virtues of the Witch Hill site for its symbolic importance, and also for the natural landscape, made up of solid bedrock and impressive vistas, that would make the site attractive. By stressing the naturally monumental qualities of the site, Upham hopes to emphasize how historical fact is outside of the discursive realm: it thrives in the very landscape around us, carved into our world by God and not by the historian. But this emphasis is, of course, ironic; ultimately, Upham is critiquing the fact that as of 1867, no monument exists. For all of nature's divine commemoration of the dead, the monument to Salem's martyrs needs the urgent breath of the historian to come to life.

Despite this irony, Upham does succeed in stabilizing the historiography that surrounds Salem. Before Upham, Mather and Calef defined Salem's past through a polarized debate. After Upham, Mather and Calef were recast as historical subjects and no longer historians. Mather became the witch hunter, and Calef the brave man of means who spoke up for truth and justice. After 1867, Upham's text became the new "foundational" Salem history, and his account was given so much credence that it is not until the late twentieth century, when Paul Boyer and Stephen Nissenbaum began to publish their sociological readings of the 1692 events, that Charles

Upham began to face the same fate as Mather and Calef: he began to figure less as a scholarly authority and more as a historical subject worthy of investigation rather than reverence. And perhaps, like the corpse of history, that is the nature of the historian. Even as he periodically invents himself as a fresh authority, he also consistently guarantees his own passing into the morgue of the past.

Boyer and Nissenbaum: Context and the Crystal Ball

It may seem like a big jump to move so quickly from Charles Upham to Paul Boyer and Stephen Nissenbaum[5]; after all, more than a century passed after Upham's history of the trials before Boyer and Nissenbaum published *Salem Possessed: The Social Origins of Witchcraft* in 1976. But in many ways, Boyer and Nissenbaum are responding most directly to Upham's scholarship. On the first full page of their book, Boyer and Nissenbaum discuss their relationship to Upham's research: "Upham's analysis ... impressive as it is, remains incomplete and ultimately unsatisfactory. Like most nineteenth-century local historians, Upham idealized the sturdy colonial yeomen who figure in his narrative, dwelling almost affectionately on their petty disputes but often drawing back from confronting the larger patterns implicit in these disputes or from analyzing them in serious political terms" (*Salem Possessed*, x). This introduction demonstrates two important philosophies behind the Boyer-Nissenbaum study. First, they aim to write a "complete" and "satisfying" history. And second, they plan to focus on the "larger patterns" and the "political" landscape of Salem. Indeed, Boyer and Nissenbaum strive to wrap up the loose ends left by Upham and others by contextualizing Salem, by placing it into a full and far-reaching sociopolitical landscape that will finally explain the core mysteries of what happened in 1692.

For Boyer and Nissenbaum, Upham is not only the most important Salem historian, he is also the model from whom other, more recent historians have worked:

> Of the modern historians of Salem witchcraft, the few who have discussed the pre– or post–1692 situations at all have continued to rely uncritically on

Upham's imperfect narrative and analysis.... So far as we can tell, Charles Upham has been the only historian of Salem witchcraft to have read through [the manuscript records of the trials]. Even Marion L. Starkey's engaging 1949 narrative of the witchcraft trials, *The Devil in Massachusetts* (which despite its occasional imaginative embellishments remains the best researched and certainly the most dramatic account of the events of 1692) draws exclusively — and superficially at that — upon Upham for its "background" sections [*Salem Possessed*, xi].

In many ways, the century-long gap between Upham and Boyer and Nissenbaum is exactly that — a gap. Boyer and Nissenbaum's critique of Starkey is also telling. They accuse her of drawing from Upham "exclusively" and "superficially." A tension exists for Boyer and Nissenbaum between a criticism of Upham's "imperfect narrative" and a reverence for his well-researched study. Starkey, then, can do no right, for she is damned for relying too heavily on his imperfections and damned for not relying heavily enough on his research. Upham's specter haunts not only Boyer and Nissenbaum's book, but also all post–1867 Salem studies; he is the sign of both voluminous, meticulous, painstakingly detailed scholarship *and* imperfect, biased, and unsatisfying story-telling.

Boyer and Nissenbaum's project is to re-contextualize Salem, to situate the witchcraft events into a sociopolitical history of the surrounding area. In discussing how this project diverges from past historical scholarship on Salem, the authors remark that "there have always been other contexts, seemingly more significant, into which the witchcraft outbreak could easily be placed" (*Salem Possessed*, xi). By way of example, they cite the history of the occult, adolescent psychopathology, and the excesses of repressive Puritanism. They also remind readers that "*The Devil in Massachusetts* ... was consciously written in the shadow of the Nazi holocaust, while Arthur Miller's 1953 play about Salem witchcraft, *The Crucible*, was of course a parable about McCarthyism" (*Salem Possessed*, xi). All of these "contexts" are set up as less complete and less "true" than the sociopolitical context that *Salem Possessed* will outline. The history of the occult, adolescent psych, and repression all figure here as somehow too sexy, too trendy, and too fleeting to capture the full picture of 1692 Salem. And Starkey's and Miller's works are critiqued here as little more than flimsy allegory: Salem co-opted to speak the truth about another era. Boyer and Nissenbaum delineate their goals: to remove Salem from the web of current-day authorial motivations, and place it back into its original context.

But Boyer and Nissenbaum do not so easily extricate themselves from the subjectivity that plagued their predecessors. Consider, for example, the first line of *Salem Possessed*: "This book, too, has its history" (ix). The Preface of this book is, in fact, a contextualizing not of 1692 Salem, but of this 1974 Salem study. At one point, they refer to their attempts to articulate their own subject positions as a kind of academic writing about the self: "Such a foray into intellectual autobiography would also have to include the experience of living through the 1960's; the decade of Watts and of Vietnam helped us realize that the sometimes violent roles men play in 'history' are not necessarily a measure of their personal decency or lack of it" (*Salem Possessed*, xiii). Though, unlike Upham, they might not extol the virtues of the sturdy colonial yeoman, Boyer and Nissenbaum do seem to exhibit a similar tendency to use their own historical period's characteristics as an explanation — if not an excuse — for the horrifying events of 1692. Their use of the term "realize" suggests that their own historical moment has illuminated a truth about Salem; this is quite different from suggesting that their historical moment produced a new way of reading the Salem events. But the paragraph that explores the autobiography of their own historical positions ends this way: "These perceptions deepened our sense of the ambiguities inherent in the events we were studying, as we watched Salem Villagers for whom we had developed real sympathy driven to instigate the deaths of their own neighbors" (*Salem Possessed*, xiii). Boyer and Nissenbaum are torn between two positions. On the one hand, they wish to acknowledge their own biases and maintain the ambiguous, irresolvable character of the 1692 events. But on the other hand, they use their biases to discover the "truth," and the ambiguity they uncover is reified into "sympathy," an emotion that can only be provoked through a full understanding of the facts. If *Salem Possessed* has a "history," it is a history that, like Salem's own historiography, is plagued by contradiction.

Boyer and Nissenbaum's most famous hypothesis in *Salem Possessed* is that Salem Village, the rural outcropping located northwest of the seaport and town, was locked in a contentious — if somewhat submerged — battle with Salem Town for religious and political independence, despite the fact that the Town and the Village had, in general, a mutually dependent relationship in terms of sharing goods and services.[6] What emerges in *Salem Possessed* is a striking metaphor that aligns Salem Village with the historical project embarked upon by the two authors. Consider, for example, this description of the Salem Village political leadership: "Both the Village meeting and the five-man Committee it elected annually were, after all, only pallid shadows of the 'town meeting' and 'Board of Selectmen' which governed full-fledged towns" (*Salem Possessed*, 50). Over and over again, the authors suggest that Salem Village functioned as both a vicarious or reproduced version of Salem Town and as a distinct, independent entity. This is also how they envision their own relationships to Salem's past. "It is impossible to recover at this distance," they write in their discussion of former Salem minister James Bayley, "what bit of gossip, what hasty word, or what real or imagined slight may have caused some Salem Villagers to turn against Bayley" (*Salem Possessed*, 50). This metaphorical link — between historical methodology and historical events — crops up several times throughout the book. In their section on Bartholomew Gedney, John Hathorne, and William Brown, Jr., three Salem Town merchants who opposed the ordination of Salem Village's own minister, Boyer and Nissenbaum critique people who lived outside of the Village for failing to understand the needs of the Salem farmers: "Outsiders in these years always seemed more ready to deplore the symptoms of the Village's malaise than they were to examine its causes" (*Salem Possessed*, 58). The "outsiders" here are the three Town merchants, and "these years" refers to the late 1600s, and in particular the dates surrounding 1687, when the three merchants advised against ordaining Deodat Lawson. But anyone who has read *Salem Possessed* would also recognize here a connection to the authors' own critique of more contemporary Salem scholarship. The lack of study and research on the *causes* of the witchcraft outbreak is, of course, the very void which Boyer and Nissenbaum aim to fill. For Boyer and Nissenbaum, the "outsiders" are not just those outside of Salem Village in the late seventeenth century, but also all of those who are separated by time from the facts of Salem's past. "These years," then, are a doubled time zone, referring both to the actual date of the historical events being investigated, *and* the date from which the historians write.

This doubled time zone reappears when Boyer and Nissenbaum consider the explicit and implicit connections between themselves and certain of the key characters in the original Salem events:

> It was in 1692 that [Putnam and Parris] for the first time attempted (just as we are attempting in this book) to piece together the shards of their experience, to shape their malaise into some broader theoretical pattern.... Oddly enough, it has been through our sense of "collaborating" with Parris and the Putnams in their effort to delineate the larger contours of their world, and our sympathy, at least on the level of metaphor, with certain of their perceptions, that we have come to feel a curious bond with the "witch hunters" of 1692 [*Salem Possessed*, 180].

The "metaphorical sympathy" bears further analysis. We can presume that the sympathy is not so much for the particular opinions of Parris and Putnam, which, no doubt, are considered (at the very least) unfortunate by Boyer and Nissenbaum. Instead, the sympathy stems from a methodological parallel that the authors note between themselves and the witch hunters: both the authors and the hunters embark in their own historical moment on a certain fact-finding mission, a mission which aims to place singular experiences into a context that can give them meaning, a mission that can transform "shards" into "meaning." One wonders, then, how "curious" the bonds between Boyer, Nissenbaum, Parris, and Putnam actually are. Of course, the authors use the word "curious" to absolve themselves from any guilt associated with the deaths of the innocents in 1692 Salem; by distancing themselves — through the use of this term — from the witch hunters, they imply that any link between themselves and those who encouraged the hangings is coincidental, accidental, and an anomaly of some kind. But the "curiosity" that emerges when Boyer and Nissenbaum are juxtaposed with Parris and Putnam is a particularly historiographical "curiosity"; in fact, it is the very curiosity that powers any historical project. The desire to make whole the fragment, to decipher or delineate the pieces of the puzzle, to reify the abstract into the concrete: it is this drive — which we might call "curiosity" — that underlies both the scholarly historical inquiry and the historical subject's own search for identity.

This connection between historical methodology and a psychoanalytic search for identity springs up for Boyer and Nissenbaum because they must provide a *why* to the question of *what happened*. Claiming, as they do, that the Salem Villagers battled with those from Salem Town because of fundamental tensions between farmers and merchant capitalists does not go far to explain why such a tension should exist in the first place.[7] Thus, Boyer and Nissenbaum turn to psychology to probe the motivations for such anxieties and conflict. "At a time when one world view was imperceptibly yielding to another," they write, "each faction must have shared enough of the other's outlook to feel its power and be drawn to it. The anti–Parris men must at times have sensed with a pang what they were giving up in turning toward the burgeoning Town and away from the Village. And the pro–Parris Villagers, for their part, must have felt deeply the lure of the forces which were transforming the Town: the very forces they feared and despised" (*Salem Possessed*, 107). Despite the sociological and even Marxist rhetoric, this passage actually indicates the focus on interior, psychological conditions. Here, the conflict between Village and Town becomes a conflict between a single man's (or many single men's) own personal demons and desires. "The Villagers," the authors write, "were not only at war with each other; they were also at war with themselves" (*Salem Possessed*, 107). Boyer and Nissenbaum's slippage between a sociopolitical reading and a psychological reading of the 1692 events mirrors the slippage that accompanies their own historical methodology; as they attempt to move further towards an original motivation for the witch hunt, they must increasingly draw on the powers of their own imaginations. The repeated use of "must have" ("must have sensed," "must have felt," etc.) reveals both their own uncertainty about the interior lives of the Salemites, and also their desire to eliminate this uncertainty. Indeed, Boyer and Nissenbaum share a similar psychological condition to the ones they identify in their subjects: a split interior psyche. Salem Villagers are caught between a sublimated desire for success in the mercantile world that is slowly strangling their senses of identity as independent farmers; Boyer and Nissenbaum are caught between a sublimated desire to provide a psychological genesis for the witch hunt even as they attempt to eliminate the individual psychological subject in favor of a broader sociopolitical analysis. This accounts for the rather schizophrenic comments from reviewers that appear on the back cover of *Salem Possessed*. "Illuminating and imaginative," raves the *New York Review of Books*, alluding to the text's twin desires to both discover and create the Salem story. "Sophisticated and

86

imaginative," praises the *William and Mary Quarterly*, calling attention to the text's ability both to "draw on an impressive range of unpublished local sources" *and* to "provide a challenging new interpretation of the outbreak." Boyer and Nissenbaum, like the Salem Villagers, are at war with themselves.

Boyer and Nissenbaum's interior war is well demonstrated in their discussion of Mary Veren Putnam, Thomas Putnam's wife, who, upon her death, angered her family by leaving everything to her stepson Joseph, who had married — of all people — a *Porter!* In this discussion, the authors suggest that hanged witch Rebecca Nurse functions as an "ideal 'substitute' for Mary Veren Putnam." They regard the accusations against Nurse as a misplaced projection of anger meant for Mary Veren Putnam. But, they write, "to be sure, there were also a number of reasons, on the conscious and 'rational' level, why [Nurse would have been accused]" (*Salem Possessed*, 148–49). Even as they attempt to locate a psychological motivation for the witch hunt, Boyer and Nissenbaum fear that this attempt is what will ultimately lead to the undoing of their "sophisticated," well-researched study; and so they retreat back to the world of the "rational," where interior mental and emotional processes are safely eclipsed by statistical demographics.

Boyer and Nissenbaum, as they fight their own internal war, also describe the internal war of the Salemites. In their discussion of the role the ritual of confession played during the trials, they write:

> In 1692, if we are correct, this familiar ritual would have taken on a particular resonance for the accusers and on-lookers, since the confession they had drawn from the mouths of the accused was surely one that on some level they themselves longed to make. By first projecting upon others the unacknowledged impulses which lay within themselves, and then absolving those they had accused, the accusers could bring such impulses into the open, gain at least temporary mastery over them, and thereby affirm their commitment to social values in which they very much wanted to believe [*Salem Possessed*, 215].

The "if we are correct" reveals the imaginative reading that accompanies such a psychological analysis; Boyer and Nissenbaum reveal their own anxiety that perhaps their reading of the confessions has its origin not in 1692, but in their own authorial biases. Perhaps Boyer and Nissenbaum project their own interior impulse — the impulse to make Salem historical subjects into autonomous, integrated human beings — onto the subjects themselves, who soon become subjects wrapped up in a quest for identity, a quest that happens to coincide perfectly with the overall sociological context already established by the authors. In this way, Boyer and Nissenbaum work to make interior and exterior, psychology and politics, align seamlessly in a narrative that not only explains what happened, but *why* it happened as well. The question remains, however, where does the psychological explanation for the events of 1692 come from: the minds of the 1692 historical subjects, or the minds of the 1974 historians?

Perhaps the best way to conclude a section on Boyer and Nissenbaum is by taking a look at the very first words of *Salem Possessed*. "It began in obscurity," they write in "Prologue: What Happened in 1692," "with cautious experiments in fortune telling.... [One of the] young girls who met in small informal gatherings to discuss the future ... devised a primitive crystal ball — the white of an egg suspended in a glass — and received a chilling answer: in the glass there floated a 'specter in the likeness of a coffin'" (*Salem Possessed*, 1). Boyer and Nissenbaum might just as well be referring to their own historical project as much as to the young girls of 1692 Salem. They begin their inquiry with the very same crystal ball that supposedly began the whole witch hysteria. The crystal ball effect here is complicated. The historians use it to look back at the pre-trial past, and then use it again to jump from that past into a future in which the hangings have already occurred. Boyer and Nissenbaum aim to rescue Salem's past from obscurity and place it into a fully legible and scrutable narrative. But to move from the obscure to the scrutable demands some trickery, both for the young girls of Salem and for Boyer and Nissenbaum. The crystal ball demonstrates that there is no solitary past moment. The future and the present are inextricably linked in the crystal ball's landscape, which is a landscape that includes both the present-day fortune-teller and the reflection of the future. And for such a reflection to exist in the crystal ball, one must imagine that it has existence, that it — in some sense at least — becomes a peculiar kind of past as it is viewed. The crystal ball anecdote suggests that the historical timeline that will be elucidated in *Salem Possessed* is not linear, but tripled, a kind of past/present/future all in one. Simultaneously, it suggests that the original Salem events did not so much unfold or develop as they did perform themselves in a pattern that was to be scripted and rescripted by many generations that had yet to be born. As much as Boyer and Nissenbaum aim to tell the story of "what happened," one senses in the background a crystal ball effect that raises the possibility that what happened *then* only took shape, gathered meaning, looked familiar and legible because of the skill of the fortune-tellers.

Pathologies of Witchcraft: A Brief Look at Psychosomatic and Biological Theories

There are, of course, many other significant historical interpretations of the Salem witch trials. In 1702, two years after his death, Beverly minister John Hale's *A Modest Inquiry Into the Nature of Witchcraft* was published. Hale, who had been at first an avid supporter of the trials until his wife was ultimately accused, completed his text in 1697, when only Cotton Mather had previously published a formal history on the trials. Hale laments the sad consequences of mistakes made, and writes from personal remorse and heartbreak about the lessons to be learned from the Salem trials. In 1764's *The History of the Colony and Province of Massachusetts Bay*, Thomas Hutchinson accused the afflicted of creating the mass hysteria. For example, he described one afflicted girl from Groton, Elizabeth Knapp, as a "ventriloqua," a "fraud" and an "impost[er]" (Vol. II, 17). In 1907, Puritan descendent George Lyman Kittredge published "Notes on Witchcraft," which was followed by the exhaustive study *Witchcraft in Old and New England* in 1929. Like Boyer and Nissenbaum after him, Kittredge sought to contextualize the Salem crisis; but Kittredge looked to Anglican England and Catholic France for examples of witch hunts that predated and dwarfed the incidents at Salem. He concludes that the belief in witchcraft is the "common heritage of humanity," and was, in the seventeenth century, "no more discreditable to a man's head or heart than it was to be ... ignorant of the germ theory of disease" (372). Kittredge absolves Salem of its guilt and even praises Massachusetts' public repentance as unprecedentedly noble. John Demos, a descendent of the Putnam family, published *Entertaining Satan* in 1982. The book, split into four parts — Biography, Psychology, Sociology, and History — is an apt precursor to Boyer and Nissenbaum, as it looked not only at individual personalities and the anecdotes of petty squabbles in Salem, but also at the underlying questions of personality development and spatial proximity. Though Demos' inquiry is primarily psychoanalytic, he is the first modern historian to use extensive maps, charts, and tables to reveal — much as Boyer and Nissenbaum do — how demographic patterns influence identity and social interaction.

Mary Beth Norton's 2002 book, *In the Devil's Snare: The Salem Witchcraft Crisis of 1692,* is the newest of the significant histories making a contribution in the field of Salem studies. Norton argues that the First and Second Indian Wars provided the context that ultimately allowed the proliferation of witchcraft paranoia in Essex County. As their economy suffered as their northern outposts fell to their Native American and French enemies, New Englanders began to wonder what had happened to the divine providence so central in the founding of the Massachusetts Bay colony. As King William's War progressed and the colonists moved further into defeat, the "assaults from the visible and invisible worlds became closely intertwined in New Englanders' minds" (Norton 297). In her meticulous research, Norton describes how Native American attacks, particularly on the Maine frontier, impacted the trial participants in Essex County. For example, Norton describes how confessed witch Abigail Hobbs explained that she had been recruited by the devil in Maine four years before the Salem crisis and just as violence was erupting on the frontier again. "Not only were their menfolk being drawn off to the frontier to fight an elusive and often victorious enemy," writes Norton, "witches in their midst had allied themselves spectrally with the Wabanakis" (301). In turn, the "afflicted girls" of Essex County worked to contain the threat of the invisible world by calling out the witches, even as their male counterparts failed to contain the threats with which the visible world was targeting New England. While Norton's book is comprehensive and innovative,[8] it has not (yet) entered the ironic category of "mythological fact," a category that permeates Salem historical scholarship. Norton is a careful historian, and she is left unable to offer a definitive answer to the question of why the afflicted girls made those accusations. Norton considers a wide variety of possibilities linked to her overall theory about the Indian Wars (including a persuasive argument about post-traumatic stress disorder as it might have been experienced by survivors of war), but ultimately leaves that question open. The text's exhaustive research is in interesting juxtaposition with the gaps that Norton highlights, among them gaps in the primary source records and gaps in her own interpretive license (13, 305–8).

Despite the status as "primary document" of texts such as Hale's, despite Hutchinson's plaintive and moving morality tale, despite the academic credibility of work by Kittredge and Demos and Norton, most of these authors have not so dramatically influenced the trajectory of Salem studies as the work done by Mather, Calef, Upham, and Boyer and Nissenbaum. But there are two other texts — one published just before and the other published just after *Salem Possessed*—which have left enduring effects on the current-day debates about what happened in 1692. In this section, I will discuss briefly the 1969 book *Witchcraft at Salem* by literature professor Chadwick Hansen, and the 1976 article "Ergotism: The Satan Loosed in Salem?" by biologist Linnda R. Caporael. Both of these texts, despite the fact that each has been in many ways discredited by competing scholarly opinion, have entered into the mainstream discussion about the trials, and both texts will demonstrate their influence when we begin to examine the fictional literature about the witch hunt that has been produced in recent years.

Though ultimately Hansen will suggest that history and witchcraft both collapse from fact into faith, he states right off the bat that he wants to "set straight" the record on the witchcraft phenomena at Salem, and that he can "see no point in employing the common revisionist technique of quarreling with [his] predecessors item by item and person by person, for to do so would be to bury the account of what did happen in an immense account of what did not" (ix). Like Upham's, Hansen's history is a body that must be rescued from an obscure death by the historian, who keeps the truth from being buried in a grave and forgotten. And like Upham, Hansen claims to work from the primary documents, avoiding the pitfalls of bias that intervening years can throw in the path of the earnest scholar. But what sets Hansen apart from Upham and other Salem historians is his provocative assertion that some of the hanged witches at Salem were guilty. "To begin with," he writes at the opening of his book, "witchcraft actually did exist and was widely practiced in seventeenth-century New England.... It worked then as it works now in witchcraft societies like those of the West Indies, through psychogenic rather than occult means, commonly producing hysterical symptoms as a result of the victim's fear" (x). First, note the subtle contradiction that infuses Hansen's language. The phrase "to begin with" competes with the adverb "actually," since "to begin with" implies that this is the foundation or origin of the debate, while "actually" is a corrective modifier that reveals a pre-existing — if erroneous — platform. Hansen, like the other historians discussed in this chapter, is caught between wanting both to create and repair Salem's history.

But more interesting than this is Hansen's desire to medicalize the condition of the afflicted girls. He argues that the hysterical fits suffered by the afflicted are symptoms of true, scientific hysteria, a condition that he describes as both psychosomatic and thoroughly real.[9] "The most cursory examination of the classic studies of hysteria," he writes, "will demonstrate that the afflicted girls of Salem were hysterical in the scientific sense of that term. It has, of course, been customary to call these girls hysterical, but only in the loosest and most popular sense of the word. Thus the same historians who have called them hysterical have also called them liars, though the terms are mutually exclusive.... With minor exceptions the girls' behavior belongs to the history of pathology rather than the history of fraud" (1–2). Hansen, then, has a distinctly anti-performative perspective on the trials, as he locates the origins of both his own history and the behavior of the afflicted girls themselves in the bodies and minds of those girls. But what is most fascinating about his attempts to naturalize and pathologize the afflictions as "disease" is the way that he describes witchcraft's efficacy:

> We must bear in mind that in a society, which believes in witchcraft, it works. If you believe in witchcraft and you discover that someone has been melting your wax image over a slow fire or muttering charms over your nail-parings, the probability is that you will get extremely sick. To be sure, your symptoms will be psychosomatic rather than organic. But the fact that they are obviously not organic will make them only more terrible, since they will seem the result of malefic and demonic power [10].

In other words, Hansen suggests that the belief in witchcraft precedes and produces the effects of witchcraft. Though he removes maliciousness and intentionality (and thus blame) from the characterization of the afflicted girls, he still maintains that their afflictions are not organic. This anti-organicism is reflected in Hansen's final warning to future generations: "In matters of malice the devil suits his actions to man's beliefs about them" (227). When Hansen suggests that some of the witches at Salem were in fact guilty of practicing witchcraft, he does not mean to imply that any magic actually transpired there. Instead, he makes it clear that witchcraft is not about the devil, but about contemporary ideology and its tangible effects on the psychology of those who believe in the power of magic — just about everyone in seventeenth-century Salem, according to Hansen. For Hansen, the "surety" of the psychosomatic, the "fact" of inorganicism, lays the groundwork for an understanding of witchcraft that is both anti-theatrical *and* highly performative. While Hansen, like Mather, suggests that the greatest culpability for the witchcraft outbreak lies with the "witches," Hansen has radically revised the definition of what a witch is. Because he is aligned with Mather in his final judgment of the trials, Hansen is often dismissed by more recent, "enlightened" historians and scholars. Most compelling about Hansen, though, is his tendency to deconstruct Mather's arguments and Upham's methodologies even as he so clearly replicates them. If the new witch is both anti-theatrical and performative, Hansen, too, is self-contradictory: he is a revisionist historian who reasserts the first judgments about the witchcraft outbreak, and he is a supporter of medical interpretations of the afflicted girls who also believes that bodily afflictions are anything but organic. The question of whether or not some of the witches at Salem were guilty is not the most salient or creative part of Hansen's argument. What is highly provocative, though, is his exploration — implicit as it is — of how history and witchcraft both function as a slippage between fact and faith, between the real and belief in the real.

The final historical reading of Salem that this chapter will consider is the hypothesis that ergot poisoning was responsible for the hallucinations experienced by the afflicted girls in Salem, a theory that we will revisit in pulp fiction form in the next chapter. As a graduate student at the University of California, Santa Barbara, biologist Linnda R. Caporael published an article that suggested that ergot (*Claviceps pupura*), a parasitic fungus that grows on a variety of cereal grains, including rye, caused an outbreak in 1692 Salem that was misdiagnosed as witchcraft. She explains that there are two types of ergot poisoning: gangrenous and convulsive. Gangrenous ergotism is characterized by "dry gangrene of the extremities followed by the falling away of the affected portions of the body" (Mappen 64). Convulsive ergotism, which is the ergotism Caporael diagnoses in Salem, "is characterized by a number of symptoms. These include crawling sensations in the skin, tingling in the fingers ... hallucination, painful muscular contractions leading to epileptiform convulsions ... [and] mental disturbances such as mania, melancholia, psychosis, and delirium." Caporael concludes, "All of these symptoms are alluded to in the Salem witchcraft records" (Mappen 64–65). Caporael cites three main reasons why she suspects ergotism in Salem: the matching of symptoms described in the witchcraft documents with known symptoms of ergot poisoning; the fact that growing conditions in late 1691 and early 1692 were perfect for producing the ergot on local Salem rye; the "localization" of the ergot-infected rye bread, which suggests that rye would have been readily available at the homes of certain afflicted girls; and tangible links between these homes and the homes of others who were also afflicted (Mappen 65–66).

All in all, the ergotism theory seems rather straightforward. Indeed, if historians often wish to approach scientific objectivity, Caporael's status as a biologist and her highly scientific methodology (dealing with the pathology of disease and the biological effects of chemicals on the body) combine to make her an appealing person to believe as far as the familiar question of "what happened" goes. And certainly, Caporael gained instant fame when she first published her findings.[10] While Hansen went so far as to treat the symptoms of the afflicted girls as authentic, Caporael went one step farther, finding an organic cause for the odd behavior that erupted in Salem. And this biological explanation has solidly entered the contemporary American consciousness. Scholarly and popular audiences alike are, for all of the reasons explored in this chapter, tempted and enticed by the idea that historical events could be explained by resorting to science.

While most Salem scholars and hobbyists are aware of the ergotism theory, very few are aware of subsequent refutations of Caporael's work. Nicholas P. Spanos and Jack Gottlieb published their critique of Caporael less than a year after Caporael's article came out. They argue, among other points, that ergot poisoning needs a deficiency of Vitamin A in the host body in order to thrive, and that Salemites, because of their access to both meat and fish, would not have had such a deficiency (Mappen 73). In addition, they take issue with Caporael's characterization of the symptoms experienced in Salem. They write, "Caporael says that 'complaints of vomiting and bowels almost pulled out are common in the depositions of the accusers.' This statement is incorrect" (Mappen 74). Again and again, Spanos and Gottlieb critique not only Caporael's findings, but also her methodology, accusing her of shoddy scholarship and even implying that she lies. They conclude their article with this scathing summation:

> The available evidence does not support the hypothesis that ergot poisoning played a role in the Salem crisis. The general features of the crisis did not resemble an ergotism epidemic. The symptoms of the afflicted girls and of the other witnesses were not those of convulsive ergotism. And the abrupt ending of the crisis, and the remorse and second thoughts of those who judged and testified against the accused, can be explained without recourse to the ergotism hypothesis [Mappen 82].

What is so fascinating about the ergotism debate is the way that it takes history to its scientific ends ... and still manages to reveal the failure of objectivity to answer questions about the past. The finalistic language employed by Spanos and Gottlieb does not bury Caporael's theory, for the ergotism hypothesis — as the discussion of Robin Cook's *Acceptable Risk* in Chapter Three will demonstrate — is alive and well today. What Spanos and Gottlieb do end is any doubt that science is not capable of solving historical ambiguities. Their final phrase highlights the irony that permeates their final "summary." To say that characteristics of the witchcraft outbreak at Salem can be explained "without recourse to the ergotism hypothesis" does not, of course, preclude the truth of such a hypothesis; what it does prove is that there are multiple competing explanations about what "really" happened at Salem.

Mather, Calef, Upham, Boyer and Nissenbaum, Hansen, Caporael, and Spanos and Gottlieb all offer the facts, all claim to speak the truth, and all set the record straight. They may disagree about the events in Salem in 1692, but they seem to agree that the events can be revealed by the right historian. But because all of them are "the right historian," they contradict their own claims about having the exclusive scoop. The history of Salem's past is fraught with controversy. This is, in part, because of the nature of the events that took place in Salem; as the fiction writers we will examine in the next chapter surely know, Salem's incidents are innately spooky, uncanny, unbelievable, dramatic. But perhaps the main reason why Salem's historical legacy remains both compelling and unresolved has to do not with what happened, but with what has been *said* about what happened. Salem's history began as a debate; it was reified into a single corpse and developed into a living-dead body, retaining properties of the grave even as it defied its own stasis; it stepped outside of its original time zone, offering up a new definition of "context" that included the past events, the present historical writing, and future interpretations; and it prostrated itself to science, a science that failed to escape from a historiographical legacy that ultimately revealed psychology and biology to be just newly minted words for "witchcraft."

THREE

Fiction and the Real
Novelists Rewrite Salem

In many ways, the fictions under exploration in this chapter are not so very far from the "facts" that were explored in Chapter Two. The novelists that this chapter will examine — John Neal, Nathaniel Hawthorne, Marion Starkey, Maryse Condé, and Robin Cook — oftentimes work directly from earlier historical accounts (such as Upham's, in Starkey's case, and Boyer and Nissenbaum's and Caporael's, in Cook's), and sometimes work from the original transcripts themselves (as, for example, Condé did). But like the historians, these writers have found gaps and silences in their "primary" sources, and have filled the unknown spaces with their own inventions. In addition, these writers provide, like the historians, more than just diverging accounts of "what happened" in Salem in 1692. They have also inquired about what it means to rewrite the past in one's own terms. They have explored the ethics, the moral imperative, the fun, and the horror of digging up Salem's history and repackaging it for a new generation. And, like the historians, they have found — even in their varying versions — that there are a similar series of questions that tend to haunt stories about Salem: Is the Salem story a ghost story? How does Salem's spookiness connect with the real living conditions of its inhabitants? What are fiction writers doing to history when they reimagine it? Can they offer, through fiction, vindication to the victims of the witch hunt? These questions, which are, of course, intimately tied to the questions of truth and origins that Salem historians have encountered, lurk just below the sometimes moving, sometimes witty, sometimes ridiculous narratives that this chapter will consider.

The question of representation is at the heart of all of these explorations of truth and origins. In the Salem transcripts, witchcraft emerges as a symbol for "representation" itself: the production of an externalized action or effect that stems from a preceding internal condition. This process of projection — combined with the simultaneous legal maneuvers that record and make official such projections — makes Salem's story a story that begins with a *reference to a pure, inner state.* The transcripts, then, by the process of *alluding* to such purity, set the tone for subsequent Salem accounts that constantly repel the very origins they describe simply because they describe them. The Salem histories are less a collection of readings that reveal the primary sources than they are a collection of readings that reiterate the reiterative game of primacy that has become the field of "Salem." To look at Salem-related novels, then, is not to explore how the truth has been perverted by authors of fiction, but to examine the process of representation that began back in 1692 when court officers began to take notes about the witchcraft events. Salem narratives are like an unending spiral: though each claims to move closer to some kind of "truth," each Salem account seems to circle around "truth" without actually hitting it. Histories, such as Upham's or Boyer and Nissenbaum's, for example, claim both to be further from the "facts" than the "original" records they uncover *and* to be closer to the overarching truth of what happened. Similarly, fictional accounts, such as those which we will explore in this chapter, claim to be less "true" than histories but somehow more able to deliver the heart of Salem's significance. This paradox posits the most derivative texts as the most "truthful," and it suggests that the categories of the "real," the "original," and the "true" are defined mainly through their representations.

John Neal's 1828 novel *Rachel Dyer* is the first novel published that focuses on the Salem witchcraft crisis, and it is significantly concerned with the question of how fiction can tell "truths."[1] With well over one hundred years separating him from 1692, Neal wonders how he can understand the major players from the trials. "We know little or nothing of the facts upon which their belief was founded," he writes of the belief in witchcraft common during the seventeenth century. He continues, "All that we know is but hearsay, tradition, or conjecture" (24). Or, one might add, "history." Neal spends the first three chapters of the novel engaged in a history lesson about the founding of the Massachusetts Bay and Plymouth colonies, and he ends his novel with a section called "Historical Facts," which provides primary source transcripts of letters written during the trials. But in between these historical brackets, Neal's novel makes some interesting departures from the "facts." Some of them are provocatively based on apocryphal mythologies, such as the myth about George Burroughs' preternatural strength, but some are even more provocatively simple inversions of fact. For example, even though George Burroughs keeps his historical name, Samuel Parris is called "Matthew Parris" in the novel, and Parris' daughter becomes "Abigail," while Betty Parris becomes "Bridget Pope." These intentional "errors" seem pointless, especially when he corrects them all at the end of the text in the "Historical Facts" section. Why does Neal depart from fact for such seemingly inconsequential yet importantly referential details within the context of a narrative that tries so vehemently to assert its historical framework?

This tension between the accurate and the invented, the speculative and the proven is at the heart of both the Salem witchcraft trials and the fictions that have been written about the trials. As Neal's characters struggle to determine what constitutes proof of bewitchment, Neal struggles to determine what constitutes a true story. "Why not say the truth?" Neal's Burroughs righteously asks the court on the behalf of an accused witch. "Why not say that where a man is charged with a crime, you are, in the very nature of things, under the necessity of taking that for proof which is not proof?" (111). And just as the kangaroo court that Neal condemns takes speculation for proof, Neal himself takes the hearsay, tradition, and conjecture — and the primary source documents — generated by the trials and makes them into a narrative. His George Burroughs not only opposes the rhetorical play that constitutes evidence in 1692, but also opposes a retelling of the story of 1692 that reinscribes such rhetorical constitution of truth. His George Burroughs does not ultimately tell the truth by failing to confess to witchcraft; instead, as Neal writes it, Burroughs stops telling altogether because he is indeed "a preacher of the word of truth" (257). In the novel's climactic moment, Burroughs tries to persuade accused witch Rachel Dyer to confess and save her life.[2] As he forcefully makes his case, the chapter ends abruptly with this line from Burroughs: "I forget what I was going to say —" (253). As the dash and subsequent blank space on the page represent, Burrough's silence is as close to truth as he or any other accused witch can get. And Neal's own paradoxical insistence on both historical accuracy and historical inaccuracy indicates the challenge of trying to speak the truth. The gaps, silences, paradoxes, and conflicts between language and truth, present and past, and speculation and evidence flourish from the very beginning of the Salem witch fiction tradition.

There is, of course, no shortage of fictional texts about Salem witchcraft. I have selected the next four texts that I deal with here for several reasons. All were or are either highly popular texts or texts by highly popular or famous writers. These texts explore not only the issues that surround certain Salem fictions, but issues that, for the majority of Americans familiar with the Salem story, comprise the dominant, collective American understanding of the witch trials. They also cover a wide range of time periods. Hawthorne's *The House of the Seven Gables*, the chronologically earliest of the texts explicated below, came only twenty-three years after 1828's *Rachel Dyer*, and was the first Salem fiction to remain popular through modern times. One hundred thirty-four years after the publication of *The House of the Seven Gables,* pulp fiction writer Robin Cook published the wildly popular medical thriller *Acceptable Risk.* Though there are a number of other important Salem fictions besides those discussed at length here, I wanted to represent a diverse chronological field. Though the four works I investigate here are by no means the definitive canon of Salem literature,[3] their diversity in approach, publication date, genre, and themes make them into lenses that each focus on a different aspect of how the Salem story gets told. At the same time, their common emphases on questions of truth and reality highlight the ways in which these texts interact with similar questions raised by the transcripts and historical accounts that have been explored in previous chapters.

The Ghostly Real: Nathaniel Hawthorne's The House of the Seven Gables

No fictional work concerning Salem has enjoyed more lasting popularity in America than Nathaniel Hawthorne's 1851 novel, *The House of the Seven Gables.* The actual house upon which the story was based still stands in Salem today, and thousands of tourists visit the site annually, sometimes to see dramatic reenactments of scenes from the novel. Hawthorne had personal ties to Salem history; his great-great grandfather, Colonel John Hathorne, was one of the judges who presided over the Salem Witch Trials. When he was twenty-six years old, Nathaniel Hawthorne added the "w" to his name to distance himself from what he considered to be a repressive, oppressive Puritan ancestry. In addition to his link to a hanging judge, Hawthorne had other personally charged connections to Salem, Massachusetts. He wrote *The House of the Seven Gables* in partial response to his dismissal from the Salem Custom House in 1849; critics generally agree that Hawthorne's attack on Judge Pyncheon is meant as a critique of the Whig politics that had cost him his job.[4] What is more interesting for the purposes of this study, however, is that the person who dismissed Hawthorne from this position was none other than Charles Upham, author of the influential historical account of the Salem witchcraft trials.[5] Hawthorne, then, had direct ties to both the actual historical subjects of the trials *and* to the historians who wrote about them. But Hawthorne did not want to write a true account of the trials. He distinguishes himself from the historians we discussed in the last chapter. "He would be glad," Hawthorne writes in the preface to the novel, referring to himself in the third person, "[if] the book may be read strictly as a Romance, having a great deal more to do with the clouds overhead, than with any portion of the actual soil of the County of Essex" (3). But this dichotomy — between the Romantic and the Real — is one that is contested and collapsed throughout *The House of the Seven Gables*.[6]

Hawthorne's preface suggests that even if his book is of the realm of the clouds, it still has a core of truth: "the truth, namely, that the wrongdoing of one generation lives into the successive ones, and, divesting itself of every temporary advantage, becomes a pure and uncontrollable mischief" (2). This "moral" (to borrow Hawthorne's own term) is articulated with diction that calls attention to its status as stable and factual. The "namely" highlights that this moral can be labeled, that its signifier and its signified are indistinguishable. The "pure" and "uncontrollable" nature of the inherited wrong doing suggests that what passes from generation to generation is not distilled or altered over time; instead, it remains elemental, unchanged, and utterly without temporal or cultural influences. But this pure, truthful moral coexists with Hawthorne's distaste for didactic art: "The Author has considered it hardly worth his while," he continues, "relentlessly to impale the story with its moral, as with an iron rod — or rather, as by sticking a pin through a butterfly — thus at once depriving it of life, and causing it to stiffen in an ungainly and unnatural attitude" (2). Like many of the historians discussed earlier in this book, Hawthorne is caught between two projects: to tell the truth and to tell the story. For Hawthorne, this doubled, paradoxical project has everything to do with the relationship of the past to the present. "There will be a connection with the long past," he writes in the beginning of the novel, "which, if adequately translated to the reader, would serve to illustrate how much of old material goes to make up the freshest novelty of human life" (6). The "new" always carries a trace of the "old," just as the "romantic" in this story has at its core a kernel of the "real" (and vice versa).

There are many places in the text where Hawthorne demonstrates how the past invades the present in direct, physical ways. As Hepzibah gazes at the portrait of the colonel in the house, she has this to say about the resemblance between the famous Pyncheon ancestor and Judge Pyncheon, whom she had just seen in the street: "'This is the very man!' murmured she to herself. 'Let Jaffrey Pyncheon smile as he will, there is that look beneath! Put on him a scull-cap, and a band, and a black cloak, and a Bible in one hand and a sword in the other ... nobody would doubt that it was the old Pyncheon come again!'" (59). Ancestral heritage in this novel comes very close to mystical reincarnation. Judge Pyncheon dies in precisely the same way that the colonel died: in the armchair, quietly, with blood on his shirt-bosom. Is Judge Pyncheon simply suffering under the same Maulean curse as his ancestor? Or, as Hawthorne speculates, was "Old Maule's prophecy ... founded on a knowledge of this physical predisposition in the Pyncheon race?" (304). Or could it be that the judge *is* the colonel condemned to relive his original death over and over again? These three possibilities, all of which are offered up as credible in the text, demonstrate how the old and the new connect: through witchcraft and prophecy, through science and biology, and through the raising of the dead.

Holgrave expounds on these old/new connections:

> "Shall we never, never get rid of this Past!" cried he.... "It lies upon the Present like a giant's dead body![7] In fact, the case is just as if a young giant were compelled to waste all his strength in carrying about the corpse of the old

giant, his grandfather, who died a long while ago, and only needs to be decently buried" [Hawthorne 182–83].

Holgrave is, no doubt, referring to his own situation as direct ancestor to the infamous Matthew Maule. But Holgrave is not just a descendent of Matthew Maule: he is also "as much of a wizard as ever he was" (Hawthorne 316). In this sense, then, the dead giant is both the proof of heritage *and* the ability to mesmerize or prophesize. In addition, Holgrave knows of the secret spring in the portrait, which, when depressed, will yield the compartment that holds the famous Pyncheon real estate papers. So the giant is also the paper that proves what generations of Pyncheons have always known (that there are vast tracts of land that belong to them). This paper is, like the biological hypothesis that all Pyncheons suffer from some disorder involving bleeding at the mouth, one way that the text reifies into fact what has previously only been considered fancy or fable. In other words, the dead giant is not just an ambiguous metaphor for the past; it is a specific description of how ancestry, witchcraft, and truth function to define what we come to call "the past."

Clifford explains the past in different terms, but terms that nonetheless define the past as a complex relationship between what has been and what currently is:

All human progress is in a circle; or, to use a more accurate and beautiful figure, in an ascending spiral curve. While we fancy ourselves going straight forward, and attaining, at every step, an entirely new position of affairs, we do actually return to something long ago tried and abandoned, but which we now find etherealized, refined, and perfected to its ideal. The past is but a coarse and sensual prophecy of the present and the future [Hawthorne 269–60].

The competing diction in this passage illustrates the way that *The House of the Seven Gables* repeatedly wrestles with a conception of the past as both over, linear, and reified, and as persistent, cyclic, and abstract or interpretive. The juxtaposition of "etherealized" with "refined" demonstrates this paradox perfectly. But Hawthorne does not simply offer philosophy; after all, he is a writer of fiction. He takes this idea of the spiral curve, of the heritage-witchcraft-truth hybrid, and weaves it into a story — a ghost story, to be precise.

When the colonel begins to build on Matthew Maule's land, Hawthorne tells us, "He was about to build his house over an unquiet grave" (9). But Matthew Maule's own grave, we find out, is not at the site of the house of the seven gables, but on Gallows Hill: the graves of the executed witches lie "in the crevices of the rocks, [and] were supposed to be incapable of retaining the occupants, who had been so hastily thrust into them. Old Matthew Maule, especially, was known to have as little hesitation or difficulty in rising out of his grave, as an ordinary man getting out of bed" (Hawthorne 189). What is interesting here is the way that Maule's grave is metaphorically relocated to the site of the house. This is not such a stretch, since the novel hints at the fact that Gallows Hill is always already a metaphor anyway. The phrase "were supposed to be" suggests that Gallows Hill is less a physical spot than it is an apocryphal landscape; what happened there is not history, but tradition, story, myth. In effect, Hawthorne resituates Gallows Hill to the site of the house of the seven gables, all the better to utilize the ghost who has found new life in the pages of his novel, a novel whose title has the same name as the newly described sepulcher: the house and the book are each Maule's grave and Gallows Hill.

So once the ghost is buried and ready to rise, what does it do? "It is wonderful," writes Hawthorne, "how many absurdities were promulgated in reference to the young man. He was fabled, for example, to have a strange power of getting into people's dreams, and regulating matters there according to his own fancy, pretty much like the stage manager of a theater" (189). In this passage, Hawthorne gives life to Maule's ghost — who has no existence outside of the text, of course — even as his diction ("absurdities," "fabled") calls attention to the fact that the ghost is decidedly not real. And this is how the symbol of the ghost functions throughout the novel: as a sign of history's relationship to myth, tradition, and superstition. But for Hawthorne, this is not a scathing, clear-cut critique of history's inadequacies. Instead, Hawthorne demonstrates how even the ghost — so distinctly indistinct, so unreal, so dead — can have real effects on both the novel's characters and its readers.

To begin to examine this question of the "ghostly real," or what Peter J. Bellis calls the "intermingling of Actual and Imaginary," I would like to look briefly at the portrait at the center of the novel (Bellis). When we first see the painting, we see at the same moment the "live" subject himself. As the party-goers squeeze into the study, they see "a large map on the wall, and likewise a portrait of Colonel Pyncheon, beneath which sat the original Colonel himself" (Hawthorne 15). The picture — supposedly the reified, unchanging, "deathlike" version of the colonel — is of course more alive than the actual colonel himself, who, it is discovered, is sitting beneath his portrait stone cold dead. From the beginning, the portrait seems to substitute for the colonel himself, not acting as a representation or copy of an original, but as a reincarnation or even a usurpation of the original subject. This collapsed hierarchy between original and copy becomes more pronounced when Judge Pyncheon and Matthew Maule discuss the possibility of turning the house back over to the Maules:

> The wild chimney-corner legend (which, without copying all its extravagances, my narrative essentially follows) here gives an account of some very strange behavior on the part of Colonel Pyncheon's portrait. This picture, it must be understood, was supposed to be so intimately connected with the fate of the house, and so magically built into its walls, that, if once it should be removed, that very instant, the whole edifice would come thundering down, in a heap of dusty ruin. All through the foregoing conversation between Mr. Pyncheon and the carpenter, the portrait had been frowning, clenching its fist, and giving many such proofs of excessive discomposure, but without attracting the notice of either of the two colloquists. And finally, at Matthew Maule's suggestion of a transfer of the seven-gabled structure, the ghostly portrait is averred to have lost all patience, and to have shown itself on the point of descending bodily from its frame. But such incredible incidents are merely to be mentioned aside [Hawthorne 197–98].

On the one hand, this passage reveals the way that the portrait stands in for the actual colonel. By nearly jumping out of its frame, the portrait seems to shrug off its limitations as "art" and enter the realm of the real. At the same time, Hawthorne situates this scenario into a context that is decidedly unreal: the context of gossip, legend, apostrophe. If the frame-jumping occurs only in the parts of the story that get described as unreliable and/or fanciful, what are readers to make of Hawthorne's ghosts? Are they to be believed or dismissed?

The ghostly pageant that occurs during Judge Pyncheon's death scene is in many ways the climax of the novel; however, the pageant itself is not so remarkable as the accompanying disclaimers that Hawthorne uses to bracket the event. "We are tempted to make a little sport," he begins. "Ghost-stories are hardly to be treated seriously, any longer. The family-party of the defunct Pyncheons, we presume, goes off in this wise" (279). This preface suggests that the entire parade is born of Hawthorne's own imagination (unlike the rest of the novel? Are we to believe all of that to be true? Is Hepzibah any more "real" than the ghost of Colonel Pyncheon?). And the parade concludes with a similar comment: "The fantastic scene, just hinted at, must by no means be considered as forming an actual portion of our story" (Hawthorne 281). In light of literary history, this sentence seems all the more amusing, since *The House of the Seven Gables* has gained fame as a ghost story. In fact, the ghosts in the text form what can only be described as the core of the novel. If Matthew Maule did not curse the Pyncheon family, if his ghost does not haunt the house, if Colonel Pyncheon and Judge Pyncheon are not living out a witch's prophecy, then what would this novel be about? The editors of the Oxford World's Classics edition of the novel summarize the story on the back cover in this way: "In *The House of the Seven Gables* Hawthorne sought to write a story which would show guilt to be a trick of the imagination." But *whose* imagination? Of course, the editors imply that Clifford and Hepzibah and, above all, the judge, are cursed more by their own broken consciences than anything else. But it is the *reader* more than anyone who is tricked by the story. You simply cannot leave this book without feeling that the ghosts had their way ... with Judge Pyncheon and with you.

Thus, what is central about the ghosts in *The House of the Seven Gables* is the way that they connect to the readers of the novel. When we first meet Hepzibah, Hawthorne tells us that her heavy sighs are "audible to nobody, save a disembodied listener like ourself" (30). Like the author, the reader here is omniscient. Throughout the text, we are brought into the story not as a character, but as sort of second author. At the end, when Judge Pyncheon lies dead and bloody in the house, as a monkey performs outside on the street, Hawthorne writes, "To us, who know the inner heart of the seven gables, as well as its exterior face, there is a ghastly effect in this repetition of light popular tunes at its door-step" (294). The reader hears things that aren't quite there (and yet Hepzibah's sighs are not quite *not* there, either). The reader knows things that the mortal characters cannot possibly know. And yet the reader, unlike the author, has not created the scene. In effect, the reader becomes a ghost of the author, a copy — like the colonel's portrait — that is able to jump its frame in order to render judgment about the action of the story. But the reader — again, like the portrait — seems to usurp its original; the author is overwhelmed by the reader's unwillingness to dismiss the frivolous, ahistorical, fanciful parts of the story. *The House of the Seven Gables* is first and foremost a ghost story: a story about ghosts, yes, but more importantly, a story told to a ghost who, like Matthew Maule and Colonel Pyncheon, is unwilling to lie quietly in its grave.

As author figures go in the text, Hawthorne creates a kind of artistic mirror of himself in Holgrave. Holgrave, like Hawthorne, is a direct descendent of a witch trial participant: Holgrave descended from an accused witch, and Hawthorne from a hanging judge. But more interestingly, Holgrave is a daguerreotypist, while Hawthorne is an author. Both claim to represent reality, but Holgrave seems to have a more direct line to the truth.[8] "There is at least no flattery in my humble line of work," Holgrave tells Phoebe. Holgrave's profession seems to have bled into his very character. "Homeless as he had been" we are told of him, "putting off one exterior, and snatching up another, to be soon shifted for a third — he had never violated the innermost man, but had carried his conscience along with him. It was impossible to know Holgrave without recognizing this to be the fact" (Hawthorne 177). Like a photograph, Holgrave is a true representation of himself; there is no gap between what his outside represents and who he truly "is." Like the portrait, Holgrave and his art seem to break out of their frames, leaving the realm of the performative and entering the realm of the elemental, the fundamental, the real. The ghostly pageant is not a "real" part of the story, but Holgrave and his work are, in many ways, "realer" than real. When Phoebe has to be told of the Judge's death, she is shown a daguerreotype — instead of the corpse, which is in the next room — of the dead man: "This is death!" she shudders when she sees it (Hawthorne 302).[9] The reader of *The House of the Seven Gables* is a ghost of the text's author, but Holgrave is an anti-ghost. As the text uses the ghostly mechanism of establishing and then (ineffectively) canceling its own truths, Holgrave functions as a kind of stable truth in the midst of this interpretive realm. His name is a doubled pun. He is a "whole grave," as he is a character who is complete, original, and true, not in spite of, but *because of,* his connections to the grave. After all, the revelation of his ancestry functions as the novel's moment of truth and the resolution of its mysteries. But the "hole" in his name reminds us — the reader-ghosts that we are — that even this daguerreotypist is caught in the novel's web of reality and romance. As Holgrave replaces the judge's corpse with the representation of the corpse, he suggests that the novel as a whole (or a hole?) has both great faith in art and great skepticism about whether or not the real exists or is relevant at all. Just as Salem itself is a series of representations that get reified into "historical fact," Hawthorne's story demonstrates the reification of romance into realism; in addition, he thematizes the attendant doubt that ultimately surfaces over whether or not representations can be so easily subordinated to and controlled by their originals. Hawthorne, then, writes a novel that is less about "a trick of the imagination" than it is about the inability of all of us — authors, readers, and characters alike — to distinguish between the truth and the fiction, the history and the gossip, the original and its embodied, its literary, or its artistic ghost.

Passions and Predictions: Marion Starkey and the Salem Story Romance

Marion Starkey's 1973 book, *The Visionary Girls*, uses the trial transcripts to add validity and verisimilitude to her amorous historical novel about the Salem witch trials. Starkey is a prolific Salem scholar, and her 1950 book *The Devil in Massachusetts* was a popular non-fiction account of the trials. *The Visionary Girls* takes up a familiar subject for Starkey, but it clearly diverges from *The Devil in Massachusetts*: "My first book was history in which I did not deviate from the records," she writes in an Author's Note to *The Visionary Girls*, "Nor do I in this so far as characters and the general course of events are concerned, but I have made use of 'poetic license' to enlarge on the records" (viii). For Starkey, "poetic license" means changing or adding to the facts in order to get at some deeper truth previously not accessible through the primary source documents: "I have invented [some] scenes," writes Starkey, "but they are what I believe really happened" (ix). Starkey uses quotations to camouflage the difference between direct passages taken from the trial records and newly invented dialogue penned by Starkey herself. Starkey's text has three main stylistic features. First, characters often speak the exact words that appear in the trial transcripts and other primary source documents. Second, characters speak in invented dialogue that reflects their emotional and psychological motivations, motivations that are not apparent in any primary sources. And third, Starkey uses background information culled from the transcripts and other histories of Salem (such as Upham's). What is compelling about the fact that this text is comprised almost exclusively of these three kinds of writing is the juxtaposition between actual records and complete fiction. It is extremely challenging for any reader to distinguish the real quotations from the invented dialogue, and Starkey cites no sources and makes no effort to point out the places where her own imagination leaves the trial records behind.

There are two major subjects that highlight Starkey's use of poetic license. She centers on the twin themes of romance and of Tituba's culpability, and both of these themes are concerned with the question of origin. In the opening of Chapter Two of her novel, Starkey explains one of the reasons that the trials happened: "Tituba's consultants," she writes, referring to the afflicted youths, "were merely young girls looking for a man, and what was wrong with that? If they had kept their secret to themselves neither they nor their village would have contributed a tragic page to history" (14). The search for "a man," then, is the impetus for the whole hysteria. Starkey reiterates this totally speculative hypothesis when she laments the fact that the young girls weren't sent more promptly to Cotton Mather, so that they could fall in love with him and therefore channel their unbridled passions into a safer avenue:

> Cotton Mather was immensely popular with the young people in his congregation, and in his work with such hysterics as came his way ... he achieved what a psychologist today would call a transference. Warming to his prayerful attentions, the girls more or less fell in love with him. All the afflicted of Salem Village, perhaps Ann Putnam and the two younger girls excepted, were ripe for love. What tragedy might have been spared the Procter family had Mary Warren been removed in time to the society of the personable young pastor [61].

For Starkey, the girls' desire for love is what propels them first to tell fortunes with Tituba, and second, to project their misplaced lust (such as Starkey claims Mary Warren has for "Procter") into unrelated situations, where it becomes toxic and malicious. Starkey effectively makes the Salem witch trials into a romance narrative, complete with unrequited love, jealousy, sexual frustration, and secret passions.[10] More interestingly, she suggests that the tragedy of Salem, like the tragedy of *Romeo and Juliet*, is not so much that romance exists in the story, but that it is not allowed to find its proper outlet and ripen to fruition. Though the literal narrative is hard to imagine, it makes symbolic sense in Starkey's world to wish that the afflicted had simply fallen in love with a minister. That way, the romance narrative can be fulfilled metaphorically by the union between Christ and his followers. But the carnal, anti-church lust that characterizes the girls' attempts to read tea leaves and break up marriages ends up destabilizing rather than strengthening the Christian system that keeps the peace in Salem. For Starkey, romance should be a happily-ever-after kind of fairy tale that reaffirms the position of God in the lives of the young, nubile girls. For the girls, however, romance is the very thing that pollutes this fairy tale. Starkey's novel is a classic romance novel gone bad, and she seems intent on showing just how easily the tragic ending could have been avoided had the rules of chaste love been followed.

If one theme in the novel centers around the corrupted romance at the heart of the tragedy, the other main theme in the novel certainly focuses on Tituba. Tituba is even, in many ways, at the center of the romance narrative, since she plays the role of matchmaker, bringing the girls together with their tea-leaf futures and married lovers. But even more than this, Tituba is presented in the book as a kind of Patient Zero, without whom the entire plague of trials and hangings never would have transpired. The first three accused (in the novel and in history) are Sarah Good, Sarah Osburne, and Tituba. Here is what Starkey has to say about Tituba's role in fanning the fires of hysteria:

> Goody Osburne, taken from her sickbed, quavered that she was "more like to bewitched than be a witch." Goody Good, defiant before authority, had one reply to all charges, "I scorn it!" Though both were held for formal trial (Goody Osburne died before it could take place) their fate would have been an obscure episode in history but for the conduct of the third prisoner. She was Tituba, and Tituba "confessed" [55].

This is, of course, a stunning statement. Would the afflicted girls have lost authority or motivation had all three of the first accused denied the allegations? Considering that Tituba herself denied the allegations at first, it seems at least possible that the hysteria would have continued regardless of her ultimate confession. But Starkey is adamant that Tituba is to blame for Salem's witchcraft past. What is most interesting, however, is the fact that Starkey blames Tituba for failing to confess the actual truth, which, according to Starkey, has to do with romance, tea leaves and fortune-telling, and lustful young girls, not with brooms, beatings, or claims of innocence:

> [Parris] beat the slave until he got a confession out of her. Not what actually happened — no one was ever to report in rational terms what went on between Tituba and the girls — but in terms of the mad logic of witchcraft [56].

In other words, Starkey faults Tituba for not coming clean about "the events in the parsonage kitchen" involving the calling out of spirits to predict the future (14). But these events, as far as anyone knows, occurred *only* in *The Visionary Girls* (and *The Crucible*, and, to a certain extent, in Upham's work), and definitively *not* in any primary source documents. For Starkey, the truth of what happened in Salem can only be revealed by fiction; *The Visionary Girls* shows what really transpired behind the lines of the trials records. Tituba stands as the figure for this fictive truth-telling, which is also the role she plays on a more literal level in the novel, telling fortunes that over and over again in the novel turn out to be true. For example, Tituba is able to foresee the hangings, even including such details as Elizabeth Procter's pregnancy that ultimately saves her from the gallows (Starkey 19). In the novel, fortune-telling functions the same way that the novel itself functions in relationship to history. Tituba's fortune-telling tells truths that seem fictive or outside of the known, just as the novel itself purports to tell truths that similarly seem made up or impossible to know. In many ways, Starkey herself becomes her own Tituba: a fortune-teller who not only holds all the answers, but who must bear all of the responsibility for the tragedy that unfolds.[11] Tituba predicts the hangings, but also causes them. Starkey explains "what happened" in Salem, but also *creates* the very past she seems to expose. Starkey's continual references to Tituba's "tranced," "hypnotizing" eyes help to mold the slave character into the voodoo priestess that she has become in popular representations of the Salem witch trials (7, 11). But the diction points to a more nuanced concept of the Tituba figure: she is both in a trance and all-knowing *and* hypnotizing and all-powerful. This is ultimately the paradox of the writer of historical fiction: Starkey both knows all of the facts about the past that she claims to represent even as she powerfully imagines a story that is all her own, hypnotizing her readers into believing that she is just a messenger speaking the truth. This hypnotizing effect allows her moralistic romance tale to flourish. Starkey can chastise the afflicted girls for their anti–Church lustfulness because she has revealed herself to be an omniscient authority; at the same time, she projects any fictionality — associated with the figure of the whore[12] — safely away from herself so as to remain, herself, chaste, pure, and truthful.

Songs and Laments: Irony in Maryse Condé's I, Tituba, Black Witch of Salem

Maryse Condé's 1986 novel *Moi, Tituba, Sorcière ... Noire de Salem* was translated into English by her husband, Richard Philcox, in 1992. Born in Guadeloupe in 1937, West Indian author Maryse Condé was educated in Paris, and has lived in independent Guinea, Ghana, and Senegal, and in the United States. Condé herself sees her novel as an attempt to give voice to a previously silenced historical subject. Before examining the text in detail, it is worthwhile to explore Condé's articulated agenda for writing the novel, and consider how this agenda fits with previous fictional and historical representations of Tituba. At the end of her novel (and I am dealing here with the 1992 English translation), Condé includes a brief historical note. After a concise summary of the known transcriptual evidence about Tituba, Condé writes, "Around 1693 Tituba, our heroine, was sold for the price of her prison fees and the cost of her chains and shackles. To whom? Such is the intentional or unintentional racism of the historians that we shall never know" (183). In an interview that is included with the English translation of the text, Condé explains that she sees Tituba as a neglected, erased figure from the past: "I got lost in the huge building [of the Occidental College Library] and found myself in the history section in front of a shelf of books about the Salem witch trials. Looking through them, I discovered the existence of Tituba, whom I had never heard of before. This story may seem farfetched. However, it is entirely true" (199). Even though *I, Tituba* follows both *The Crucible* and Starkey's books, all of which were extremely popular, Condé reveals that to her, Tituba's history is a forgotten one. "This story may seem farfetched," she writes, and I wonder, which story? Tituba's or Condé's? For most American readers of Condé's novel, it seems more unlikely that someone could have knowledge of the witch trials and never heard of Tituba than it does that Tituba existed and played a role in the trials. In fact, most American readers have what I might call "Tituba overexposure"; she has been so mythologized throughout American history, and her role in the trials so dramatically and creatively expanded, that in many ways Tituba has become the central figure in Salem fiction and history.

Bernard Rosenthal, in his article "Tituba's Story," claims that Tituba has been "branded the instigator of the crisis as early as 1702," when John Hale wrote that "the success of Tituba's confession encouraged those in Authority to examine others that were suspected, and the event was, that more confessed themselves guilty of the Crimes they were suspected for. And thus was this matter driven on" (Rosenthal 4, Hale 415). Since then, writes Rosenthal, "her story has taken on nothing short of mythical dimensions"; he even equates Tituba with Eve, arguing that both women were responsible for an "originary myth of the Fall," and that both "carried the burden of having introduced sin and loss" (1). Early narratives such as Hale's, Daniel Neal's, and Thomas Hutchinson's suggested that Tituba's confession spurred the hysteria and ultimately laid the foundation for further accusations.[13] But beginning in the early 1800s, Tituba's story grows more intriguing. Writer and reformer John Neal's 1828 novel *Rachel Dyer*, which, as noted previously, is the first novel written about the Salem witch trials, depicts Tituba as "a woman of diabolical power" who seems, mysteriously, to be around whenever the young children take ill (Neal 59). In 1867 when Upham published his history, he expanded on Neal's intimations and began the myth that Tituba had imported strange religious practices from her homeland and that she had met with a small group of the afflicted girls and sparked their imaginations about the invisible world. Since so many American writers, including Miller and Starkey, dealt directly with Upham's text, Tituba has continued to be refigured in the image of practitioner of the black arts.

Even more interesting than the fact that Tituba's main characterization emerged more than a century after the trials were ended is the fact that historians and writers have refigured her race at the same time as they altered her personality. In his 1974 *New England Quarterly* article, Chadwick Hansen traces her transformation from Indian to half Indian to half "Negro" to "Negro." Bernard Rosenthal points out that not only is there no evidence to suggest that Tituba was brought by Parris from Barbados, but that she is *consistently* referred to as "Indian" in all trial records, records which do a solid job of delineating between native "Indians" and people who were imported in the slave trade. Thus, Tituba has emerged through history and fiction as a black slave imported by Parris who practiced Barbadian voodoo and was married to John Indian.[14] None of these "facts" is supported by primary source evidence. Rosenthal concludes, "Those despising Tituba and those celebrating her all ultimately return to the same invented narrative" (3). Though there are certainly many people who know little or nothing about the Salem witch trials, it seems likely that those who have some awareness of the 1692 events have heard something about Tituba. What is compelling about Condé's approach to the character is that despite her assertions that she is doing something new by writing an invented Tituba back into the historical record, this is precisely the Tituban methodology; practically every writer before Condé has placed Tituba at the center of the Salem story, and practically every writer has done it, like Condé, with more imagination than fact.

But it is not the case that Condé's novel simply continues the trajectory of Salem studies that blame Tituba, whatever her cultural heritage, for the witch hunt. Condé's work does something very different with Tituba than, say, Starkey's or Arthur Miller's. Starkey and Miller both claim to work closely with historical records; and Condé, too, claims a sort of direct historical connection. As an epigraph to the novel, Condé writes, "Tituba and I have lived for a year on the closest of terms. During our endless conversations she told me things she had confided to nobody else" (vii). Condé claims that her novel comes from the most primary of primary sources: the mouth of the actual Tituba.[15] Like Condé's Tituba, Condé herself is apparently able to communicate with the dead, to raise them up and speak to them as if they were still alive. And yet, in a 1996 interview, Condé says, "Tituba's spirit did not come to me. The epigraph was just for fun" (Pfaff 59). This contradiction points to the irony that infuses *I, Tituba*. Condé puts it this way: "What some critics did not understand is that the book is ironic. It is also a pastiche of the feminine historic novel, a parody containing a lot of cliché's about the grandmother, the sacrosanct grandmother, and about women in their relationship to the occult. I split my sides laughing while writing the book.... I don't see how people could read *I, Tituba, Black Witch of Salem* with any seriousness in the first place and make Tituba into something she is not" (Pfaff 60). Though Condé's irony can be difficult to delineate (we shall examine it in some depth below), she sets her project apart from Miller and Starkey by locating parody and humor in the tragic story of Tituba. Though on the one hand, Condé is concerned with bringing Tituba's story into the light and using actual trial texts to illustrate her presence in Salem, she is also interested in challenging the serious academic notion that Tituba can be located at all. Condé's use of parody and irony continually intersects with her desire to expose a forgotten truth of the past, and this paradox between methodology and political agenda adds a dimension to her work that sets her apart from previous writers whose form and content have been intentionally seamless.

Condé's irony is first established in the way her novel utilizes and alters known facts about the trial history. Tituba, as a character, is clearly aware that the question of how she relates to the actual, historical Tituba permeates the entire novel. In jail after being accused, Tituba has a premonition about the way history will remember her role in the witch hunt:

> It seemed that I was gradually being forgotten. I felt that I would only be mentioned in passing in these Salem witchcraft trials about which so much would be written later, trials that would arouse the curiosity and pity of generations to come.... There would be mention here and there of "a slave originating from the West Indies and probably practicing 'hoodoo.'" There would be no mention of my age or my personality. I would be ignored.... There would never, ever, be a careful, sensitive biography recreating my life and its suffering [Condé 110].

This projection is, of course, reminiscent of Condé's own opinion of what actually did occur with the historical writings produced on the subject of the trials. But as Tituba forecasts this erased history, she also corrects it, for the "careful, sensitive" biography — or autobiography —*has* been written, is being written as she launches her critique. In other words, Tituba establishes herself as both a past, forgotten historical subject and a present, authoritative, historical biographer. By looking forward into the future — which to us, as readers, manifests as a look back into the historiographical past — Tituba manages to inhabit an ironic, tripled temporal position. She is past, present, and future, and she is erased/powerless and visible/authoritative.[16]

If Condé plays the powerful fictive Tituba against the disempowered historical Tituba, she also plays with the specific facts of the history itself, inverting recorded events to shift the overall mythic significance accorded to the Salem story throughout history. Consider, by way of example, the character of Rebecca Nurse, who in historical records and writings before Condé has been described as a pure martyr, noble, pious, and fully good. Condé, however, challenges this characterization of Nurse, suggesting that she, too, would have been as petty and vindictive as any other accusing Salemite:

> I was deep in thought about my terrible dilemma when I heard Rebecca Nurse murmur: "Tituba, can't you punish them? It's those Houltons again who forgot to tie up their hogs and they've ruined our vegetable garden once more...." For a moment I didn't understand. Then I realized what she expected of me. I was seized with anger and let go her arm, leaving her all askew in front of a fence. Oh no, they won't get me to be the same as they are! I will not give in. I will not do evil! [Condé 69].

Though Nurse does end up as a martyr figure in *I, Tituba*, she is presented as contradictory and complex, not wholly pure.[17] At the same time as Nurse is made fallible, Tituba is raised to the status of pure, innocent heroine. Her subsequent corruption into one who would name names and therefore "take revenge" becomes the fault of the (white) "they" that drags her down to their level. This "they" is inclusive; it refers to the magistrates who rape Tituba to procure her confession, Sarah Good and other accused witches who betray her in jail, everyday Salemites who wished all along that Tituba would be a witch (and therefore capable of doing their evil bidding), and Hester Prynne whose bitter brand of "feminism" encourages spite in the face of oppression.

Though Condé has asserted many times that Hester's encounters with Tituba are meant to be parodic, critics still take issue with the anachronistic quality of the scenes. Robert H. McCormick, Jr., for example, complains that Condé's imagination has grown "too fertile" in the Hester-Tituba scenes (277). One of the most contested passages in these sections is a dialogue between Hester and Tituba, about Hester's wish to found an all-female utopian community:

> "I'd like to write a book where I'd describe a model society governed and run by women! We would give our names to our children, we would raise them alone...."
>
> I interrupted her, poking fun: "We couldn't make them alone, even so!"
>
> "Alas, no," she said sadly. "Those abominable brutes would have to share in a fleeting moment."
>
> "Not too short a moment," I teased. "I like to take my time."
>
> She ended up laughing and drew me close to her.
>
> "You're too fond of love, Tituba! I'll never make a feminist out of you!"
>
> "A feminist? What's that?" [Condé 101].

Condé parodies white lesbian feminism, a distinct political and social movement of the 1970s and 1980s.[18] Her Hester is a man-hating separatist. And unlike Tituba, she seems cut off from her own sexuality. While Tituba masturbates, adores John Indian's penis, has sex with her surrogate son, and returns from the dead to have sex as frequently as she did while alive, Hester even abhors her own child, the "offspring of a man [she] hated," and sees pregnancy as a sign of women's submission to men (Condé 15, 19, 169, 97). But she does give Tituba a night of "bodily pleasure," as well as several sexualized kisses to the neck, etc. (Condé 122). Interestingly, however, Hester is so sexually repressed that even her lesbian desire can only emerge after her suicide, when she is just a ghost. The spiteful, repressed Hester is still a savior figure for Tituba. Tituba's only regret to accompany her to the afterlife is that she doesn't see Hester often enough, since Tituba is in Barbados while Hester is across the sea near Salem (Condé 178). What emerges with Hester is another irony; Hester is not just a parody of white feminism, but also a deadly serious homage to white feminism.[19] Just as Rebecca Nurse is both fallible *and* a martyr, Hester is allowed in the novel to be both ridiculously comedic and tragically inspiring. These paradoxes characterize Condé's particular brand of irony. Hester's fictionality — for readers are clearly supposed to recognize her as a character from *The Scarlet Letter* — is undercut by the way that she instructs Tituba on how to respond in her deposition; and this deposition is reprinted in the novel directly from actual trial transcripts. And Hester's anachronistic quality (neither *The Scarlet Letter* nor lesbian feminism are "actually" coterminous with 1692) is undercut by the novel's placement of Hester in jail for committing adultery; Hester's behavior in *I, Tituba* is consistent with both the conditions of *The Scarlet Letter* and the rationale of lesbian feminism. Though together, Condé's novel, Hawthorne's novel, and current-day feminism seem out of alignment, Condé makes sure that there is a certain kind of consistency between the three landscapes. This misaligned consistency is precisely what makes the parody function so delicately: the real and the fictive, the comedic and the tragic, the past and the present, all are wound so tightly in the scenes between Hester and Tituba that focusing on just one aspect of their dialogue or tone could make the entire novel unravel into loose threads of over-earnestness or silliness.

Throughout the novel, Tituba is searching for her song, a song that society has told her over and over again does not exist. Christopher puts it bluntly when asked:

> I touched him on the shoulder. "And what about me, is there a song for me? A song for Tituba?"
> He pretended to listen hard, then said: "No, there isn't!" Thereupon he began to snore [Condé 153].

But after her death, Tituba discovers that she does have a song, and that it inhabits the island, shouting itself out whenever Tituba "take[s] the trembling spirit of a dead person in [her] hands" or reunites someone alive with someone who has passed away (Condé 175). Tituba's song is, in many ways, the novel itself, which is mainly concerned with introducing living readers to a historical character long since dead. But this joyous song, which crosses the boundaries between past and present, is juxtaposed with Tituba's other song, a song that recurs several times in the novel during Tituba's most vulnerable moments: the moonstone lament. The lament is about a lovely girl ("I," she is called by Tituba) who drops her moonstone into the river. A hunter happens by, offers to dive for it to end her weeping, and is drowned in his attempt. The moonstone lies "glimmering at the bottom of the water," easy to see and seemingly easy to retrieve (Condé 113). But appearances are deceiving, and the stone ends up, like a mirage, just out of reach of the girl's fingers and the hunter's dive. The lament, unlike Tituba's other song, does not collapse boundaries; instead it erects or reinforces them. Tituba sings the lament for her and Hester's dead children, symbolizing that they will never know anything about these children and "what does it matter really?" (Condé 113). On the one hand, Tituba sings a song of joy, echoed back to her from the future, about the ability of the past to remain present. On the other hand, she sings a lament to those who will never hear her, about the inability to recapture that which has been irretrievably lost. The twin songs of Tituba, like the other paradoxes and ironies that saturate Condé's story, ultimately comment on Tituba's own place in history. In this novel, she is alive, present, and fictive, even as she is dead, past, and forgotten by the same history she helps to rewrite.[20]

The Price of Research: Science and History in Acceptable Risk

Robin Cook's 1995 pulp fiction novel *Acceptable Risk* was, like many of his novels, a *New York Times* bestseller. Cook, a graduate of Columbia Medical School who did his postdoctoral work in medicine at Harvard, is famous for high-octane medical thrillers, and his previous works have featured wild but current-events-oriented plots: the use of murder to obtain organ donors; a doctor accused of malpractice who discovers a vast conspiracy; the dark — even evil — side of managed care. *Acceptable Risk* takes on another "hot topic," the overconfidence Americans have in prescription psychotropic drugs such as Prozac. But the novel has as much to say about how we think about our historical past as it does about what we think about the present state of U.S. psychopharmacology. In this novel, a neuroscientist isolates a drug with promising psychological effects, and at the same time, he manages to unlock the mystery of the Salem witch trials. Drawing on trial transcripts and recent historical and biological scholarship about Salem, Cook uses science as a panacea to cure what ails us; practical problems and identity crises are alleviated by the drug his characters discover. And yet, at the same time, a dark side lurks below the surface, an intimation that science can lead to fading memory and dehumanization even as it promises a link with the past and a heightened civility. For Cook, science is a cure-all and a root cause of the very problems it claims to — and indeed can — solve. And for Cook, science and history are inextricable.

As discussed in Chapter Two, the ergot-poisoning hypothesis was extended by Linnda R. Caporael, and it claimed that a fungus which comes from the mold *Claviceps purpurea* infected rye bread in Salem, and, when it was ingested, the symptoms caused the fits and hallucinations experienced by the afflicted. Edward, Cook's fictional neuroscientist, explains it to his girlfriend Kim — a descendent of the (invented) Elizabeth Stewart, a hanged witch — this way: "Remember that Beatles song, 'Lucy in the Sky with Diamonds'? Well, it would have been something like that because ergot contains lysergic acid amide, which is the prime ingredient of LSD" (Cook 42–43). Edward is keen to prove that the Salem afflicted were poisoned. He tells Kim as he gathers dirt samples from Elizabeth's former basement, "If I find *Claviceps purpurea* down there ... I know one thing that information will do: it will rob a bit of the supernatural out of the story of the Salem witchcraft trials" (Cook 66). For Edward, science and the supernatural are at odds, and he aims to replace witches with mold spores. In addition, he wants to redeem the reputations of accused witches, and prove once and for all that they were not guilty of cavorting with the devil. "If I can prove that ergotism was at the heart of the Salem witch craze," he says, "it would remove any possible remaining stigma people felt who were associated with the ordeal, particularly the Stewarts" (Cook 73). The shame that Kim and her mother feel about Elizabeth's death is palpable, and neither will openly discuss the matter at the beginning of the novel. Kim's lessening shame is directly related to Edward's scientific discoveries and his overall scientific curiosity. Cook, then, suggests that science cannot only illuminate the truth about history, it can also change our psychological experiences of such interior emotions as shame and resentment. If Prozac in the text represents a kind of scientifically engineered emotional health, then Ultra, the ergot-based drug Edward invents, links this same mental health to the process of history; Cook creates a triangular relationship between science, history, and psychology.

In many ways, this triangle appears to be a solid working relationship throughout the novel. Kim and Edward function as two points of the triangle; Edward is mainly concerned with the scientific work of Ultra while Kim focuses on the archival history of Elizabeth's story.[21] Both Kim and Edward meet at the third point — the psychological point — and for Kim, the psychological well-being that she finds through her historical research functions as a kind of self-actualization. Edward says to Kim as he looks at an old portrait of Elizabeth, "What's so damn striking about it ... is that it looks a lot like you, especially with those green eyes" (Cook 64). Kim begins to sense a connection between herself and her ancestor: "It's as if Elizabeth were trying to speak to me over the centuries, perhaps to restore her reputation" (Cook 65). On the day that Kim moves into Elizabeth's house, she finds Elizabeth's diary and opens automatically to an entry about the day *Elizabeth* moves in to the very same house. But more than appearances and coincidences, Kim senses a connection between her wronged, shamed ancestor and her own insecurities. "The reality was," Cook writes, "Kim had not allowed her own interests and aptitudes to chart her course through life" (Cook 357). The daughter of an overbearing, hard-to-please father, Kim ended up a nurse and let her real passion (for interior design!) fall by the wayside. Over and over, the text makes issue of Kim's shyness, her failure to stand up for herself, and her willingness to be a doormat to the men in her life. Kim speculates that Elizabeth may have been abused by men, too. Though there is no evidence to back it up, and though it is finally completely disproved, Kim suggests that Ronald, Elizabeth's husband, may have had her hanged so that he could marry her sister. As Kim builds a psychological parallel between herself and Elizabeth, she begins to uncover Elizabeth's story as much to vindicate and declare herself as to absolve her ancestor of the title of "witch." At the end of the novel, when all historical questions have been answered, Kim believes she sees Elizabeth's portrait smile,[22] and she vows "to live the rest of her life for both of them" (Cook 385). For Kim, the novel seems to have a happy ending, and the implications are that good historical research will change not only the ontological facts that can be known about the past, but also the subjective, or psychological, experience that would-be historians have of the present.

Of course, science and history cannot be so easily separated in this novel, and Kim's discoveries depend upon the knowledge that she gets from Edward about the ergot. Asked by Kim if he thinks ergot was responsible for the witchcraft outbreak in Salem, Edward replies, "Without a doubt ... [ergot is] the Salem devil incarnate" (Cook 167). But if ergot leads to self-actualization for Kim by solving the historical dilemma of the outbreak and absolving both her and Elizabeth of guilt, it offers self-actualization to Edward in a different way. Edward creates an ergot derivative that he calls "Ultra," and takes it to improve his psychological state. Though the drug at first makes him feel "bitten," "pinched," and "chok[ed]" — clearly references that solidify his argument that this compound caused the Salem crisis — it also makes him feel "clairvoyant" and "euphoric" (Cook 101–102). But more than this, Edward loses his stutter, becomes more tolerant, less shy, and downright assertive, a feeling that he loves and recollects from his days on Prozac. The clairvoyant effect is particularly interesting. We are told that Edward's previous work, before Ultra, had the "overall goal of elucidating the mechanisms of short- and long-term memory," and Ultra causes its users to recall long-forgotten phone numbers and "remember all sorts of things with startling clarity" (Cook 68, 177, 147). Cook reminds us that just as Kim's historical work was intimately tied to the science of Edward's lab, Edward's scientific discoveries are linked to the past in direct and symbolic ways. The triangular relationship between science, history, and psychology seems to deliver Edward, just as it did Kim, to a place of total contentment.

What all of this suggests is that the book uses the ergot-poisoning theory as a sacred cow, an indisputable scientific discovery that solves the problems of both past and present. But the happy ending and the general upturn in the psychological health of the characters are completely undermined by several events in the novel. For one thing, the nature of the "evidence" that convicted Elizabeth Stewart back in Salem in 1692 shifts the way we read the novel's ending. Readers are told about this evidence in the novel's opening scene, and yet they must wait until nearly the end of the book before they find out precisely what the evidence *is*. At the outset, the evidence is described as "real," "strong," "shocking," "horrifying," "compelling proof" (Cook 21–22). As Kim searches through documents, she finds many mentions of the evidence, but no exact description of it. The deferral, which of course provides much of the novel's suspense, functions to establish the evidence as the central mystery surrounding Elizabeth's death. Once solved, the mystery should answer the historical questions that linger for Kim around the events of 1692. The evidence, then, seems to be the key to providing closure to Kim's hunt, and indeed, when it is found, it both confirms Edward's scientific hypothesis that Elizabeth was poisoned and concludes Kim's historical search for answers. *But* the nature of the evidence also undermines both of these "happy" endings. Kim discovers the evidence in a tiny Harvard museum. It is brought out and she observes it: "Crammed into a large glass jar filled with brown-stained preservative was a four-to-five-month-old fetus that looked like a monster" (Cook 354). The deformed fetus, with its hoof-like fingers and fish-like tail, "could easily have been taken for the devil incarnate. Indeed, copies of woodcut prints of the devil that Kim had seen from that era looked identical" (Cook 355).[23] The fetus functions both as the answer that exonerates Elizabeth and proves Kim's and Edward's work worthwhile *and* as the hideous symbol of the monstrosity that they have brought back to life.[24] The fetus is a symbol of the past, present, and future: past because we witness its birth in the old documents that Kim unearths; present because we watch with Kim as it is pulled down from a Harvard shelf on a busy, present-day afternoon; future because the unborn child — itself a kind of symbol for (sick and unrealized) potential — has, in the words of Cook's Cotton Mather, been "preserved at the College for the edification and instruction of future generations" (Cook 198). Thus, the fetus stands in the text as a symbol for historical-scientific success and its attendant horrors.

These horrors reach their height when it is revealed that Ultra is slowly turning Edward and his colleagues into murderous animals. Like ergot, its predecessor, Ultra eventually causes collective panic and death. When Kim visits the lab and notes the new "buoyant" atmosphere, she gets "the uncomfortable feeling that some degree of group hysteria was occurring" (Cook 249). As the researchers test the new drug on themselves, their sense of their own improving memories is undercut by their increasing forgetfulness. Edward brushes his teeth twice in a row and forgets to feed his beloved dog repeatedly (Cook 276–77). But worst of all, the researchers are discovered to be roaming at night, ferreting through garbage, killing and eating small animals, and even murdering a man and consuming half of his body. It is as if, one researcher explains, "we'd experienced retroevolution.... [We're] functioning on our lower-brain centers alone. [We're] like carnivorous reptiles!" (Cook 327). They hunt primarily via a heightened sense of smell, and snarl and behave like animals when encountered. The loss of memory and the animalistic behavior both directly counter the book's original argument that the science-history-psychology triangle can deliver society to a clearer understanding of the past and a more civilized and advanced human self-identity. Though Edward's disintegration is more grotesque, Kim also senses a kind of danger in her own quest to identify with Elizabeth: "With a shudder, Kim wondered if a fate similar to Elizabeth's was in store for her" (Cook 282). Though Kim technically gets a happy ending and Edward gets institutionalized (in a specially designed science lab!), she does in some ways end up with a fate like Elizabeth's: she will live out her days in Elizabeth's house, smiling at Elizabeth's portrait that looks so much like her, knowing that both she and Elizabeth have had their true selves exposed by the historical-scientific process of the novel. The book, then, claims to restore the health of the triangle even as the "shudder" lurks underneath. The "one thing" that Kim takes from the horrifying events of the novel is that "all drug taking, whether steroids for athletes or psychtropic drugs for character enhancement, is a Faustian contract" (Cook 378). Indeed, for Kim to have her happy ending, she too has made a deal with the devil. Ultra is not the only drug in the novel. As Kim addictively rummages through primary sources and hunts through museum holdings, she invents a historical question that can only be answered by a dead fetus, a symbol of the hideous side effects of finding out "the truth." Cook's novel presents historical and scientific inquiries as risky endeavors. For Kim, the risks turn out to be "acceptable." But the happy ending that follows scenes in which Edward eats both his own dog and a passing stranger might make readers — if not Edward — think twice about the price of such research.

Each of these novels is interested in the pursuit of historical truth, and in each novel, "truth" is not so much something that is discovered or arrived at, but something which gets constructed by the characters who seek to locate it. For Hawthorne, even the ghostly past, long dead and perhaps even a product of human imagination, haunts the "real" world and the people who inhabit it. For Starkey, "truth" finds its clearest expression in storytelling, and novelists both create and recount the past in much the way Tituba the fortune-teller recounts and creates the futures she prophesies. Maryse Condé fully realizes this kind of irony as she picks up the character of Tituba, and positions her as both a conduit to the past and as a figure who has tragically and irrevocably lost so many who were dear to her. What is the risk of trying to tell the truth about what happened in the past, whether that past be 1692's Salem or any other historical moment? It is that a truth-teller will never be able to tell the truth without also simultaneously telling a story.

FOUR

A Dramatic Tale

Salem on Stage and Screen

If Salem novelists remember history through the lenses of irony and invention, Salem texts written to be staged (plays, films, television shows) make explicit the distance between history and fiction by calling attention to the perimeter that constructs the text *as* a text. As discussed in Chapter One, many of the trial transcripts echo the performative and theatrical elements that become culturally associated with the witch trials as staged versions of the events become popular. While Chapter One of this book does not locate performativity in the transcripts as a way of demonstrating the primacy or originality of that characteristic in Salem's witch history, it is compelling to note that the explicit theatricality of these staged Salem texts is not so much a quality that accompanied the transition to the stage as much as it is a quality of the history that has been made explicit by these performed versions. What happens when Arthur Miller uses the theatrics of the transcripts to script a play that would become one of the most enduringly popular Salem texts? In what ways do playwrights, moviemakers, and television writers and executives develop the Salem narrative that has been so multiplicitously shaped by primary sources, historians, and novelists? In this chapter, we will examine six main staged versions of the Salem story: Longfellow's short 1868 play, "Giles Corey of the Salem Farms"; Arthur Miller's famous 1953 play, *The Crucible*; two films from the 1930s and 1940s, *Maid of Salem* and *I Married a Witch*; and two more recent television episodes, from *Bewitched* and *Sabrina, The Teenage Witch*. Compellingly, what these texts will make *most* explicit is how language is constructed, and how rhetoric functions both to reify and to destabilize that most confused category of "witch."

126

The Politics of Witchcraft and the Production of Proof: Longfellow and the Real

"Giles Corey of the Salem Farms" is a short play by Henry Wadsworth Longfellow, written and first published in 1868, seventeen years after *The House of the Seven Gables*. Hawthorne, who is no stranger to scathing social commentary of the sort found in *The Scarlet Letter*, has a partner in critique in Longfellow, who portrays in his play the hysterical tenor that characterized the witch trials. In the prologue, the Chorus describes the leadership of colonial Salem: "The Minister and the Magistrate/ Who ruled their little realm with an iron rod,/ Less in the love than in the fear of God" (Longfellow 562). What is most interesting about his critique, however, is the way in which he mixes methodological analyses. On one level, Longfellow launches a political analysis that cites concrete racial, economic, and gendered reasons why the witch hunt gathered such power and momentum. On another level, though, Longfellow examines how more abstract philosophies colored the hunt; specifically, his play considers the relationship between the spectral and the real, and between lies and the truth, and he blurs the foundational lines that supposedly separate the witch from the hunter.[1]

Like Arthur Miller's play about the witch trials, which I will discuss later in this chapter, Longfellow's drama begins with Tituba. Though we might expect Tituba to function as a scapegoat for the 1692 events (as, in some ways, she functions in both Marion Starkey and Miller), what Longfellow does with this character is rather extraordinary. As she gathers herbs "in the woods near Salem Village," she ruminates about the plants she collects: "I know their secrets,/ And gather them because they give me power/ Over all men and women. Armed with these,/ I, Tituba, an Indian and a slave,/ Am stronger than the captain with his sword,/ Am richer than the merchant with his money,/ Am wiser than the scholar with his books,/ Mightier than Ministers and Magistrates,/ With all the fear and reverence that attend them!" She concludes, "Thus I work vengeance on mine enemies,/ Who, while they call me slave, are slaves to me!" (Longfellow 362–63). Tituba flips the prevailing power differential in Salem, commenting both on how her status as slave presumably places her below the ruling classes of the colony *and* on how her status as a witch allows her to step outside of her social position.

The ability of witchcraft to affect social status arises again in a scene between Martha and Giles Corey. Giles has lost his saddle, and Martha, who knows where it is, teases Giles and will not tell him the location of the saddle; she hopes he will stay at home instead of riding to town to get tied up in the witchcraft chaos. Consider this exchange between the husband and wife:

> COREY: Have you seen my saddle?
> MARTHA: I saw it yesterday.
> COREY: Where did you see it?
> MARTHA: On a gray mare, that somebody was riding/ Along the village road.
> COREY: Who was it? Tell me.
> MARTHA: Some one who should have stayed at home.
> COREY: *(restraining himself)* I see! Don't vex me, Martha.... I'll ride down to the village/ Bare-back; and when the people stare and say,/ "Giles Corey, where's your saddle?" I will answer, "A witch has stolen it." How shall you like that? [Longfellow 576–77].

Corey's threats prompt Martha to fetch the saddle, but they also serve to illustrate how witchcraft relates to the power relationship between men and women, husbands and wives, in Salem. Longfellow demonstrates here that witchcraft can be a containing agent that works to cement the status quo whenever it threatens to collapse.

Tituba and Martha, then, are two contradictory examples of how witchcraft functions. For Tituba, it works to release her from her slave identity; for Martha, it works to ensure her subservience to her husband. But despite this apparent paradox, there is also a dramatic commonality, for both Tituba's and Martha's cases suggest that witchcraft has less to do with magical power than it does with social power.[2] Though Tituba asserts that her herbal talents are what make her powerful, there is no evidence in the text that her conjurings actually have any result. For example, when she meets up with a lost Cotton Mather in the woods, she tells him that she will lead him the way out if he lets her climb atop his horse with him. Though he is pleased to meet this "penitent confessor" (for she has presumably already saved herself from execution by confessing her sins), he is appalled by the thought that he, a prominent reverend, would be seen riding with a witch. Rebuked by his attitude, Tituba retorts, "I do not need a horse!/ I can ride through the air upon a stick,/ Above the treetops and above the houses,/ And no one sees me, no one overtakes me!" (Longfellow 565). Immediately the scene ends. When the next scene opens, Mather is comfortably seated in Justice Hathorne's living room. How did he get there? Did Tituba really fly, leading him out of the woods by broomstick? We don't know. The play relegates all acts of "witchcraft" to the invisible realm — that is, the spaces outside of the play itself. What we know for sure about Tituba's exchange with Mather is not that she rode through the air on a stick in front of him, but that she used her identity as a witch to deny his attempts to scorn and belittle her. Though Tituba uses witchcraft to free herself from her slave identity while Martha has witchcraft used against her to force her to accept her wifely duties, Longfellow seems to suggest that witchcraft was used in seventeenth-century Salem as a tool for establishing hierarchies of power.

This suggestion arises again in the relationship between John Proctor, Giles Corey, and John Gloyd, Corey's hired man. Proctor accuses Corey of burning down his house in retaliation related to an ongoing dispute. A village farmer explains it to Corey like this:

> FARMER: He said you did it out of spite to him/ For taking part against you in the quarrel/ You had with John Gloyd about his wages....
> COREY: I'll not be slandered at a time like this,/ When every word is made an accusation,/ When every whisper kills, and every man/ Walks with a halter round his neck! [Longfellow 579].

The wage dispute is at the core of the compromised rapport between Proctor and Corey. Gloyd himself discusses his complaints about Corey. When told by a local man that Corey seems a good master, Gloyd replies, "If hard work and low wages make good masters,/ Then he is one. But I think otherwise./ Come, let us have our dinner and be merry,/ And talk about the old man and the Witches" (Longfellow 594). In the ensuing discussion, Gloyd makes it clear that he is skeptical about the actual witchcraft charges launched by the afflicted girls: "Oh, those Afflicted Children," he says, "They know well/ Where the pins come from. I can tell you that" (Longfellow 595). But despite his skepticism, he is happy to joke and make merry about the accusations, nap calmly after Martha is seized, and jockey for a good seat in the courtroom so that he can best enjoy the spectacle of the trials. Gloyd demonstrates that class stratification provides good kindling for the witch hunt, and the Proctor-Corey dispute shows how accusations of witchcraft can grow from socioeconomic roots. Race, gender, and class all provide the soil from which witchcraft grows, and witchcraft itself functions as a cover — possibly only a semantic cover — for the contests over power that rest underground.

A metaphorical parallel exists between the witchcraft/politics relationship and the relationship of the spectral to the physical. In the play, witchcraft works hard to contain and diffuse political conflict, even as it actually gives voice to the radical power differentials at work in Salem. Similarly, "reality" in the play keeps surfacing as characters attempt to explain — and thereby annihilate or solve — the spectral mysteries at issue during the witch hunt. But just as witchcraft exacerbates political strife, the intrusion of "reality" simply serves to call into question the strength of the divide between the spectral and physical worlds. Consider this exchange between Justice Hathorne and the Reverend Mather about their visit with afflicted girl Mary Walcot:

> HATHORNE: You now see/ With your own eyes, and touch with your own hands,/ The mysteries of witchcraft.
> MATHER: One would need/ The hands of Briareus and the eyes of Argus/ To see and touch them all [Longfellow 570].

Mather's reference to these two mythological creatures (the first a many-armed and the second a many-eyed monster) is interesting in its reliance on fictional, non-biblical creatures. Indeed, in order to make witchcraft real and tangible, one must be oneself *unreal.* Mather clearly means to establish a tautology here: witchcraft can only be seen and touched by those who themselves can neither be seen nor touched. But the play continues to explore the desires of those involved in the Salem events to find a way to make witchcraft into a physical rather than a spectral event.

These desires come to a head at the end of the Mary Walcot scene:

> MARY: Look! Look! there is another clad in gray!/ She holds a spindle in her hand, and threatens/ To stab me with it! It is Goodwife Corey!/ Keep her away! Now she is coming at me!/ O mercy! mercy!
> WALCOT: *(thrusting with his sword)* There is nothing there!
> MATHER: *(to HATHORNE)* Do you see anything?
> HATHORNE: The laws that govern/ The spiritual world prevent our seeing/ Things palpable and visible to her./ These spectres are to us as if they were not./ Mark her; she wakes....

MARY: [I am] weak, very weak. *Taking a spindle from her lap, and holding it up.* How came this spindle here?
TITUBA: You wrenched it from the hand of Goodwife Corey/ When she rushed at you.... *(Picking up a bit of gray cloth from the floor)* And here, too, is a bit of her gray dress,/ That the sword cut away [Longfellow 571–72].

Walcot thrusts at "nothing" ... and strikes it! This "nothing" embodies the characteristics of the spectral world: real and yet not real. The gray cloth and the spindle function as reified proof of what could not otherwise be proven. If the specters "are ... as if they were not," then at least the cloth and the spindle simply *are*. But what is most interesting is the way that this reification is enacted. After Hathorne explains that the spectral world cannot be visible to the unafflicted (in fact, he implies that it cannot *be* at all to the unafflicted), he remarks, "Mark her; she wakes." This indeed "marks" Mary's return from the spectral world, and also "marks" what was previously unmarked: the specters themselves. Hathorne's rhetorical marking pulls the spectral evidence into the realm of legal evidence; and who better to do this "marking" than Justice Hathorne, who has previously noted to Mather that he cannot use ministry or religion to combat witches, but that he, "as a Magistrate, must combat them/ With weapons from the armory of the flesh" (Longfellow 566). And doubly interesting is the fact that it is Tituba, a professed witch, who holds the key to explaining the legal proof that surrounds the scene of Mary's affliction. Of course, we are provoked to wonder (as Gloyd wonders) whether the whole affair was orchestrated by Mary and Tituba, whether the cloth and the spindle are proof not of witchcraft, but of deceit. In other words, the legal proof that nudges aside spectral mystery in this scene is produced as much by the magistrate as it is by the witch (Martha Corey), and reveals the court's desire to harness and control witchcraft as much as it reveals the presence of witchcraft itself.

Legal proof and spectral evidence come together at the end of the play in a way that they never did during the actual trials. As Corey is on the stand confronting real-life witnesses such as Gloyd who testify against him, a startling thing happens: ghosts who have been wronged by Corey in the past rise up to testify against him as well. Mary Walcot shouts out:

> MARY: Look! Look! It is the ghost of Robert Goodell,/ Whom fifteen years
> ago this man did murder/ By stamping on his body! In his shroud/ He
> comes here to bear witness to the crime! *The crowd shrinks back from
> COREY in horror.*
> HATHORNE: Ghosts of the dead and voices of the living/ Bear witness to
> your guilt, and you must die! [Longfellow 606].

Mary's "Look! Look!" is familiar to the audience, as it is the exclamation
she shouted when she was rushed by a spectral Martha Corey; it calls attention to the play's interest in the invisible world, and the desires of the characters to make the spectral physical, and therefore visible. The "testimony"
of Robert Goodell is only given through Mary Walcot. Indeed, he is never
actually made "visible" in the drama. And yet he has real repercussions,
causing the crowd to shrink back and ultimately assuring Corey's death.
The question that the play — especially in written, rather than performed,
form — refuses to answer is: are these ghosts real? What the play suggests
is that the reality of the specters is not half as important as the effect that
they have, an effect that is fully achieved through the rhetoric of real, living characters. Witchcraft remains in the play an invisible, even non-existent, *yet highly potent* rhetorical act that depends on the willingness of the
characters to mark — to notice, to see, to touch, and to explain — what
might not be there at all. Witchcraft, then, is solidly tied to the real world
in that it stems from real power dynamics and can be used as legal proof.
But this real world efficacy is evidence less of witchcraft's undeniable existence than it is of the desires of Salem's occupants to express, challenge,
and validate their own hopes and fears about their relationships to each
other and to the spectral world. In the same way that Hawthorne explored
the connections between his romantic ghost story and his "real" narrative
of events in *The House of the Seven Gables,* Longfellow blurs the boundaries between the world of the specters and the world of everyday Salem
folks and their power struggles.

History and the Whore: Arthur Miller's The Crucible

Arthur Miller's 1953 play *The Crucible* is currently the most famous
of all fictional writings about the Salem witchcraft trials.[3] Originally

penned as a response to Senator Joseph McCarthy's hunt for communists and traitors amongst American citizens, the play is still performed frequently in this country and abroad. Miller himself has been called on often to explain his authorial relationship to the original trials. *The Crucible* was first published with a running commentary by Miller himself, a commentary that exists to inform readers and actors — but not necessarily the play's spectators — about how the action of *The Crucible* connects to historical fact.[4] Just before Act I, a preface of sorts entitled "A Note on the Historical Accuracy of This Play" appears in the written text. Miller writes in this preface, "This play is not history in the sense in which the word is used by the academic historian." "However," he continues, "I believe that the reader will discover here the essential nature of one of the strangest and most awful chapters in human history" (2). Miller sets up a dichotomy here between real historical fact and fictionality. But the dichotomy as he describes it is changeable, less than solid. For although his play is fiction, it (and not "real" history) contains the "essential nature" of what happened. In other words, Miller tries both to offer a disclaimer about the imaginative aspects of his work, and to claim a higher level of veracity for the play's authority. He concludes his preface by stating that the characters in his play "may therefore be taken as [his] own, drawn to the best of [his] ability in conformity with their known behavior, except as indicated in the commentary [he has] written for this text" (2). This implies that the commentary will be responsible for marking the places where Miller's imagination diverges from known historical fact; this, as we shall see, is not at all how the commentary actually functions.

Before we get to the commentary that focuses on individual characters and their "real" vs. "dramatic" lives, I would like to look briefly at the opening comment in the play, which has been inserted by Miller in between the opening stage direction and the first lines of dialogue. This commentary, which runs for more than four pages, sets the scene, and establishes the connection that Miller claims to have with the events of 1692. In this passage, he outlines the relationship between fiction and history:

No one can really know what their lives were like. They had no novelists — and would not have permitted anyone to read a novel if one were handy. Their creed forbade anything resembling a theater or "vain enjoyment" [4].

In order to know what the lives of seventeenth-century Salemites were like, Miller implies, we would have to have access to fiction or drama; letters, historical tracts, journals, and legal papers, all of which are in existence from the period, would not give a sense of what things were *really* like back then. Here, Miller reveals his bias: that only fiction has the ability to reveal the true essence of history. And Miller also makes it clear that his fiction, *The Crucible*, is not only a conduit for essential historical truth, but also a *producer* of this truth. In discussing the contradiction between a pro-community theocracy and its own tendencies to exclude and prohibit, Miller has this to say about the events in 1692: "The Salem tragedy, which is about to begin in these pages, developed from a paradox" (6–7). Yes, the paradoxical nature of the unified theocracy divided against itself is of importance here; but equally as important is the paradox that Miller reveals between his own desire to accurately reproduce historical fact *and* to imaginatively produce history's truer, emotional story. In many ways, then, Miller suggests that history is as much a product of the contemporary fiction writer's pen as it is a stable set of events in the past. For Miller, the Salem tragedy really *does* originate "in these pages."

Another example of this contemporary, fictional production of history pops up in the middle of Act I. Miller occasionally interrupts his dialogue with commentary about the scene being played. When Putnam and Parris are discussing whether or not the afflicted girls are suffering from an attack by the devil, Miller interjects a few words on Putnam, whom he describes as a man made bitter by the failure of his candidate for minister, James Bayley, and by his failed attempt to contest his father's will, which left a disproportionate inheritance to a stepbrother. Miller writes, "So it is not surprising to find that so many accusations against people are in the handwriting of Thomas Putnam, or that his name is so often found as a witness corroborating the supernatural testimony, or that his daughter led the crying-out at the most opportune junctures of the trials, especially when — But we'll speak of that when we come to it" (15). The dash here doubles — and even triples — the time zone, a phenomenon that we have seen over and over again in our discussions about Salem's presence in history and fiction. On the one hand, Miller's dash suggests that there are past events that have actually happened in the world; they exist whether or not they have been written down. In order to "come to" something, it needs to exist before one arrives at it. But at the same time, the dash here demonstrates that Miller's narrative, the story he is writing about Salem, has an order that must be obeyed. Miller's fiction effectively removes past events from the past, and places them in the present and, in this case, in the future. Thus, although Miller calls attention to the past as if it were stable and real, he also rhetorically deconstructs that past and absorbs history into the master narrative that he himself is creating.[5] History, then, is both that which exists in a real world outside of the fiction, *and* that which can only exist as the fiction itself takes shape.

The supplanting of past historical fact with present fictive writing comes to fruition in the commentary about John Proctor. Up until this point, the commentary accompanying the play has served to provide historical background to the events happening on stage. Most of this background comes directly from the trial transcripts, through which Miller assiduously poured. For example, the commentary on Putnam concerning Bayley and his stepbrother's inheritance all comes directly from primary sources. Though Miller initially stated that his commentary would help delineate the fact from the fiction, in general what it has done thus far is to demonstrate the seamlessness between what actually happened in Salem and Miller's dramatic account. But the Proctor accompaniment radically shifts the function of the commentary itself. Here is the first half of the first Proctor commentary:

> Proctor was a farmer in his middle thirties. He need not have been a partisan of any faction of the town, but there is evidence to suggest that he had a sharp and biting way with hypocrites. He was the kind of man — powerful of body, even-tempered, and not easily led — who cannot refuse support to partisans without drawing their deepest resentment. In Proctor's presence a fool felt his foolishness instantly — and Proctor is always marked for calumny therefore [Miller 20].

Although those of us familiar with the primary source documents available relating to Proctor might agree with the general gist of this comment, there are certainly places where Miller seems to be beginning to diverge from fact. Each sentence here gets progressively further away from historical record.[6] That Proctor was a farmer in his middle thirties is absolutely written in stone in the court documents. But skip to the final sentence above, and we get pure speculative fiction. Did fools feel more foolish around Proctor? Was Proctor a marked man? These questions can certainly not be answered with any degree of certitude by examining primary sources. And the second half of the commentary on Proctor seems to build from these speculations:

> But as we shall see, the steady manner he displays does not spring from an untroubled soul. He is a sinner, a sinner not only against the moral fashion of the time, but against his own vision of decent conduct. These people had no ritual for the washing away of sins. It is another trait we inherited from them, and it has helped to discipline us as well as to breed hypocrisy among us. Proctor, respected and even feared in Salem, comes to regard himself as a kind of fraud. But no hint of this has yet appeared on the surface [Miller 20–21].

Of course, Proctor's feelings of being a fraud stem from his affair with afflicted girl Abigail Williams. And this affair happens *only* in *The Crucible*; there is no evidence anywhere in any primary source documents that Proctor ever cheated on his wife with anyone. Considering that Miller's spoken objective with his commentary is to articulate when he is diverging from known fact, it seems amazing that he slips in this commentary about Proctor without alluding to the fact that he made it all up. If we go back to the preface again, we can find a whole list of facts that Miller claims to have altered in writing his play: the number of afflicted girls has been reduced, Abigail's age has been raised, the judges have been worked into two composites (Miller 2). But nowhere does he mention that the affair has been fabricated. Below, I will discuss the implications of the affair between Abby and Proctor, but here, I would like to call attention not so much to the substance of Miller's fictive addition, but to the way in which it is made. By using the commentary, which he has established as the voice of truth, the place where actual history and the drama at hand converge, Miller manages to inject the affair back into the original historical record. In other words, the contemporary drama rewrites history, and the suspense of *The Crucible* becomes not just a case of dramatic tension but of solving a historical mystery at long last. Whether or not Miller is attempting to deceive his audience seems to me to be irrelevant; what is much more salient is the way that he redefines history as an imaginative trajectory that shoots both forward and backward. When he says that "no hint" of Proctor's self-doubt "has yet appeared on the surface," Miller again triples his time zone: he inserts Proctor's fraudulent identity back into the "real" past, he establishes dramatic tension in the present, and he alludes to the future moment when the truth will erupt.

This "truth," that Proctor and Abby have had a sexual relationship, is at the core of *The Crucible*. For Miller, this affair becomes the *raison d'être* of the witchcraft trials themselves. Why sex? What is it about the witch hunt that brought Miller to his chosen "sexplanation" of why the trials happened? I would argue that it is the connection between truth, nudity, and sex that makes the Abby-Proctor affair an apt explanation for what occurred in Salem.[7] That Proctor's "abomination" is at the heart of the witchcraft hysteria is apparent in the play. As Elizabeth Proctor is being hauled off to jail, the Reverend Hale begs of Proctor to reveal the real reason God is so displeased with Salem. Hale doubts that Abigail would accuse Elizabeth just to be spiteful. Hale says, "Proctor, I cannot think God be provoked so grandly by such a petty cause. The jails are packed — our greatest judges sit in Salem now — and hangin's promised. Man, we must look to cause proportionate. Were there murder done, perhaps, and never brought to light? Abomination? Some secret blasphemy that stinks to Heaven? Think on cause, man, and let you help me to discover it" (Miller 79). Of course, when readers or an audience — or Proctor himself — hear such a plea from Hale, we all know immediately that the secret abomination at the root of the trouble is Proctor's infidelity. For Hale, the secret abomination brings God's wrath, and causes Him to allow the devil into Salem. But the audience and Proctor know an even deeper truth: the devil is actually Abigail Williams, who torments Elizabeth and others because she has been displaced as Proctor's lover. The fact that the abomination is a "secret" seems overly obvious; of course an affair is generally concealed. But the secrecy of the affair, its hidden quality, is precisely what allows the hysteria to mount in the play. And when Proctor attempts to admit the truth — that he has "known" Abigail — he is undermined by Elizabeth's attempts to preserve his reputation. What emerges is a complex web of lies and revelations centering on this one sex act. The affair is less important than the process that it spawns of stripping bare one's soul, revealing one's core identity, and telling the truth (and conversely hiding one's status as fraud and telling lies).

When Proctor convinces Mary Warren to confess her duplicity, he seems to allude to the fact that he, too, will come clean. "Peace," he tells her, "It is a providence, and no great change; we are only what we always were, but naked now" (Miller 81). Nakedness is linked both to Mary Warren's sin and to Proctor's. Mary Warren was with the girls who danced naked in the woods when they played at conjuring spirits. For Proctor, nakedness stands for his sin of lechery with Abigail. But nakedness is also Mary Warren's confession that she was only "sporting," not really under the influence of any witch. And nakedness is also Proctor's confession to his affair. Nakedness, then, is a doubled marker of both guilt and confession, both duplicity and truth. When Mary Warren tells the court that she lied about being afflicted, Judge Danforth replies, "We burn a hot fire here; it melts down all concealment" (Miller 89). This "hot fire" is, of course, the "crucible." In the crucible, all dishonesty and disguise are melted away until only the naked truth remains. This naked truth is vexed, however, in that it always contains traces of its own corruption. Mary Warren's nakedness always revives the naked girl dancing in the woods, just as Proctor's revives his carnal lust in the barn with Abigail. Thus, when Proctor claims that it is fraud for him to die a martyr, that his "honesty is broke," he reveals the inability of confessional nakedness to overcome the mark of the original sin (Miller 136). "Nothing's spoiled by giving them this lie that was not rotten long ago," he tells Elizabeth (Miller 136). Confession is either the effective confessing to a lie (that he is in league with the devil, which would save his life) or the ineffective confessing to a truth (that he is an adulterer, which once articulated, fails to save him or Elizabeth and fails to diminish Abigail's authority). In these scenarios there is no pure nakedness, no confessed state that can redeem Proctor or the situation in Salem.[8] When Proctor goes to his grave, it is with the hope that in another world, outside of the landscape of this play, there can be a truth, a nakedness, unmarked by sin and deceit.

The "naked truth" is a vexed and conflicting state both within the landscape of *The Crucible* and in the relationship between the play and the history it purports to tell. Proctor strips naked again and again in the play: to bed Abby, to admit that he "knew" the girl, to confess that he is a witch, to confess that his confession was a lie. Nakedness fluctuates from sin to redemption and back again. Similarly, Miller's own relationship to historical fact shifts wildly from one form of nakedness to another. At first an essential but fictive account of the trials, the play gradually replaces historical fact with authorial fancy, and that fancy gets played out as not only *true*, but as *the truth* that explains the whole enigma that surrounds the Salem witchcraft trials. That enigma is, of course, *why did they happen at all?* The figure of the "whore" haunts the whole play. Abigail is not a whore until late in the proceedings, when it is clear that she will go to whatever lengths she needs to in order to destroy Elizabeth and elevate her own status in the village; even when Elizabeth initially puts her out of her house, Abby manages to be a sympathetic character — both in Proctor's eyes and in the audience's — until the hangings get out of control. What this suggests is that what makes a *whore* is not so much the sex act but the betrayal of truth.[9] The whore, then, symbolizes a world upside-down, a fraudulent nakedness, a rhetorical truth established that flies in the face of the true essence of things. Miller's final answer to the central questions — What happened in 1692? And why did it happen? — is "Abigail Williams." She represents all that is diseased in men's souls and in society's laws. And she also represents, perhaps unintentionally on the part of Miller, how historical fact can only be "known" in one way: the way that Proctor "knew" Abby in that dank, dark barn. Miller quite literally fucks (with) history, and his whore, Abigail Williams, relegates any pure "Elizabeth-an" fact to the position of the moral, wronged, and ultimately bereft wife. When we are told in a note at the end of the play that "legend has it that Abigail turned up later as a prostitute in Boston," we are no doubt supposed to feel that Abby has gotten her due punishment for her lewdness and her betrayals in Salem (Miller 146). But the prostitute, despite Miller's attempts to demonize and control her, has a very successful run of it in *The Crucible*, and even at the end, she keeps on whoring instead of getting killed off.[10] No primary source documents, and no legend that I can find in writing, suggest that Abby actually became a prostitute. As Miller absorbs this speculation into the fabric of his final commentary, he proves once and for all that history is a prostitute: there to be used to help the customer achieve a particular desired outcome. Miller manipulates Abby seemingly without regard for her autonomy, dignity, or real lived experience. *But* this does not mean she is not effective, powerful, and very much alive; Abby's refusal to behave (both within the play and after the curtain falls) becomes evidence that the "prostitute" — whether she be "history" or a woman — can have unexpected motives and effects that cannot be controlled by the customer she "serves." Charges of sexism that are often launched against Miller may be short-sighted, in that his Abigail reveals the subversive potential of the whore[11]; Miller's Abigail is both a figure for how truth can be manipulated and how the ensuing manipulated results can be infused with the power of truth. As did Hawthorne and Longfellow, Miller reshapes the category of "truth," creating reality — much of which has come to represent all that many Americans know about the Salem witch trials — out of shreds of concrete evidence and sexy invention.

Black and White Witches: Salem Mythology and the Limits of Patriarchy

Arthur Miller's Abigail Williams is ironically cast in his play as both a serviceable whore and a subversive agent. As we turn our attention from the theater to the big screen, we will further investigate the curiously doubled category of the witch under patriarchy. The focus here will be on two films from the 1930s and 1940s, *Maid of Salem* and *I Married a Witch*, that center on two Salem witches, and on the question of what a "witch" is. In both films, as in 1692 Salem itself, the witch is both frightfully powerful and obsessively contained, and she threatens subversion of the patriarchy even as that patriarchy works to turn that subversion into a perfect reinscription of its own patriarchal authority. In this era of black and white filmmaking, the question became how "black and white" the category of "witch" actually was for the Salem women who occupied it.

Durward Grinstead, author of the 1929 Salem novel *Elva*, shares screenwriting credit for 1937's *Maid of Salem*.[12] In the film, Barbara's (Claudette Colbert's) transgressions against the Puritan standards of feminine behavior are responsible for the accusations of witchcraft that are ultimately levied against her. At the beginning of the film, we see that her friend has brought her a decorative new hat that she ordered from Boston; it is so out of step with the austere fashion of the film's 1692 Salem, that Samuel Parris' only sermon in the film takes it as its central topic. "I tell you that a female that will fritter away her time trimming and tricking herself out in such a fashion," he preaches as he looks straight at Barbara, "is a mere gizzard of a trifle, the epitome of nothing, and very apt prey for the devil" (*Maid of Salem*). The problem with Barbara's trimming is that at its center, it is empty, and this emptiness figures, as the female lack generally does, in a paradoxical way: it is both worthless and vacant *and* attractive and desirable. The film suggests that witchcraft inheres in this complicated double play, as the sexually desirable woman (the attractive lack) is also the woman who is most susceptible to the devil (the vacant lack). In other words, witchcraft is the doubled and paradoxical state of the woman as subject — who *makes* men's minds wander — and the woman as object — that is penetrated and overtaken by Satan himself.

Barbara is accused of witchcraft, and the climax of her trial happens when young Mercy Cheeves is called to the stand to testify about a poppet that Barbara has made for her. Mercy's own mother is both physically and verbally abusive to the young girl, while Barbara is gentle and maternal. When she enters the courtroom, Mercy pulls away from her mother's arms and runs to Barbara. The court wonders if it is because Barbara is loving and kind or because she has bewitched the child. Again, Barbara's identity is paradoxically doubled: she is both a nurturing mother and a demon feeding on the young and innocent.

Maid of Salem demonstrates a pointed anxiety about women's "trimming and tricking." Through adornment, transgression of gender roles (such as when Barbara role-plays the part of King William in order to pardon her fugitive suitor), and complicated doubled identities that both reinscribe and undo conventions of both Puritan maids and matrons, Barbara's trimming is taken for trickery, and she is accused of being a witch. The final deus-ex-machina that frees her has to do with Roger Coverman, Barbara's fugitive suitor. After leading an anti-tax rebellion against the crown, Roger flees to Salem to hide out, and in this way, his name, "Coverman," is a pointed pun. Roger is continually associated with hiding and dressing up. One day in the forest, he meets a drunk cow herder; in order to avoid being discovered, Roger tells us that he "threw [his] cloak over [his] head and bellowed like a demon" (*Maid of Salem*). In addition, we know that after his first meeting with Barbara, he immediately decides to repair his clothes and shave his beard so as to make himself more attractive to Barbara. In these ways, he offers an interesting parallel to Barbara. In the film, he is both lawless fugitive and righteous revolutionary, the preening prig who, because of his reckless cavorting, is responsible for the charges against Barbara and the plainspoken hero who returns to set the record straight. When he bellows at the cow herder, the viewer knows that Roger is not literally a demon, but of course, the thing he is covering up by bellowing — his fugitive identity — stands in stark contrast to the law-abiding citizenry of Samuel Parris' Salem. And the bellowing also becomes the originating spark that ultimately sets the witch trials in motion, as the drunkard rushes back to report that he has seen a demon in the woods; and in this way, surely the innocent masquerade has horrific consequences, especially for Rebecca Nurse and others who are hanged as a result of the hysteria.

Roger rushes into the court to save Barbara. At issue is the fact that villagers have seen Barbara cavorting with a mysterious figure, who they assume, because he is unknown to them, is a specter. "Am I not flesh and blood?" he asks as he runs into the meetinghouse (*Maid of Salem*). Indeed, the implication is that all of his layered performances "covered" the man underneath. Once he is stripped bare, he is able to relieve the tension that existed between his demonic and heroic selves. It seems that his fugitive status simply evaporates as he testifies in court; the thing he feared all along — exposure — turns out not to matter at all, as he is celebrated for coming forward and reunited with his now-free bride-to-be. In truth, there is nothing left to expose, as the flesh-and-blood Roger fully undoes the previous fellow and all of his complexity. By extension, Barbara's paradoxes — subject or object, desirable or demonic, masculine or feminine, corruptor of youth or maternal protector — simply melt away when Coverman's do. She is revealed to be both wrongly accused and fully feminine as her suitor literally rides in on his horse to save her. In keeping with her newly simplified position, the previously outspoken Barbara speaks not one word after Roger's heroic rescue. We can be assured that the scene to follow the film's final shot will feature a wedding, and the scene after that will show Barbara as, at long last, not a witch but a *real* mother, unchallenged in her natural maternal abilities.

Like *Maid of Salem*, 1942's *I Married a Witch* is interested in the relationships between domesticity, feminine power, and witchcraft. The film was adapted from the 1930's Thorne Smith novel *The Passionate Witch*. When Smith died before finishing the novel, it was finished by Norman

Matson, who ultimately helped to shape it into the film version, *I Married a Witch* (Gibson 195). The novel went through many alterations on its way to the big screen. The film's story begins with Jennifer (Veronica Lake), a Salem woman accused of witchcraft by Jonathan Wooley (Frederic March). Jennifer curses Wooley for accusing her, and dooms him and his male ancestors, that "all their marriages and love be disastrous" (*I Married a Witch*). Jonathan laments that perhaps he accused her without enough proof that she was actually a witch. His mother responds that of *course* she was a witch: "Our cows turned pink and blue, and our sheep danced the minuet" (*I Married...*). In light of this rather startling evidence, it seems astounding that Jonathan would be feeling remorse over his accusation. From the beginning, the film expresses a rampant anxiety about feminine power, as men are repeatedly shown to be humiliated, controlled, and manipulated by evil women who can't be subdued. Jonathan is saddled with the blame for accurately accusing a *real witch* of witchcraft, and suffers the curse as a result.

When Jennifer's spirit is freed by a flash of lightning from the grave where it had been trapped for hundreds of years after her execution, Jennifer wishes that she had a body again: "It would be nice to have lips, lips to whisper lies, lips to kiss a man and make him suffer" (*I Married...*). This is the emasculating force that defines womanhood in the film, and interestingly, it is intimately related to Jennifer's father, Daniel. Daniel was burned at the stake with Jennifer, though we don't know any more details than that. When both are released as puffs of smoke from their gravesites, Jennifer asks, "Father, why cannot I have lips?" In an inversion of biological reality, Jennifer's new body will be birthed by her father. "Father," she begs, "give me a body." But he doesn't want to, so she teases him: "Thou canst not give me a body. Thou wouldst not even know how to begin" (*I Married...*). She pricks his ego, and in order to prove his potent power, he creates a body for her; Jennifer's manipulation has emasculated her father, recasting him as a mother figure and setting him up for his continued ironic positioning in the film, where his phallic, paternal power is reified as it is simultaneously compromised by his own daughter's machinations.[13]

Wallace Wooley, descendent of Jonathan, is running for mayor, and is also about to be married to Estelle. "She has the look of a shrew," Jennifer says of Estelle. "Each Wooley must marry the wrong woman," she brags to her father about the curse she has placed. He replies, "Ha! What a curse! Every man who marries marries the wrong woman" (*I Married...*). Daniel, servant to his daughter as he is, certainly married the wrong woman; though we don't hear much of Jennifer's mother, the fact that Jennifer was the offspring demonstrates the way that marital procreation leads to the future doom of the hapless father, a doom that is, as will be argued later in this chapter, echoed at the end of the film.

After falling in love with him as a result of a love potion that she mistakenly takes herself, Jennifer convinces Wallace to leave Estelle and run away with her. In their wedding bed that same night, Jennifer realizes she has to confess her true identity as a witch to Wallace; she is concerned that if they have children, the children will be witches. When she confesses, he replies, "Of course [you're a witch.] I've been under your spell since I met you" (*I Married...*). In order to convince Wallace that she is really a witch, she decides to throw the mayoral election in his favor; of course he has no non-magical way of winning, since he has just left his fiancé at the altar and run off with a strange unknown woman. When he wins, he realizes the truth about his witchy wife, but also realizes the advantage he now has, given his wife's power. Jennifer started out as a nuisance: she was pesky and irritating to Wallace, much like his shrewish fiancé. For no apparent reason, Wallace changes his mind completely about her, and in loving her, harnesses her power for his own benefit. Women occupy three possible roles in the film: demonic — yet bungling — tormentors who try to cast spells on men but only doom themselves, shrewish nags who hound their husbands mercilessly, and steadfast, loyal wives who stand behind their men. Jennifer manages to be all three through the course of the film.

At the end of the film, Jennifer lays dying after a car crash; she asks Wallace to "remember me as just an ordinary girl" (*I Married...*). Indeed, the message of the film is that witchcraft is not really about potions and spells, for Wallace never drinks a potion, and the whole Wooley curse is, as Daniel told us, no worse than the curse of every married man. The *real* witchcraft in the film is the way that women can morph from blushing maidens into shrewish wives. At the end, the film seems willing to admit the unappealing nature of this confined track for women, and so it offers a "way out": instead of nagging your husband and making him look bad publicly (as Estelle did, for example), smile pretty and help him win elections.

Daniel, Jennifer's father, is conned into relinquishing his fatherly role in favor of a motherly one, and then is ultimately completely emasculated by becoming an impotent drunk, unable to remember spells or do magic. At the end of the film, the revived Jennifer traps him in a booze bottle and locks that in a cage over the fireplace mantle. The phallic shape of his container is ironic, caged and powerless as it is. Its position on the mantle reinforces the film's ultimate statement about domestic life. The effect of the witch on patriarchy is complex: she emasculates her men even as she shores up their symbolic power, their status as fathers, husbands, mayors. If the living room and the public sphere both function under the gaze of male power, that power is radically constrained by the witch that has won her husband and won her husband's election, overthrown her father, and birthed a new generation of witches to doom yet another generation of men.

Both of these films are about the anxious backlash that accompanies the appearance of female power. I say "appearance" because, in both films, the anxiety works to contain this power. In *Maid of Salem*, the "witch" is a paradoxical category that allows women to evade definition as either subject or object, desirable or demonic, masculine or feminine, corruptor of youth or maternal protector; but the end of the film safely replaces the "witch" with a "woman," who is clearly only a desirable feminine object and a good mother. In *I Married a Witch*, a paradox is allowed to endure: "witches" — who might be defined as "all women" — tease and challenge the patriarchy even as they ultimately reinscribe it. In other words, all of the horror generated by the body and spirit of the female witch, all of the suffering of the men who endure her, all of the threat she posits to the family, the state, the court, and the village, all of these things ultimately and ironically render her an indispensable tool of these institutions, absorbing their nightmares and resolving them at the same time. In some ways, the patriarchal reinscriptions that witchcraft and witchcraft trials seem to gesture towards are subverted by the doubled nature of the witch, who at times manages to be as powerful, horrifying, and inscrutable, as she is disempowered, contained, confined, executed, or exonerated.

Back to Salem: Samantha, Sabrina, and the Mock Trial

Both *Maid of Salem* and *I Married a Witch* interrogate the category of "witch" by drawing parallels to the category of "woman," and considering how both categories function within and against a patriarchal environment. We will turn now to two more recent texts, as we also move from the big screen to the small one. In the two television episodes discussed here, from *Sabrina, The Teenage Witch* and *Bewitched*, the emphasis shifts from an interrogation of womanhood into an interrogation of identity itself. Both episodes work to compare real witches with those who are wrongfully accused and named as witches, and a similar sense of paradox and irony emerge as emerged in the two films discussed above. In all cases, the category of "witch" becomes one that only exists in a state of tension, with competing definitions of the term always in play against each other. In a 1997 episode of *Sabrina*, Sabrina — who is indeed a "real" witch — and her high school classmates go to Salem, Massachusetts, on a field trip. Each student is given an index card at the beginning of the trip, and they are told by their teacher that several of the cards have the identity "witch" written on them, and it is the job of the students to figure out who amongst the group are the witches. The trials begin when Sabrina's nemesis, Libby, accuses Sabrina's best friend, Jenny, of being a "witch." As they did in 1692, the trials get out of control and others — including Sabrina who tries to defend Jenny — are accused. At the end of the episode, the teacher reveals that *nobody* had a "witch" card, and that she was just teaching them a lesson about persecution and hysteria, and about how people react against those who are thought to be different. On the bus ride home, Sabrina finds her index card, takes it out of its sealed envelope, and finds that — mysteriously — it says "witch" on it.

Interestingly, this episode is not entitled "The Salem Witch Trials," but "The Crucible," which calls attention to the layers of performance that comprise its plot. The episode is couched in layer upon layer of reenactment. First of all, the students don't travel back to 1692 Salem, but to a recreated tourist village. Sabrina's aunts, real witches themselves, tell her not to worry about visiting the site of the 1692 persecution: "Salem had nothing to do with real witches three hundred years ago," they tell her, "and today you have nothing to fear there but overpriced souvenirs" ("The Crucible"). In 1692, the aunts remind Sabrina, the people accused of witchcraft were not actually witches; they maintained their innocence and never displayed any true signs of doing witchcraft. And today, Salem has been co-opted by a tourist industry that has ironically reified this non-witchery into a commercial endeavor. The episode pointedly reiterates that the students aren't hunting "real" witches, but those who are playing witch based on their scripted identities. Over and over again, the episode collapses the idea that there is such a thing as a real witch, either in 1692 or in the "present."

Of course, this collapse is rendered ironic by the unassailable fact of Sabrina's true identity. While Jenny takes the accusations against her in stride, and declares "it's just a game," Sabrina is horrified by the reenactment. "What if you were a witch," she asks Jenny, "and this wasn't a game?" ("The Crucible"). Sabrina's question illuminates what is most complex about the episode. Salem in 1692 is portrayed as a community creating a fiction based on hostility to difference. Salem in 1997 is portrayed as a derivative tourist site. The student activity is portrayed as a performance. But at the core of each of these theatricalized events is the real witch who fears for her life and/or her self-esteem. At the height of the mock trial's energy, when Sabrina is most under fire for being a witch, she cries out against her accuser, "Libby, the only witch in this room is you!" ("The Crucible"). She points at Libby and a ball of light flies from her fingertip and jets around the room. In this moment, there is a complicated aporia. At the same moment that Sabrina's accusation against Libby constructs Libby as a nasty witch and Sabrina as wrongfully accused, it also — because of the fireball — defines Libby as an afflicted girl and Sabrina as a witch after all. The category of "witch" becomes an impossibility, containing as it does both the afflicted and the accused, both the non-witch and the real witch.

But after Sabrina throws the fireball, the science teacher steps in to explain it away. "That was ball lightning," he tells the students, "a very rare and unusual phenomenon" ("The Crucible"). Thus the concrete proof that reveals Sabrina's true identity is morphed into a harmless educational lesson, part and parcel of the field trip's educative mission. This seemingly relieves the aporetic paradox that evacuated the meaning of the term "witch," but the end of the episode reveals the paradox has still survived despite the teacher's best efforts. At the end of the trial, Jenny is found guilty, but Sabrina, despite the fact that she confesses, is found not guilty. As Libby demands just punishment for Jenny, one of the teachers tells her, "you can pretend we hanged her" ("The Crucible"). This angers Sabrina, who, for the first time, hexes Libby for real by placing a monkey on her shoulder that is only visible to Libby. "Now I REALLY see a monkey," exclaims Libby, which leads Sabrina to interject, "See, she was making it up before!" ("The Crucible"). Again, the irony is produced when the real hexing begins; instead of it revealing Sabrina's witch identity, it reveals the falseness of the witchcraft accusations. Witchcraft becomes the thing that illuminates the "real witch," who, ironically, is not the girl casting the spells, but the girl who is bewitched.

At the end of the episode, Sabrina's teacher tells the class that there were no witch cards. "I didn't create the witches; you did," she explains, as part of a pathos-laden speech about the persecution of difference ("The Crucible"). But what does it mean that the class created the witches themselves? What the episode demonstrates is not that witchcraft is a cover for stereotyping and oppression, but that witchcraft is an odd rhetorical category, one that constructs itself in a dialectical play with its own opposite. Set as it is in the context of such a performative landscape, the episode reimagines the idea of "authenticity" where witchcraft and Salem are concerned. It's no longer a question of settling the facts about what happens, but an example of how facts and truths and identities get produced by the representations that enter into discourse. Sabrina says at one point, "I don't know who I am; I lost my card" ("The Crucible"). In this episode, named so aptly not for the 1692 hysteria, but for a *play* about it, identities — witchy and otherwise — are scripted and enacted, rather than created or developed. And when Sabrina brings a "kitchen witch" home to her aunts to hang over their cauldron, the episode suggests that the thin line that separates the true witch from the tacky souvenir is as porous as the line that separates afflicted from accused, guilty from innocent, and the real from the performed.[14]

At one point during the *Sabrina* episode, Sabrina laments, "Why couldn't we just have recreated Thanksgiving?" ("The Crucible"). In an interesting conflation, a 1967 episode of *Bewitched* finds Samantha, Darin, and Tabatha returning to 17th Century Plimoth Plantation, where they celebrate the first Thanksgiving and suffer through a trial in which Darin is accused of being a witch. Despite the fact that the presence of both Myles Standish and John Alden in the episode sets the show in *Mayflower*-era Plimoth, it's clear that the episode draws heavily from apocryphal Salem history. When Aunt Clara mistakenly zaps Samantha, Darin, and Tabatha to Plimoth, Darin worries about his wife's safety: "They burn witches in the 17th century." Samantha replies, "The ones they *thought* were witches, not the *real* ones" ("Samantha's..."). The set-up for this episode, called "Samantha's Thanksgiving to Remember," reminds us of the Sabrina episode in many ways. First, the plot revolves around the question "What makes someone a real witch?" Second, the main accused person in the *Bewitched* episode is Darin, not the real witch, Samantha. Both shows deflect the witch hunt onto the non-witch, which highlights the way that witches get constructed by the trials that put them on display, not by nature or the divine or the demonic. But as the real witches defend the accused, they use their witchcraft to incriminate the accusers. Sabrina uses a fireball to ultimately reveal that Libby was lying (and therefore that she is a witch of a sort), and Samantha also uses fire to suggest that Phineas, Darin's accuser, is a witch.

Darin's flight backward in time has made him susceptible to the charge of witchcraft; when he unwittingly lights a modern match (just one of his many anachronistic blunders), he raises the villagers' suspicions against him. Samantha and Aunt Clara, though, are able to meld seamlessly into Puritan society despite their true identities as witches. In the *Sabrina* episode, the emphasis was on reenactment, but here in *Bewitched*, the emphasis appears to be on total immersion — method acting, if you will. But Darin's inability to play the role perfectly highlights his performance, and this, in turn, confers the identity of witch upon him. A "witch" then, is not someone who does witchcraft (as Samantha and Aunt Clara do), but someone who is "strange," foreign, an interloper. This association of the foreign with Darin's inability to play-act has important repercussions in the episode. When Samantha defends Darin, she argues,

> Take not the fault upon thyself. 'Tis more a comfort to place it on another. How do we decide who is the witch? Doth someone speak different than thee?' Tis witchery. Doth he show different mannerisms?... If one examines

one's neighbors closely, one will find differences enough so that no one is safe from the charge of witchery ["Samantha's..."].

A witch, then, is anyone who is deemed different, and since everyone is different from everyone else, everyone may be a witch.[15] As Sabrina accused Libby, the accuser, and simultaneously revealed that witchcraft is a self-constructing rhetorical maneuver, here Samantha reveals that to equate witchcraft with the foreign is, for a "new world accepting of all differences, of our common humanity," a way of perpetuating oppression and, ironically, a way of evacuating meaning from the very term that simultaneously oppresses ("Samantha's..."). This paradox in which a witch is persecuted while "witch" ceases to exist as a distinct identity category manifests itself in more concrete terms when Samantha proves that Darin's match tricks weren't witchery. She takes the used match and passes it to Phineas, who expects — as do viewers — that he won't be able to make fire. But Samantha casts a spell, and as Phineas strikes the match, it sparks and lights. Just as Sabrina used witchcraft to put the monkey on Libby's shoulder as a way of highlighting Libby's false accusations, Samantha uses witchcraft to reveal that Phineas the afflicted, who in this scene is certainly hexed, has been lying about being bewitched. Both of these episodes are, like 1692 Salem, obsessed with the question of what a witch is. We recall the famous exchange in Bridget Bishop's examination, in which she pleads, "I am innocent to a witch. I know not what a witch is," and Judge Hathorne retorts, "How do you know then that you are not a witch?" (Boyer and Nissenbaum, *Salem-Village*, 39). The episodes here use a parallel rhetorical play to establish the paradox at work in the construction of the term, a term which is also confused by the use of witchcraft to illuminate witches by ironically causing the accusers to appear guilty.

The performance of witchcraft, thematized in one way by the very fact that these texts explicitly *stage* the Salem story in some way or other, generates paradox over and over again. Whether it be the dichotomy between the spectral and the real, witches and witch hunters, or the powerful witch and the powerless "witch," all of these plays, films, and television shows wrestle with the contradictory nature of the rhetorical category of "witch." As discussed in Chapter One, this kind of contradiction haunts Salem's primary sources, as accusers become accused, as confessions retract and invert, and as cross-examinations produce solipsistic definitions of witchcraft. In the Salem histories, we saw key dialectics — such as the one that emerged between Cotton Mather and Robert Calef— shape Salem discourse and American memory of the trials. And in novels about Salem, irony and fundamental tension between truth and fiction define the texts' approaches to telling Salem's tales. As we move from history, fiction, and drama into a discussion of tourism in contemporary Salem, Massachusetts, many of these paradoxes and ironies will find expression in the museums, monuments, and attractions that, like these other texts, recreate and even invent Salem's storied past.

FIVE

Selling the Story

From Salem Village to Witch City

Sitting outside on the pedestrian mall in Salem, Massachusetts, during any warm contemporary afternoon, one can watch as streams of tourists flock to hotdog carts, purchase t-shirts at sidewalk sales, and follow their Chamber of Commerce maps from site to site.[1] With scheduled regularity, each day at a precise moment a commotion breaks out on the mall. Like clockwork, gathering crowds of families with fanny packs encircle the outbreak, and watch as a verbal battle unfolds. Though the players vary from day to day, and one actor might play many parts over the course of a season, the outbreak always goes something like this:

"What do you mean, Goodman? Are you to imply that she was bewitched?" A young man in Puritan dress will shout at another, older man.

The older man will shout back, "I know not about such things, but it is clear she is not right, and for you to deny it casts doubts upon you as well."

Though the two men will wear seventeenth-century clothing, they will always hold a stack of glossy, mass-produced brochures as well. A study of the gathering crowd will reveal a compelling juxtaposition: poised video cameras held by tourists, side by side with several less vocal "Puritans" with brochures who have subtly mixed into the group. Tourists snap photos of the "early Americans," inevitably capturing in their shots images not only of the performers, but also of other tourists taking pictures. This phenomenon happens over and over again in Salem, as tourists record the actions and words of performers who mix in with the general crowds. Della Pollack, editor of *Exceptional Spaces: Essays in Performance and His-*

tory, explains how this process of photographing other photographers works to establish "seeing" as the very object under view. "If all the subjects are ... masked by cameras," she writes, "There is nothing left to see but *seeing*; nothing left to appropriate *by* seeing but the act *of* seeing. *Seeing* thus becomes its own object" (7). As performers in Salem mix with tourists, and, perhaps even more notably, as they involve tourists in their productions by asking them to participate, tourists have the tourist gaze — the interpellating glance that casts the object in sight as a "site" — cast back upon themselves. In this sense, then, the act of *seeing* also becomes the state of *being seen.* Throughout one's time in Salem, it becomes clearer and clearer that being a tourist in "Witch City" — Salem's current-day nickname — will not be a simple matter of appropriation; it will be a complex relationship between audience and actor in which the divisions between object and agent will be confused and blurred.[2] In much the same way that historians and fiction writers have invented the "true" story of what happened in Salem, Salem's tourist industry supports a dynamic system in which "facts" are created by the interaction between site, viewer, and a nebulous character called "the past."

In this particular routine outbreak on the mall, this confusion — over where the locus of control for the production actually inhered — will continue to mount, and before long, nearly a dozen "Puritans" will be discussing the matter of Bridget Bishop's guilt, sometimes with each other and sometimes with the amused tourists; the "Puritans" will raise their voices, attract more onlookers, and deftly give out brochures to anyone who will have them. "History Alive presents *Cry Innocent,*" the brochures read, "It's April 1692. Bridget Bishop is on the witness stand, and *YOU* are on the jury. Play your part in history" (*Cry Innocent* brochure). Flipping over the brochure reveals the fine print: "From the moment you enter Old Town Hall, you are treated as a Puritan living in Salem, 1692.... As a member of the jury, you may cross-examine witnesses, argue with the defendant or give testimony yourself. Our actors will respond to your comments in character, revealing much about the Puritan mind" (*Cry Innocent* brochure). After witnessing the outbreak and perusing the brochure, tourists will be swept away by the Puritan-infiltrated crowd, propelled along towards the ticket booth outside Old Town Hall, where they can purchase an admission to the show for six dollars.

Salem today is a raucous clash of time periods, as Puritan history and current-day tourism provoke and define each other in a constant web of mutual influence. *Cry Innocent* is an apt place to start, since the way it blurs the line between the real and the performed is central to Salem's approach to doing history. As the actors mix into the crowds in the street, the production abandons its scripts, explodes through the fourth wall, and brings history "alive," making it spontaneous, new, and seemingly "real." As the "live history" begins its downstream journey to the theater, the tourists are cleverly absorbed into the play; the performers neatly begin the process of usurping the natural feel of the pre-show ad-lib and using it to fuel the credibility of a more fully staged drama. The tourist becomes, in this theatrical experience and in most Salem tourism, both passive audience member and active shaper of the experience, and performers are both reincarnations of Puritans past and creators of a constantly evolving truth. Through performance, Salem's tourist culture reinterprets not only the past, but also the very means by which we access — or reinvent — this past. In one recent performance of *Cry Innocent* that I attended, the audience sided with history: we decisively voted that Bishop seemed guilty and should be held over for trial.[3] "Hang her!" one man shouted from the audience at the end of the show. In Salem, the tourist drive is not necessarily about moral lessons, historical education, or commemoration; often, it is about the entertaining thrill that accompanies the macabre side of Salem's story: the corpse swinging from the tree limb, the old witch casting spells on her neighbors, the fear — and hope — that the devil was — and might still be — afoot in Salem. The desire for spooky thrills and the desire to tell the truth for the moral betterment of society make uncomfortable but profitable bedfellows in Salem, and the disjunction between a drab seventeenth-century outfit and a slickly produced, full-color brochure is an appropriate metaphor for the general disjunction that characterizes Salem's historical tourism. This chapter will explore how this disjunction plays itself out, and how Salem's varied and competing goals — to make money, to educate, to commemorate, and to entertain — actually work together to ensure the survival of each individual tourist site in the city.

It is worth noting before the discussion turns to Salem in particular, that while education and entertainment are often thought to be conflicting goals in the world of tourist sites, the linking of learning with amusement has a long-standing past in the history of American museums. For example, in 1776, Charles Willson Peale began keeping a small gallery of portraits (mostly of distinguished men of the Revolution) in a small building behind his Philadelphia home; this was not unusual at the time, but in 1786, he enlarged his gallery to become a "Repository for Natural Curiosities," one of the United States' first exhibits that displayed items other than paintings (Bank 37). In 1794, the exhibit was moved to the American Philosophical Society, and the Society and Peale's collection became a full-fledged museum open to the public. Interestingly, this move to larger, more established quarters closely followed the lifting of the Philadelphia Theater Ban in 1789, and it seems that Peale aligned a visit to his museum with a visit to the theater. Rosemarie K. Bank writes, "Although Peale believed his museum had a crucial part to play in creating a 'universally educated public,' he contextualized instruction in 'useful knowledge' as a form of 'rational amusement'" (38).[4] Bank points out that the entertainment side of curiosity-related museums became so pronounced that "well before the Civil War, learned societies retreated even 'from public exhibitions and the collection of antiquities other than books and paintings'" (Brigham in Bank 38). The union between education and entertainment was present in museum and tourist culture long before Witch City came along, and even the tension between high, educative sites and low, entertaining sites has a long history that predates today's Salem. But Salem engages with this union and its attendant tensions more explicitly — and more profitably — than many other American sites of historical tourism.

"As mayor," writes Salem politician Stanley J. Usovicz, Jr., in the 2002 *Official Guidebook* to the city, "I invite you to enjoy all that Salem has to offer. Stroll the streets of the historic district to see the mansions of the sea captains who were America's first millionaires. Enjoy the beautiful works of art in the famed Peabody Essex Museum. Explore the harbor and see how Salem helped launch the great age of Sail and enjoy the restaurants and shops of Pickering Wharf" (2). What happened to "Salem, Witch City?" To hear from official Salem — i.e., to visit the Salem Visitor's Center or to hear from Salem's leaders — is to experience a strange kind of parallel universe: one in which Salem's witch history is nearly completely obscured by its maritime past and its non-witchcraft-related educational attractions. In the 2000 *Official Guidebook*, Usovicz makes absolutely no mention of witchcraft in his opening remarks.

In the revised 2002 *Guidebook*, the mayor adds this brief tagline: "Walk the Heritage Trail to learn about the infamous Witch Hysteria of 1692 and to visit the House of Seven Gables, inspiration for Salem's native son, Nathaniel Hawthorne" (*Official Guidebook*, 2002, 2). Witchcraft is mentioned after a bevy of sea-related issues, and it is not even allowed to occupy the final, privileged position in the welcome; this spot is saved for Hawthorne, who of course had much to say about witchcraft, but who is celebrated by official Salem simply as a native, not as a commentator on the witchcraft era.[5] But Usovicz concludes his remarks with this contradictory salutation, "Welcome to the bewitching seaport of Salem, Massachusetts — enjoy your visit!" (*Official Guidebook*, 2002, 2). Usovicz's mayoral message illustrates the tension that infuses contemporary Salem's tourist industry. On the one hand, educational and high art museums and sites battle to de-emphasize Salem's witch past, which gets marked as entertaining, tacky, and trivial. At the same time, however, the city is witch-crazy; tourists are obsessed with witches, the Wiccan community is thriving, and witchcraft-related attractions continue to draw the greatest crowds in Salem. Salem's seaport gets constructed as the valuable, significant, educational, and "true" historical past, while witches get constructed as a kind of bogus and even fraudulent historical narrative. But Salem's seaport remains "bewitching," as witch history continually thwarts the efforts of maritime history to leave it silent and buried. This war, between classy and tacky tourist sites, between education and entertainment, between truth and fiction, is what drives and ultimately sustains Salem's tourist industry.

Of course, no one would dispute that Salem is a city "originally built not upon witches but upon maritime trade" (Salem Witch Village Tour). Originally called *Naumkeag* by natives, Salem's first English settlers arrived in 1626; Salem became part of the burgeoning Massachusetts Bay Colony in 1643. By the time of the American Revolution, Salem was one of the "new world's" largest cities, and as the war ended, Salem was immersed in highly successful trade with the West Indies, Europe, and the rich East Indies. Codfish went out and Indian silks, Sumatran pepper, and other profitable imports arrived, and Salem's upper classes built mansions along the harbor that had made them rich. Salem was incorporated as a city in 1836, and it began to develop into a hub of manufacturing and retail; leather and shoe factories sprung up, and immigrants first from Canada and Ireland and later from Italy and Eastern Europe arrived to provide labor for the new industries. Sylvania and Parker Brothers Games arrived and gradually replaced Salem's declining leather and shoe companies, but the most dramatic shift in Salem's recent economic landscape came in the 1970s when tourism supplanted all industrial, mercantile, and fishing businesses as Salem's number one moneymaker (*Official Guidebook*, 2000, 4). Until the 1970s, the witchcraft history was a just one of many blips on Salem's commercial radar, and its seafaring past had yet to be revived as a tourist industry.

In his comprehensive survey of Salem guidebooks, Stephen Olbrys Gencarella describes a complicated back-and-forth tension between Salem's commercial tourist industry and its educationally oriented historians:

> From the 1850's to the bicentenary in 1892, a loose affiliation of historians and businesses met with relative comfort as the tourist market emerged. Divisions arose from 1892 to the 1920's as the witch theme became dominant in public representation of the city; the tension between those favoring rampant commodification and those resisting it was apparent in public discourse for the city's tercentenary in 1926. The 1930's and 1940's created opportunities for local historians to mollify or repel the witch association and advance other aspects of Salem's history in an effort to forefront preservation rather than commercialization. The 1950's and 1960's brought a renewed interest in the supernatural and the Trials that inspired new alignments and contests for power, but the historians maintained the upper hand through the 1970's. In the 1980's local representation ceded as burgeoning national interest in the Trials returned for the Tercentenary. Since 1992, sharp divisions have again arose in reaction to a greatly-intensified reliance upon the witch theme [Gencarella 283].

Today, when Salem's history is narrated, the commercialized witch trials seem to compete with the historian-favored, sea-oriented past. After a brief explanation of the witchcraft events, Salem's *Official Guidebook* explains, "Thanks to its burgeoning codfish trade with the West Indies and Europe, and despite the disruptive impact of the Witchcraft Trials of 1692..., the town grew and prospered" (*Official Guidebook*, 2000, 4). The impact of the witch trials disrupts not only Salem's journey toward prosperity, but also Salem's own self-history. Treated as a problematic inter-ruption in an otherwise sensible historical narrative, the witch trials are relegated to the margins of Salem's own understanding of its evolution. Interestingly, however, for more than thirty years now, Salem's major indus-try has been tourism, and the witch trials' "disruptive" effect on prosperity has surely been revealed as a fallacy. Today's Salem seems caught between its past, in which the trials functioned as an obstacle to progress, and its present, in which its very survival depends upon the revival of its witch his-tory. If Salem was "originally" a port capital and not a witch city (though precisely when Salem "originates" — in Naumkeag? in 1643's "Essex County"? in its incorporation as a city? — is surely not a resolved question either), it seems that today its "true" history and its commercial history are at odds.

When one enters the National Park Service Regional Visitor Center at the heart of Salem's historic district, one is struck by the total absence of witches. Large dioramas illustrating important scenes from Salem's his-tory are dotted throughout the enormous main lobby. At the center is a tremendous trade ship, complete with small-scale sailors, a busy dock, and tiny packages waiting to be unloaded. There are also displays on Salem's Armory Drill Shed, the neighboring town of Ipswich, Salem's textile indus-try, and the life of early settlers (pre–1692). A display on African-Ameri-can heritage features Salem's notable eighteenth- and nineteenth-century blacks, but no mention is made of 1692 or of Tituba, who has come to be known — perhaps erroneously — as Salem's most notable "black" woman. Where are the witches? In the lobby area, they are in two places: in the gift shop, and in the minds of the tourists who are visiting.

In the gift shop, approximately 50 percent of items for sale are witch-related. This includes everything from books about the witchcraft trials to key chains and other mementos. In Salem, witches are good business, and even the most "educational" of sites stock their share of coffee mugs featuring witches on broomsticks. Interestingly, this commercialization — which might seem to posit tourists as nothing more than unthinking con-sumers of goods — actually stems from a history that viewed tourists as part of a "heroic undertaking." Scholar Judith Adler writes,

> The kind of seeing first consciously cultivated by the methodologists of a
> post–Renaissance secular art of travel was intimately bound to an overarching
> scientific ideology which cast even the most humble of tourists as part of ...

the impartial survey of all creation. Such seeing, strikingly reminiscent of the taking of inventory, was accompanied by significant collecting activity, as travelers transferred antiquities and other natural and manmade "curiosities" from many parts of the world to the private estates and scientific academies of their home countries [24].

In other words, as tourists load up on tarot cards and witch mugs, they both consume — some might say "swallow" — the packaged, commercialized version of the past that is fed to them at the same time as they *appropriate* that packaging, taking it in and recontextualizing it into their own landscapes. Whether they purchase out of parody or earnestness, consumers in Salem use souvenirs to establish a link between themselves and the city. This link is parallel to the link that Salem works to establish — via the use of reiterative performances not unlike the hundreds of mugs that line the Visitor Center shelves — between itself and the past. As the Visitor Center struggles with a shame about its own investment in witches while simultaneously investing heavily in witch souvenirs, it highlights a common phenomenon in Salem: souvenirs seem to signify both Salem's superficial failures to lift itself out of the pit of low entertainment *and* Salem's slyly successful deployment of commerce to help connect visitors to the past.

The fact that the "commercial" sections of the Visitor Center are quarantined to the corner of the building demonstrates how Salem's high tourist sites discourage patrons from focusing on the witch trials. Tourists interviewed in Salem consistently reply to the question *"Why are you in Salem?"* with just one word: "witches." Charles and Nancy Pappas from Wilmington, Illinois, tourists interviewed outside of the Visitor Center, had their "misplaced" attractions to Salem corrected upon their arrival. "What I had heard before I came here was the witch thing," said Charles, "But I learned right away that that was only a small, tiny, minute part of it" (Pappas). Mr. Pappas' emphasis on the diminutive importance of the witch trials in Salem history is a direct result of his "education" in Salem, particularly, he said, the education he received from the Visitor Center film, *Where Past is Present.*

"Our story is about much more than the infamous witch trials," a "local" voice narrates at the beginning of the film, "It's about cultural evolution and change" (*Where Past*). The fact that the trials are "infamous" seems to be the main reason that they are so systematically de-emphasized by the Visitor Center. In fact, in the entire film — which runs nearly an hour in length — virtually no description of the trials is given. The film focuses on maritime trade and the fishing industry, with smaller segments on millwork and early entrepreneurs. Despite the fact that "what happened" during 1692 is not described, the film is not completely silent on the subject of witchcraft. "The Puritan treatment of natives, and later their behavior during the witch trials, have become unforgettable symbols of intolerance," the narrator intones (*Where Past*). As in Usovicz's statement, where the witch trials are syntactically subordinated to Hawthorne, here the trials are both validated and overshadowed by the dominant phrase regarding Puritan-Native relations. The film, which spends significant time examining Native culture and the effects that European settlement had on native populations, uses the Native issue to both eclipse and make educational the witch issue. This is not to say, of course, that I believe that the genocide of the Native people of Essex County should not receive more emphasis than the hanging of a handful of settlers for witchcraft,[6] but what is so compelling is the way that these two historical events get assigned value based not on the number of lives lost, but on the seemingly "intrinsic" educational value each event has.

Despite the film's condemnation of the negative impact of Europeans on Native people, it still works hard to vindicate the Puritans as far as the witch trials are concerned. "In [the Puritans'] defense," claims the narrator, "they truly believed that witchcraft existed as a terrible threat.... One positive outcome [of the trials is that] to this day the witch hysteria reminds us to be on guard against intolerance" (*Where Past*). What is important about the witch trials to the National Park Service, who produced the film, is that the trials can function today as a learning tool and a codifier of proper moral behavior. Unlike the Native genocide, which is allowed to stand as an atrocity, the witch trials must be recuperated and rescued from the realm of history. Transplanted from historical narrative to moral lesson, the witch trials become a symbol of the process of education itself. In this way, the Visitor Center separates the witch trials from the desire to discover the past, and relocates it into a present-day behavioral issue. The title of the film, *Where Past is Present*, is particularly evocative where the witch trials are concerned, since the film effectively wrestles the 1692 events out of their original context and places them into the current day. The end of the film reflects this present-ing maneuver. The narrator concludes, "As you explore our places, attend the voices of our past. You may find them hauntingly familiar. Our history may be an echo of your own story being told" (*Where Past*). This conclusion is significant for many reasons. First, the film implies that visitors to Salem create the history around them, which functions like an echo of current-day subjects. If the past is truly the present, the witch trials — presented as they were with no detail and plenty of moralizing lessons — can be safely removed from the realm of the devil, however real he may have seemed at one time, and inserted into the realm of tolerance, the new moral legislative code that replaces religion in Salem's Visitor Center. But like Usovicz, the film cannot resist the lure of the spooky side of Salem. For the mayor, Salem's past was "bewitching." For the film, it is "hauntingly" familiar. Both the film and the mayor slip into a touristic manipulation of Salem's witch lure despite their attempts to steer visitors away from any witch-related history.

But if there is one site in Salem that attempts to remove itself *completely* from the realm of tourism, it would have to be the Phillips Library, part of the Peabody Essex Museum. For a single admission fee, visitors can access both the Peabody Essex Museum — with its impressive collections of Asian ceramics, furniture, and whaling and seafaring memorabilia from Salem's early days — and the library building. The museum stresses the familiar high-tourist themes in Salem: fishing and maritime trade ... not witchcraft. My recent visit to the Peabody Essex illustrates how difficult it is to find witchcraft-related items amongst the museum holdings. I knew from a past visit that the museum holdings included four objects related to the witch trials: two canes, a sundial, and a chair, each allegedly owned by witch trial participants. At the front desk of the museum, I asked a museum staffer where these items were located. She looked surprised that anyone would ask her about witchcraft artifacts, and she claimed she didn't know where they were; perhaps, she guessed, they had been put away while the museum was undergoing construction. In one of the museum's exhibit halls, I asked a guard the same question and received the same answer. Finally, down the street at the Phillips Library, I asked the front desk attendant if he knew where the items were. Once again, he told me they were probably put away during the construction. As I paced the library lobby while he checked me into the reading room, my eye fell on a glass case adjacent to his desk. In the case were the two canes and the sundial, and next to the case in a large glass box nearly six feet tall was the chair. The items were probably less than two feet from the desk attendant. The museum seems intentionally and actively to try to erase this collection from the public view, even when the collection itself is fully exposed; the result is that at the Peabody Essex, witchcraft history is not easily accessible to tourists.

This inaccessibility is both supported and undercut by the way that the library's holdings are handled. In the Phillips Library, most of the original witchcraft documents that have survived can be viewed by just about anyone. But this viewing is controlled in such a way so as to discourage casual tourism and to encourage scholarly research interests. First, one must register at the front desk. At this point, a list of forbidden items is given to the visitor, and this list contains two of the tourist's best friends: the "camera" and the "fanny-pack." The very fact that they mention "fanny-pack" seems to suggest that the library expects tourists to desire access, and also that these tourists must be stripped of their touristic identities before entering. When one finally makes it upstairs to the reading room, one must register again at yet another front desk. The museum's doubled front desk demonstrates how the institution always keeps its visitors on the outside; even as one passes through one front gate, another is established to prove that the interior is always someplace else.[7] Indeed, the reading room contains little else than indexes, computers, and desks. All valuable documents are housed behind doors clearly marked off-limits to visitors. The reading room registration requires that guests explain both their "research subject" and the "purpose of research." Subjects that can be checked off include: "Family history," "Local history," "Maritime history," "China," "American Literature," and "Other." Though the most famous holdings of the library are the witchcraft documents, they are subsumed under "Local history" or the ubiquitous "Other." Purposes include "Term paper," "Thesis," "Dissertation," "Article," "Book," and "Other." There are, of course, no boxes to check for "Sheer curiosity," "Tourism," or "Want to get spooked." The registration form also asks for one's institutional affiliation. The process of gaining access to the Phillips Library demonstrates the library's own goal of weeding out tourists or morphing tourists into researchers via a series of well-regimented steps. This may not differ from the project of most research libraries, and it is not necessarily a negative thing. But the Phillips is in an interesting position, situated as it is not in the center of a university community or in a metropolitan area, but right at the heart of one of New England's most popular tourist epicenters.

Once one gains access to the Phillips Library, which is one of the few places open to the public in Salem that does not appear on the Visitor Center map, one can actually hold the original witchcraft documents in one's own hands. After filling out a request sheet, patrons wait while a librarian retrieves the witchcraft boxes that contain the documents. After signing out a particular document, a librarian hands the patron a manila folder with a single document inside. The patron reviews the document at one of two permitted tables, and then returns the document to a librarian who signs it back in. Some of the documents are two or three words long, as they are just handwritten names. Some are just lists of witnesses. But no matter how small, random, or inconsequential a document is, patrons can only view one at a time. During my weekday visit to the library, I found that on average, the retrieval and sign-in/-out process took about four minutes per document. To read the hundreds of documents on file would take hours and hours of administrative work — much of which must be done by librarians and not the researcher her/himself. In addition, tourists looking to visit with some of the more dramatic documents — such as the dual examination of Tituba and Sarah Good — would have to know quite a bit about the trials in order to request the appropriate folder for viewing. No browsing is possible with the actual documents. Few people would take issue with the tight security at the library; after all, these are the "originals." But if they are so valuable, why are visitors allowed to hold the parchments in their hands without the use of gloves, protective glass, or page turners? The library seems to imply that their holdings will be protected more by assuring that they are viewed by the appropriate people than by legislating contact precautions that would be taken by all patrons.

During an interview with California tourists outside of the Salem Witch History Museum, which reproduces many scenes from 1692 using mannequins and animatronics, one young man summed up his reaction to his Salem visit as "disappointed." "For some reason," he said, "I had these great ideas that there would be all this old stuff to see here, but there isn't anything that's really old" (tourists). When asked if he had heard of the Phillips Library, he said no. Though he had spent about an hour at the Peabody Essex Museum, he had left in search of witchcraft-related history, since that was what he had come to Salem to see. He was never informed that the original documents and artifacts could be viewed by any interested party just a few feet down the road from both the Peabody Essex and the Witch History museums.

Why does the Phillips Library work so hard to secret away its wonderful witchcraft-related resources? To a certain extent, it is probably a preservationist impulse that desires to protect primary source material from further decay. But the Phillips Library self-marketing materials (or lack thereof) and protocol for use suggest that the library wishes to cater to researchers and not to tourists. Witchcraft is considered by the library to be a tourist industry, and as a result, witchcraft objects are all but ignored by the museum, and witchcraft documents are unmentioned in tourist publications and the library's own literature. The library website is set up for research visitors rather than Salem tourists, and mention of the witchcraft documents are buried on inner pages about manuscript collections. An overview of the collection covers the specific holdings in several categories, but you have to read down to the fine print to find this note: "The library's best known holdings are undoubtedly the records of the special 1692 Court of Oyer and Terminer, better known as the 1692 Salem Witchcraft Trials" (http://www.pem.org/museum/lib_strengths php). In order to find out that there are primary sources related to the witchcraft trials at the Phillips Library, one would probably need to arrive at the website with prior knowledge, since nothing in the site's navigation would lead a tourist down the path to this discovery.

The purpose of this discussion is certainly not to condemn the Peabody Essex Museum for elitism, nor even to critique its lack of accessibility. What is intriguing to me about the Phillips Library is its participation in a process by which "original" history is erased or obscured because it has been identified as touristic. In this case, the original documents begin to get coded as derivative, as part of a representation of the past rather than as the past itself. Salem's "educational" sites tend to make primary sources into secondary representations, and as a result, Salem's witch history is left without an original story. One wonders whether or not the "originals" that are hidden in the Phillips Library would fully establish the events of the witch trials; clearly this book argues that Salem's "facts" were always already performative, and that Salem's history is more about historiography than ontology. But even if the very category of "originality" is treated with skepticism, this does not alter the fact that Salem's educational tendencies function to elide the "original," phantom though it may be. But as this elision is enacted, a simultaneous *production* of this same original occurs. First of all, the documents in the Phillips Library (and the sites in Danvers that shall be addressed later in this chapter), only *become* original when the copies of it are produced. As Peggy Phelan puts it, "The meaning of originality is dependent on the copy, the forgery, the counterfeit" (9). Salem's tourist sites produce the "originality" that makes notable and primary the "primary sources," and then these sites lodge these "originals" in mostly hidden library archives.

But Salem's tourist sites also produce more visible and accessible "originals" that serve the purpose of validating the very copies that preceded them. Because most of the "primary sources" are hidden from public view, the Salem tourist industry functions to construct alternative "originals" that usurp the primary source positions and add credibility to the derivative tourist attractions that ironically developed both the idea of "originality" and the new "originals" themselves. A prime example of this can be seen at Salem's Witch Dungeon Museum. The attraction is actually one part live performance and one part conventional museum. Visitors enter into an old church, which is set like a theater. After taking a seat in a pew, visitors watch a guide in period dress mount the stage steps and deliver an introduction. "What you are about to see is a live reenactment," our guide, Cay, tells us. She sets the scene by explaining some of the surrounding context for the witch trials (Indian attacks, smallpox, charter problems, etc.). She tells about Tituba's "stories of witchcraft and ... magic games." Finally, she exhorts the audience, "Let your thoughts wander back now to a morning over 300 years ago. Most of the dialogue you are about to hear was taken directly from the trial transcripts" (Witch Dungeon Museum). The curtain rises, and a scene plays out in which afflicted girl Mary Warren examines the accused Elizabeth Proctor. Right from the beginning, the Witch Dungeon is caught between its desire to establish authenticity and its desire to be as dramatic as possible. The very notion of a "live reenactment" expresses the tension that the Dungeon wrestles with. On the one hand, it is live, spontaneous, current, and on the other hand it is reenacted, scripted, past. It wants both to tantalize and entertain and to educate and explain. Though much of the dialogue does in fact come from the transcripts, the fact that Mary Warren examines Elizabeth Proctor directly without the intervention of judge or magistrate turns their play into something more intimate and more personal than the trials. One gets the feeling that a soap opera is unfolding as the private conversation gets broadcast for the public. The play — which occasionally features alternate cases, but always has just two actors — effectively takes the legal questions involved in the trials and makes them psychological and interpersonal. But there are others on stage with the two main actors during the play: judges and jury are represented by mannequins who sit along the upstage wall. The mannequins, who do not move, are set up in dramatic positions: reaching out, falling over, standing up with a gavel, as if to suggest that they are frozen in their most heightened action. As the play walks a line between authentic dialogue and dramatic soap opera, it also balances between a kind of static photograph (frozen mannequins) of the past and a dynamic dramatizing (mannequins in motion) of that same past.[8] The play seems to want to lasso Salem's original past, but at the same time, it wants to emphasize its own highly entertaining rope tricks.

This fluctuation between trying to grasp and claim an original and true Salem history and trying to entertain its modern audience is even more prominent when the play ends and the guide reappears — this time to take visitors "down to the Dungeon." "Before we go," says Cay,

> I want to tell you a few facts about our Dungeon. This is a recreation, not the original Dungeon. The original stood about 500 yards from here on Federal Street. The telephone company stands there today. About fifty years ago, they were digging a new foundation for a new phone company and they came across the remains of the original dungeon. They did save a few artifacts from it. Most of them are at the Peabody Essex Museum, and we have one beam downstairs from the original that I'll point out when we go down [Witch Dungeon Museum].

The 1957 unearthing of the original dungeon by the New England Tele-phone Company yielded mostly wooden beams, and those donated to the Peabody Essex are, as one might suspect, not on display at the museum. But the Witch Dungeon makes the most of its minor acquisition. Just before the conclusion of the tour, in a kind of pièce-de-résistance maneu-ver, the tour guide reveals the original beam, bolted about five feet off the ground, and conspicuously not serving to hold up the walls or roof of the Dungeon. "You're welcome to touch the beam from the original dungeon if you like," Cay tells us, "But if you turn into a frog, I'm not responsi-ble" (Witch Dungeon Museum). Visitors line up behind me and we rub the beam just before we leave the site. The Dungeon, despite its status as a total reproduction, focuses most of its emphasis on this "real" beam. But the beam, de-contextualized and impotent as it is, seems to be more a symbol of the Dungeon's own unoriginality than it is a direct connection to the past. By situating it into a spooky context (it hangs alone in a dark room, and its only company is a subtle soundtrack of ghostly, howling wind noises) and by warning visitors to beware curses as they touch it, the Dun-geon takes even its most "original" object and places it securely into the landscape of its own performance.

Another example of the Dungeon's dissociating split between the "original" and its "context" has to do with the building itself. The Dun-geon certainly does not try to disguise the fact that it is not the actual 1692 dungeon, but the way in which it reveals its own (lack of) connection to the original site is both confusing and fascinating. On the outside of the twentieth-century Witch Dungeon building, there is a large plaque that reads: "Here stood the Salem Gaol Built in 1684, used until 1813, razed in 1957. During the witchcraft persecution of 1692, many of the accused were imprisoned here. One of them, the Aged Giles Corey (b. 1611) was pressed to death on these grounds." Beside this metal plaque is a smaller, plastic sign that reads: "This plaque was originally located on Federal Street, The Old Jail Site, Two Blocks North."[9] At 4 Federal Street, the actual site of the jail, there is no marker at all. Here, the "originality" of the Salem jail site is contained not in the beams or the ground of that old prison, but in the contemporary plaque that marks the spot where it stood. The marker functions perfectly effectively even without the presence of the original thing it marks. The Witch Dungeon highlights how originality gets performed at Salem attractions. Despite the general lack of artifacts, despite its removal from the "real" 1692 jailhouse, despite its use of drama, the Dungeon generally considers itself to be both educational and authentic.

"You are there," reads the Witch Dungeon Museum brochure, "In Salem Village 1692, and you are guaranteed a unique educational experience with a chill or two" (Witch Dungeon brochure). The "you are there" tagline is especially ironic, for of course the fact of the matter is that you are not there (you might be close to there, but the phone company is actually there). And the mix of education and chills again emphasizes the museum's use of both a diction of authenticity and a performative methodology. The "Dungeon" itself contains cell after cell of imprisoned mannequins, and, it is reiterated, these are the "actual size of the cells." As opposed to being the actual cells, these reproduced cells can only claim authenticity by way of copying or comparing; they gain their authenticity precisely because they are like the originals but not the originals. Even Catherine "Cay" Trefry, a guide who has worked at the Dungeon for sixteen years, advertises herself as "original" by way of being a copy or derivation: she herself is "a descendent of Giles Corey, eight generations down" (Trefry). Though Cay has an ancestral connection back to an "original" trial participant, she also has some more direct experience with Salem's 1692 inhabitants: she has heard them haunting the Dungeon after hours. In a private interview, Cay revealed the following:

> In September of last year, I had the oddest experience. I was up here [on the landing by the museum's exit] and I heard humming coming from down there. It was a woman's voice. I said, "Who's down there?" There wasn't anyone down there. And afterwards it occurred to me that it was the anniversary of the hanging of Bridget Bishop, and I said, "All right, this is going a little too far." It's strange because every so often I'll see someone go by out of the corner of my eye, and I say, "If you're not gonna bother me, I'm not gonna bother you" [Trefry].

The question that arises from Cay's spooky story is why would the ghosts of 1692, in particular the jailed and executed accused witches, choose to haunt the Salem Witch Dungeon Museum? Wouldn't it be more likely that they would haunt *the phone company?* Cay's story reveals how the reproduction site, by way of its use of horror stories, at last ends up supplanting the "original" site of the "dungeon." The hauntings, the descendent tour guide, the plaque, the impotent and threatening beam, all produce a new kind of "originality" that co-opts and ultimately replaces the actual, original Salem jail and the prisoners it held.

Salem's most popular museum, the Salem Witch Museum, has no artifacts from the past on display. Unlike the Witch Dungeon, which works by a process of reiteration to link itself back to the "original" dungeon that it finally replaces, the Witch Museum functions by performance alone, choosing to use as its "original" not an object from the past or a 1692 site, but a "true story" of what transpired during the witch hysteria. The Witch Museum is the most noticeable building in Salem: "Located in a memorable gothic revival building on Route 1A at Salem Common," the brochure reads, "we are easily accessible from all major routes" (Witch Museum brochure). The building's architecture is symbolic of the museum's approach to history. As a "revival," the style alludes to the past but includes its own distance from that past. And *when* is the past to which it alludes? Puritan architectural style is sometimes referred to as "First Period" or "Post-Medieval," but though this style shares some similarities to the Witch Museum building (such as the batten doors or multiple gables), the enormous scale, fortress-like columns, and detailed ornamentation of the Witch Museum building do more to recollect Dracula's dramatic castle in a mythic Transylvania than they do to invoke images of simple Puritan dwellings (*Architectural Guide*). Thus, the gothic "revival" revives Salem's mythic past — caught up as it is with tales of witches, vampires, and horror — and not its historical past. Even more interesting is the fact that the building was not erected to house a witch museum, so the way in which it exudes an authentic, innate "witch-ness" is more irony than intention. According to a staff member at the museum, it began life as a church, before being turned into a car museum, and ultimately, after being renovated in the wake of a fire, being turned into the Salem Witch Museum (Michaels). The museum's physical presence is a tangle of "revivals" that are marketed to symbolize Salem's past, but which actually establishes the museum's own reification of "the original" as a completely mythologizing process.

"You are there," begins the brochure to the Witch Museum, recollecting the Witch Dungeon literature, which contains the same phrase. The brochure continues, "Witness the testimony of the hysterical girls, the suffering of the blameless victims, and the decisions of the fanatical judges who sent innocent people to their deaths" (Witch Museum brochure). The brochure begins by claiming to transport visitors back to 1692. It explains, "This presentation is based on actual trial documents." It seems as if, as with the Dungeon, "originality" will be of primary importance. But the brochure continues, "With 13 stage sets, you'll enter the web of lies and intrigue of the Salem Witch Hunt, one of the most enduring true stories in American History" (Witch Museum brochure). This tension between the stage sets and the truth, a familiar tension to us at this point, sends a mixed message to readers, who might be asking as they read, "Will what we see at this museum be real?" The truth is offered up, but it will be dramatically performed. And the truth has more to do with enduring stories of Salem — i.e., Salem's apocryphal past — than with original transcripts; the presentation, by way of example, spends significant time on both Tituba's voodoo and Giles Corey's dying words, "More weight," both of which are "facts" produced by Salem's histories of itself, not by any primary source materials. A band of large letters at the top of the brochure reads, "Was the Devil at work?" The written response: "19 innocent people were hanged in Salem in 1692." This response is notably ambiguous; does it mean *yes* or *no* to the question about the devil? This ambiguity characterizes the museum's approach to history. It wants to vindicate the innocent victims by declaring that the devil had *not* possessed them, but it also wants to deploy the attraction that the devil wields over tourists. Though it claims to tell the truth (and it certainly does, in many ways), the museum invests the story of the trials with such abundant spookiness and drama that it points to how the "true" story of Salem has become not just about transcripts, but about mythology as well.

As the lights go down in the large, bare room that is the museum's theater, a red circle, emblazoned with the names of the hanged, glows on the floor at the center of the crowd of visitors. A soundtrack of howling wind accompanies the voice of the narrator, who sounds like a cross between Vincent Price and Lawrence Olivier. He moans out that he is going to tell the "true story" of a time when the "Prince of Darkness ... frightened us all with eternal damnation" (Witch Museum presentation). "Do you believe in witches?" he asks, and as he narrates, a serpentine dragon lights up near the ceiling of the room, and its eyes glow red. Though the presentation purports to demonstrate just how concrete and corporeal the devil was to Puritans, it is clear by the number of crying children who get escorted from the theater at this point that the presentation is also quite scary. Throughout the show, life-sized mannequins are lit by stage lights, as diorama scenes appear one by one around the upper perimeter of the room. Tiny fragments of dialogue from *The Crucible* are interspersed with passages from the transcripts and accounts that clearly recall Calef and Upham. The entire event is a head-spinning mélange of fact, history, myth, and theater. When it is over, visitors are asked to "exit through the gift shop."

The Salem Witch Museum is Salem's most-visited museum for many reasons. Its building embodies the kind of gothic, dramatic authenticity that tourists associate with the witch trials. Its presentation uses theatrical techniques to tell the "true" story of Salem — a story that reads as "real" to those who are familiar with the most popular historical, fictional, and apocryphal accounts of the trials. And its moral lesson appeases those looking for didacticism, while its packaging of this lesson appeases those looking for a thrill. By way of examining this moral lesson, consider the final moments of the presentation. The narrator tells the audience that we can rest assured that Salem's witch hysteria was never as bad as Europe's. He concludes, "Who is the Devil? On whose side was he fighting? On whose side does he fight even now?... We may take pride in the fact that we gave but once and briefly to our fears" (Witch Museum presentation). The moral lesson — that giving way to intolerance and fear is a sign of weakness and should be resisted — is packaged in a kind of perverse homage to the Prince of Darkness, who at any moment, it is implied, might swoop down and afflict us all. Looking around the audience during my last visit to the museum in the summer of 2008, I noted the throngs of campers and counselors and the large number of families with children at the presentation. As kids shrieked with fright, it was clear that they (mostly) enjoyed the horror of the entire event. But there is a reason why most of the groups who visit the Witch Museum do not visit the Nightmare Factory or Terror on the Wharf; the museum manages to wrap its thrills in a cocoon of morality and historicity that makes its heightened drama into a methodology for education in the eyes of its visitors.

An accompanying exhibit called "Witches: Evolving Perceptions" is housed in the Witch Museum, and visitors are encouraged to walk through it before or after the main presentation (and once again, one must pass through the gift shop to reach the exhibit hall). This exhibit is another example of how the Witch Museum uses the thrilling moral lesson to please its guests. "Are you sure you know what the word 'witch' means?" asks the information sheet that accompanies the exhibit. "This exhibit will show you how the meaning of the word has changed over time" (Salem Witch Museum). The exhibit focuses mainly on "misconceptions." According to the informational sheet, the "stereotypical witch" is a "negative stereotype" created by "politics, religion, and superstition." And, we might add, by the Salem Witch Museum, which uses as its logo an image of a witch in a pointy hat holding a broom and standing beside a black cat; this image is on its sign in front of its building and on all of its brochures. It is uncanny for the way that it parallels the model of the "negative stereotype" presented in "Evolving Perceptions." This paradox is at the heart of what makes the museum so marketable: it perpetuates myths in order to correct them, and both the perpetuation and the correction are enjoyable to the museum's visitors. The exhibit ends with a large wall chart:

Fear	Trigger	Scapegoat
God/Devil	Dr. Griggs	150 Townspeople
Japan	Pearl Harbor	Japanese-Americans
Communists	HUAC	Black List
Infection	AIDS	Gay People

The chart shows the ultimate moral lesson of the museum: to contextualize the witch hunt into a historical narrative that illustrates how fear and intolerance function to oppress. By using the witch hunt as a lesson on proper ethical behavior, the museum removes the 1692 events from the past and makes them part of a contemporary moral code. Though it is a common saying to "learn from the past," this phenomenon really works to elide the past, absorbing it into a cyclic story that has less to do with time gone by than it does with the current moment. Thus, the Salem Witch Museum's theatricalizing — scripted and stilted as it is — actually engages visitors by locating the witch trials into the landscape of the visitors' own historical period. This effectively establishes a kind of doubled mode of operation:

Past	*Present*
Origin	Script
Education	Entertainment
Morality	Thrills

Despite the focus by the museum on history, truth, teaching, and ethics, the way the museum actually functions is by utilizing theatrical techniques and entertaining tricks. Salem's "real" past does not get warped or ignored as much as it gets made into a cover for the actual business of the museum: to do business. The grand success of the Witch Museum depends upon both the educational packaging and the delivery of the thrilling goods.[10]

Another museum that fuses an educational package with a thrill-related attraction is the Salem Witch Village. Distinguished from its sister attraction, the Salem Wax Museum of Witches and Seafarers, and other Salem sites by its affiliation with the Wiccan community, the Witch Village is comprised of a tour through the history of witchcraft — including 1692 Salem; the museum also hosts related events such as "pagan classes, workshops, open circles, readings and lectures by practicing witches" (*Official Guidebook, 2002*, 21). The entire attraction, including the gift shop, is managed and staffed by practicing witches. The kind of "education" offered by the Witch Village is slightly different from that offered by the Peabody Essex or the Witch Museum. At the Village, real witches work to salvage the reputation of the "witch," and to redefine witchcraft in the eyes of popular America. "Learn the truth behind the legends and tradition," the ad literature invites, "And then decide for yourself what being a '*witch*' really means" (*Official Guidebook, 2002*, 21). From early on in the tour, our guide, Donna, makes it clear that the Village is not intended to thrill or entertain, per se. "This village is not haunted," she tells our tour group, "Just educational. Nothing will jump out at you. We'll start by meeting Hella" (Salem Witch Village presentation). Donna points out a mannequin of a skeletal zombie in a chair. "Normally at Halloween, Hella would be plugged in and ready to scare you, but since this is an educational tour, today she is just a Nordic guardian here to bid you welcome and guide us on our journey" (Salem Village Guided Tour). Hella is symbolic of the fundamental irony at the core of the Witch Village, an irony that emerges most explicitly when the Village's history is revealed. Originally, Donna tells me in a private interview, "The Village was a haunted house, and it had kind of a negative reputation with us witches. So the high priest and priestess from PRANCE [a Pagan resource group] created this tour. In October, it's still a haunted house since that's what everyone's looking for then. But hopefully, the rest of the year we correct some of the misconceptions from the other attractions" (Donna). In other words, Hella and her friends in the Village were designed to thrill and scare tourists; one month a year, that's just what they do. But the rest of the year, with very little alteration to the site, the Village claims to be an educational experience.[11] The result is a collection of witches, zombies, dragons, and torture devices presented in a dark maze that winds across "Halloween swamp"; the collection, which contains just about everything one would expect to see in a haunted house, is narrated in such as way as to explain how the myths and traditions of each object or identity came into being. For example, a torture rack that shows a mannequin being grotesquely stretched apart becomes not a scare tactic, but an opportunity for Donna to discuss the history of torture in medieval Europe.

The Witch Village is perhaps the most obvious example in Salem of the battle — and partnership — between education and entertainment. The attraction demonstrates how a single site can contain two deeply divided purposes despite the fact that both purposes are enacted in the same way. What the Village highlights is how marketing and packaging — from brochures to the narrated tour — can alter a site's placement on the continuum between "classy" (or educational) and "trashy" (or entertaining). Though in Salem, the Witch Village, especially because it is owned and operated in conjunction with the notoriously tacky Wax Museum, is considered to be far less educational than the Peabody Essex, most locals in Salem — including the Wiccan community — feel that the site is primarily an educational attraction. In effect, the Village overwrites its educational mission onto a previously established core of commercialist entertainment. The educational mission then gets aligned with the superficial, surface level of the site, while the underneath, the origin, and the foundation of the Village remains purely entertaining. This reverses the standard conception of how education and entertainment are thought to function; generally, museums work to make learning fun, to incorporate or add entertainment to their primarily educational mission. A brochure published by the Peabody Essex claims that "this guide will help you find and enjoy" the off-site properties owned by the museum (*Architectural Guide*). It suggests that the artifacts, houses, and gardens themselves are not enjoyable, but that enjoyment is a layer to the attractions that is furnished by the function of the museum. The Witch Village, in contrast, suggests that the duty of a museum is not to provide the entertaining layer, but to manufacture *education* to accompany an already entertaining collection of objects. Thus, though its structure reverses the structure of museums such as the Peabody Essex, the Witch Village engages in a similar process of layering to attract and teach visitors. This layering effect is common to most of Salem's witch history sites, whether their primary goal is education or entertainment. By peeling away the entertaining layers around its witchcraft artifacts and documents, the Phillips Library effectively erases itself as a Salem attraction. To flourish in Salem as a tourist destination and profit center, sites must encourage these levels and layers of meaning to work together to attract the public.[12]

If the Phillips Library, unlike the Witch Village and Witch Museum, attempts to strip away any layers of entertainment surrounding Salem's witchcraft past, there are also sites in Salem that strip away all educational impulses. Like the Phillips Library, neither Boris Karloff's Witch Mansion nor Salem's Museum of Myths and Monsters: Terror on the Wharf are as frequently visited as the Witch Museum, Dungeon, or Village. But nonetheless, many sites like these survive, and together they define Salem's commercialized, spooky side.[13] By purchasing a Fright Pass, visitors in the early part of this decade could access both the Karloff and the Wharf haunted house attractions, which were operated by the same company. The ads for the sites read, "Vampires, Ghosts, Werewolves: Do they really exist? Take our animated journey into fear and beyond. We'll delight in your fright! Salem's *Only* Ticket to Terror!" (*Welcome to Salem*). Salem's haunted houses provide the needed fodder for the corrective measures espoused by sites such as the Witch Museum — and even the Peabody Essex. Surely the haunted houses take gross advantage of Salem's history, capitalizing on the deaths of the accused and ironically reinscribing devilish affliction back onto the history of Salem, a history that had been wiped clean of actual witchcraft by the centuries of curative accounts of the type first launched by Robert Calef. But in some ways, the haunted houses simply make explicit many of the techniques used by more "educational" sites to attract tourists and capitalize on Salem's past.

In the summer of 2002, I visited Boris Karloff's Witch Mansion. After walking through the haunted house as a tourist, I asked to walk through again, this time with the lights on and with a running behind-the-scenes commentary from the tour guide. In the Mansion lobby, cases hang on each of the walls displaying masks and props from movies such as *Nightmare on Elm Street* and *Dracula.* From the outset, the Mansion reveals its reliance on the theatrical, its immersion in the performed. And as one enters the Mansion, it is clear that no dramatic flourish will be spared. Bob, my tour guide, is the only live person in the Mansion as the tours proceed. He flits with agility from spot to spot throughout the Mansion, ducking through secret passages to remain ahead of the tour. In the first room, Karloff's "living room," he pushes a button and a recorded voice moans that this is the Karloff Mansion, a "psychic magnet" that had "stood empty" for years until an "eccentric collector of the strange and macabre here in Salem bought the empty house and moved it to this very spot" (Boris Karloff guided tour). The Mansion establishes a complicated relationship to its own "origins." First of all, the idea that the Mansion is an *empty* psychic magnet is compelling; despite its ability to attract a seemingly infinite amount of paranormal energy, it paradoxically remained empty. This idea of the magnetic, empty site is an apt metaphor for Salem's haunted houses, which draw volumes of visitors but which remain adamant in their fundamental "meaninglessness," their overall refusal to deliver "true content" such as history or education. Instead, the sites revel in their surface play, in the campy frivolity and momentary frights they supply. The idea that the Mansion is even a "mansion" at all, that it was moved from its original site to Pickering Wharf where it now stands, is also a befuddling claim. After all, anyone standing on the street can see that the building is a long, low, contemporary strip-mall type building that houses shops and boutiques in addition to the Karloff attraction. Why does the voice bother to suggest that the house is "real," that it was "moved?" The suspension of disbelief required by visitors is so enormous as to be impossible for all but the youngest of tourists. But the museum's success relies upon its deploying of precisely these over-the-top, fraudulent claims; it is this high drama — which makes no bones about its inauthenticity — that makes the site so appealing. By referring to the Salem collector who "imported" the Mansion, the museum seems to poke fun of its own commercial desires. At the Karloff Mansion, theatrics, camp, and profit are front and center, and visitors are required to celebrate them all.

When I ask my tour guide if it's true that the Mansion was moved to this spot, Bob, who is a young man dressed a long, black robe holding a black hood that he has removed to speak to me, answers, "Nah, it's not true. The real Karloffs do have a part in this, but other than that, it's all made up." He looks disappointed for a minute before he adds, "'Course if it was real, it'd be cool" (Bob). In general, Bob has a surprising attitude about his work at the Mansion. He occasionally expresses this kind of wistfulness about the Mansion's failure to actually provide its visitors with real ghosts and demons. This manifests itself not only as a desire for his attraction to be "real," but also a frustration with the faulty mechanics of the exhibits. "That guy over there," he tells me, pointing to a ridiculously grotesque mannequin in a rocking chair, "That's Boris' ghost, and he used to rock back and forth, but the chair kept moving and banging against the wall, so we just said 'the hell with him'" (Bob). Despite the aloofness (and irony) of the curse, Bob seems to resent the fact that the haunted house needs to be plugged in, needs trouble-shooting, to continue to haunt its audience. Later on in the tour, we enter a room filled with glass jars that contain the dismembered body parts of Boris' victims (which happen to glow purple in the black light). In this same room is a television screen, and on the screen, a twenty-something guy in a t-shirt and soccer shorts shadow boxes and chats idly. There is absolutely nothing horrifying about the video, but it does seem wildly out of context. Bob comments: "I usually say to people that this guy has been trapped in there for 300 years because he called Boris a sissy or something. The recording says he's been there for 300 years. But I tell the people, 'It doesn't look like that, does it?,' and they're like 'Noooo.' It's supposed to be jar or a test tube but it just looks like a TV, which it is" (Bob). What is Bob to do, faced with the dilemma of explaining to tourists all of the places where the museum fails to be realistic? What he does is adopt an hysterically bipolar approach; at one moment he is shouting in a mangled voice, "You've been cursed! Now come this way to the lab-OR-a-tory!" and at the next moment he is speaking in his normal voice, despondently telling visitors that a particular exhibit is silly. Although I don't think Bob particularly studies the complexities of his own position, his bipolar approach is in perfect keeping with the Mansion's whole atmosphere. At once fully committed to following through even its most outrageously ridiculous claim and *simultaneously* reliant on highlighting its own parodic inauthenticity, the Mansion ends up delivering just what it promises: an empty site that thrills, chills, and entertains.[14]

As I enter the final hallway of the Mansion, Bob tells me to put on my 3-D glasses. "I can't see 3-D personally because my eyes are deformed," he moans. "I have cat's eyes. But the 3-D is the best part, so put them on if you dare" (Bob). As I put them on, black lighted skulls and bones rise out of the walls by an inch or two. I ask Bob if his eyes were cursed by Karloff, and he responds, "No, this isn't part of the haunted house. My eyes really are deformed, see?" He walks up to me, stands nose to nose, and stares into my eyes, and I can see that his pupils are long and narrow instead of round. Bob's delivery of his given script, despite his regular lapses into blood-curdling screams and agonizing groans, is so similar to his own "real" conversation, it is often hard to tell where one ends and the other begins. The personal, lighted tour that I took with Bob was most interesting for the similarity it held to the real tour with a group of tourists. In both cases, Bob saw no conflict between scaring the hell out of us at one minute and criticizing the inauthenticity of the attraction at the next. Again, this bipolarity functions to expand the scope of Bob's own authentic voice, as both his moans and his critiques are expressive of his true feelings about the haunted house. His "deformed," cat-like eyes seem to symbolize the way he views the Mansion as a whole: through the eyes of someone who sees in only two dimensions. For Bob, his utter respect and love for his Mansion is not compromised by but *enhanced by* his desire to point out its flaws. The fact that he lacks any kind of sense of parody about the attraction works beautifully to help those of us who visit the Mansion to see it that much more clearly. And since the Mansion cannot actually deliver the real ghosts, it works by enabling our perception of the site as fraudulent and parodic, and therefore highly entertaining.

Salem's witchcraft-related tourism functions through this layering on of teaching and thrills. At the core of most attractions lies a deferral, an elision, or an absence. Except for witchcraft-related sites that work hard *not* to be sites at all, such as the Phillips Library, most Salem attractions are not based on original objects or artifacts, but on a complex of performances. Like the "magnetic" Karloff Mansion, most Salem sites are both highly attractive and ultimately "empty." But "empty" does not imply that they are always meaningless; on the contrary, sites that begin as generic or meaningless, such as the Witch Dungeon, manufacture significant meaning through their performances. But this meaning is based not on a previously existing core, but on the layers of production that surround the absent center. This phenomenon is especially noticeable in the commemorative sites in Salem, such as the Witch Trials Tercentenary Memorial and the graveyards. The Memorial, designed by architect James Cutler and artist Maggie Smith, is bordered by the Old Burying Point Cemetery, the Salem Wax Museum, and the Salem Witch Village, a telling landscape that highlights the tensions between Salem's actual past and its interpretive sites. But what is most striking about the Memorial is the way that it engages with the questions of absence so central to Salem's witch attractions.

"Cutler and Smith's design," writes architecture critic Marion Knox, "grew from the four words that characterized for them the injustice of the witchcraft trials—*Silence, Deafness, Persecution,* and *Memory*" (24). Each of these words, and the way the designers have inscribed them into the site, indicates a kind of loss. For "silence," the designers carved a trough into the rectangular site that leads to a break in the surrounding stone wall. This break, which reveals the gravestones from the cemetery behind the site, is filled in with iron palings. Looking at the graves through the bars leaves the viewer "at eye level with the gravestones of the Salem community who turned their backs on their own innocent" (Knox 24). The trough, the gap, and the implied ignorance of the Salemites all point to the idea of a thing that is supposed to be there that is *not* there. With "deafness," carvings of the accused witches' words disappear under the granite walls of the memorial; again, there is the implication that there is another space, a true space, where the proper things exist, but here in this memorial landscape of loss, these proper things are missing. For "persecution," the designers "planted six black locust trees, believed to be the hanging trees growing on what came to be called Gallows Hill.... The trees [are] the first to lose their leaves in the fall, [and they] cast their shadows on the space" (Knox 24). The trees point to an absence of knowledge, being symbolic more of the fact that nobody knows where Gallows Hill is or what trees grow there than they are of the actual Gallows Hill site. They are also chosen for the early loss of their leaves; in addition to recalling the lives cut short, the leafless trees also remind us of the loss of factuality that comes with the passing of time. To transport Gallows Hill into the memorial space is to transport the central symbol of Salem's historical loss into a space that mourns the death of the past itself. Marion Knox describes the site's incorporation of "memory" this way:

> Sitting down [on one of the Memorial's benches], I naturally sit beside the engraving [of the accused's name], not on it. This is *Memory*.... What speaks loudest here is what is missing: the gaps and intervals articulate disjunction. Space enclosed by walls, transgressed by the sidewalk, straddled by the ancient tree that buckles the wall around it. A wall broken as if to allow a view — but not a passage — between the memorial space of the executed and the cemetery of their persecutors. Next to me on the bench is an inscription: "Rebecca Nurse, hanged July 19, 1692." I am in the presence of absence [27].

The Memorial commemorates not just the innocent victims of the past, but the past itself, and the absence that it invokes is not just a loss of life, but a loss of access to those lives. Memory, then, is both a function that reifies the dead into stone tablets *and* a function that mourns the irreversible passage of time that inevitably removes us from what happened before. To slide over on the bench so as to avoid Rebecca Nurse's carved name is to look through an iron fence at her history. The carving acts like the fence; her name offers a teasing hope that the real Rebecca can somehow be recalled and revived, but its status in stone reminds us that her name is not herself, and that the commemorative process demands absence in order to make its meaning.[15]

Despite Salem's obsession with the bodies of the dead — practically everywhere you go in Salem you encounter mannequins swinging by their necks from ropes, gravesites pretending to mark the site of their buried bodies, reconstructed Gallows Hill pits with plaster skeletal remains poking out — the most noticeable absence in Salem is the lack of victims' bodies. Gallows Hill, where most of the dead are thought to lie, has not been discovered. As Bridget M. Marshall explains, "The remains of only one witch has been found and identified — those of George Jacobs — and these accidentally by his descendents who were digging on their family land when they discovered a skeleton" (16). She continues:

> The absent center of [Salem's headstones] is remarkable. Presumably a gravestone indicates the location of a body beneath it, but this is not the case for the witch memorials. On the Nurse Homestead in Danvers, I visited the monument erected in her honor in 1885; however, her body is not located here. The marker, which would normally indicate the location of a grave, is located in a graveyard where other markers do point to graves, including that of George Jacobs. But the Nurse monument, and others like it, is made to indicate the very absence of that grave; it points to an absence, as well as to another (unknown, unknowable) location [16].

Though it is generally accepted that Nurse's family removed her body from the Gallows Hill pit and re-buried her on the Nurse Homestead, her body has not been located, despite the marker that was erected. The Nurse Homestead website tells us that it was "undoubtedly here that Rebecca Nurse was secretly buried by her family," which alerts critical readers that, of course, there is doubt involved in the location of her body (Rebecca Nurse Homestead). The obsession Salem has with dead — whether spooky or commemorative — always centers on a phantom body, a body that, in an ironic reminder of the original accusations against it, has become a shadow of its "real," true self — at long last, a specter.

Today's Salem is a series of performances that function both to displace and to reproduce the "original" events of 1692. And though Salem tourism is thriving, and the most inauthentic attractions and happenings are wildly popular, visitors who come to Salem to view artifacts or sites related to the actual witch hunt are sometimes puzzled by the utter lack of objects and buildings that directly connect with the past. But they keep coming back, pleased by the extensive services offered to the Salem tourist, from well-managed museums and haunted houses to fine dining to good hotels to the easy-to-navigate Salem trolley. Tourists in Salem don't just enjoy the historical- and entertainment-oriented sites, but the total web of visitor services that combine to ensure the comfort and satisfaction of those who have traveled to Salem. This web of services functions to attract visitors to Salem despite the nearly total lack of the (seemingly) most important thing of all: a true historical link to the witchcraft events. A short car ride to the town next door to Salem illustrates just how important this web is.

In 1692, Danvers, Massachusetts, was called "Salem Village," while today's Salem was called "Salem Town." It wasn't until 1752, long after the witch trials, that Danvers and Salem became two totally independent towns. Today, there are over a dozen original seventeenth-century houses still standing in Danvers; many of them are open to the public, and many of them have direct links to the witch trials. For example, in Danvers, one can visit the Nurse Homestead, actual home of Rebecca Nurse and, as previously mentioned, probable site of her burial. One can visit the Putnam House, where Joseph Putnam, uncle of Ann and public critic of the trials, lived in fear of being accused. In Danvers, one can stop by the site of the Salem Village Parsonage, focal point of the witchcraft events, where Parris lived with his wife, his daughter, his niece, and his slaves. The site was excavated in 1970, and the original foundation still exists and is now accompanied by interpretive signs. The Samuel Holten House was the home of Sarah Holten, who testified against Rebecca Nurse. The Putnam Burial Ground contains the unmarked graves of afflicted girl Ann Putnam and her famous parents. Ingersoll's Ordinary, which was one of the earliest spots where accused witches were examined, still stands. Watch House Hill, which served as a lookout for Indian attacks, was also where a church was erected in 1700, a church that became the site for Ann Putnam's infamous confession. The Osburn House was the home of Sarah Osburn (sic), one of the first three accused. The Wadsworth Burial Ground has the headstone — and assumedly the body — of Elizabeth Parris (complete with epitaph written by Samuel Parris). This is just an abbreviated list of original sites in Danvers, all of which are within easy driving distance (and sometimes even walking or biking distance) of Salem. But no tourists I have spoken to over the years in Salem were planning a trip to Danvers; in fact, most had never heard of Danvers, and none knew of its connection to the Salem witchcraft events. And even though the Danvers Archival Center houses the Brehaut Witchcraft Collection, which is the "largest collection of imprints relating to the 1692 Salem Village Witchcraft," the Center regularly hosts far fewer researchers and browsers than the Phillips Library in Salem (*Welcome to Danvers*).

What is so compelling about Danvers is the way that it highlights what it is about *Salem* that is so appealing to tourists. Though most tourists would get a thrill from standing in the exact place that Sarah Osbourne once lived, the promise of this thrill is not strong enough to overcome the promises that Salem can make. By scripting and then staging history, Salem can produce an authenticity that Danvers fails to provide. Authenticity demands not an "original" site, but a *performance* of originality, just the kind of performance at which Salem excels. While Salem does have some "original" artifacts (the sundial, the beam, the documents), they are either intentionally eclipsed by more "authentic" performances (the sundial can't begin to compete with mannequins who quake and moan), or re-contextualized to support the performance at hand (the original beam only enhances the spookiness of the totally un-original Dungeon). Though Danvers has its supporters, particularly amongst researchers and scholars, Salem continues to be the center of historical tourism related to 1692. As it produces originality and performs the past, Salem attracts even those visitors who seek an authentic historical experience. In many ways, today's Salem is like the phantom bodies that its sites produce: the dead are raised as mannequins, as fake gravesites, as live performers. These bodies, like Salem itself, are attractive, entertaining, satisfying. Danvers, on the other hand, is like the real dead bodies of the 1692 victims: original, real, unmarked, and generally invisible. Though these Danversian bodies have a kind of generic appeal, this appeal is usurped by the spectral Salem bodies as they impersonate and ultimately replace any representations of the real dead.

Jonathan Culler explains this paradox this way: "The dilemma of authenticity is that to be experienced as authentic it must be marked as authentic, but when it is marked as authentic it is mediated, a sign of itself, and hence not authentic in the sense of unspoiled" (137). He elaborates, "Tourists pay to see tourist traps while the real thing is free as air. But the 'real thing' must be marked as real, as sight-worthy; if it is not marked or differentiated, it is not a notable sight" (133). Though Danvers does have a number of markers, the vast majority of its sites are free to enter, and nearly all of them lack the kind of web of services that surround Salem's attractions. In other words, Salem's markers are not just the phony plaques and eager tour guides, but also the very fabric of tourist accompaniments (gifts shops, visitor's centers, public restrooms, trolley rides) that mark Salem itself as a notable site. Danvers gets positioned, against Salem, as the free, unmarked, real site of the trials ... and this keeps the tourists away. But this does not necessarily imply, as Dean MacCannell might have it, that tourists are somehow duped by the system or filled with, as he puts it, "touristic shame" (10). For the other remarkable thing about Salem is its own explicitness about its lack of "originality" and the avidness with which many Salem tourists embrace the parts of Salem that are least "real."

Michael S. Bowman, in an article about antebellum home tours in the South, comments on the phenomenon of "Ye Merrie Olde-ing," in which Great Britain's emphasis on historical tourism has produced inventions of quaint, old British shops, pubs, and town centers where none originally existed. He continues, "Chadds Ford, Pennsylvania, ... [is] a community struggling to become the image of itself made popular by Andrew Wyeth. Tourists go to Chadds Ford expecting to see the widely circulated Wyeth images of the area, and the residents know that economic loss would result if they and their surrounding environment failed to live up to those images, failed to *be* like the paintings" (Bowman 146). Great Britain and Chadds Ford — and Salem, Massachusetts — realize that authenticity is not intrinsic or original to the tourist site; instead, it is constructed over time by historiography, art, and commerce. Tourists, then, *do* get the "real" experience of the witch trials when they visit Salem, for, despite Danvers' connection to the past, Salem is the place in which 1692 authenticity currently inheres. Tourists in Salem, perhaps more so than those visiting other spots, seem aware that this produced authenticity is different than the kind of authenticity that inheres in a primary source document from the period. Clearly, tourists know that the Witch Dungeon is not original, that the mannequins are not alive, that the Witch Village is just a didactified haunted house, that seventeenth-century Puritans didn't hand out brochures. But tourists still flock to Salem instead of visiting the sites in Danvers. Tourists still stop into Terror on the Wharf or some other quick-to-open-and-close-and-reopen haunted house even as they take in the Peabody Essex. Salem not only manages to overcome its overwhelming lack of a direct connection to the past, it also manages to manipulate this lack into precisely the thing that keeps tourists satisfied.

This successful manipulation surprises many people, who assume that Salem's outrageous tackiness will turn visitors away. Linda Hutcheon suggests that this kind of denigration arises from a conception of parody as "parasitic and derivative" (3). In her analysis of parody, Hutcheon claims that it is often seen as the "philistine enemy of ... vital originality" (4). This same charge is leveled against Salem by historical researchers and by those who work in Salem's maritime tourist industry; Salem's witch attractions are seen as copies, as frauds, and as lacking in originality. But Hutcheon recuperates parody's reputation by demonstrating how anti-parodyism is itself a historical construct, generated by a Romantic privileging of creativity, genius, and individuality, all of which are linked, at the core, to the notion of originality. She traces this Romantic bias through to Harold Bloom's modern work, *The Anxiety of Influence*. According to Hutcheon, it would make sense that Salem would be maligned by some scholars as too performative, too derivative to be of real value to society. But Hutcheon would understand why it is that the disappointed, the judgmental, and the critical of Salem's sites are in the vast minority of those who visit Salem.

"Parody," writes Hutcheon, "is a form of imitation, but imitation characterized by ironic inversion, not always at the expense of the parodied text" (6). If most of Salem is parodic, most people would agree that no sites in Salem actually parody the events of 1692. Instead, the parody in Salem represents what Hutcheon calls "repetition with critical distance" (6). By acknowledging the temporal and spatial distance between itself and the "facts" that it represents, Salem comments on the past as much as it performs it. And this commentary is generally designed not to "make fun of" the past, but to revive it, to make meaningful that which has ceased to mean, and to wrestle the long-dead past into the present day. Ironically, Salem's lack of originality and its own celebration of this lack are what make it real, authentic, and popular. Far from being duped, tourists are attracted to precisely that which would *alert* them to the very performativity that would seemingly be repellant.[16]

Salem's success at this parody has been building gradually over the years since the seventeenth century. From the moment Cotton Mather began to write about the witch trials, the events of 1692 were recreated by a series of representational maneuvers. As histories, fictions, films, and tourist sites all told "truths" about the events, Salem's past became increasingly defined by its subsequent representations. Even the "primary sources" that have survived from the period reveal that the story of what happened was figurative, symbolic, scripted, and represented right from its supposed "beginning." Kashmir Shaivism, a form of Hindu religion, has a saying: "The experiencer himself continues to exist always and everywhere as an object of experience" (Waldner prologue). In many ways, this is how Salem works. Seemingly an agent of its own history, Salem is, in actuality, an object of itself, produced by the very "truths" that it purports to generate and reveal. Salem past is not so much the blueprint for Salem present as it is a backward-looking reflection of a constantly updated present moment. And Salem continues to flourish — both as a center for tourism and as an American symbol — precisely because it so eagerly nourishes the sometimes competing mythologies that circulate within and about it.

Notes

Introduction

1. Mark Minelli, president of Minelli Inc., told *The Boston Globe,* "The witch history has always been an important part of the city and always will be, but [Salem] has sort of gotten known very narrowly in terms of the Halloween thing" (Burge).

2. The site of the Plimoth Plantation attraction is not located at the original site of the Plantation.

3. Of course, one might not feel overwhelmingly comfortable accepting Snow's identification of these patrons as "transvestites." Could they have been transsexuals? Drag queens? Female impersonators? It is outside the scope of this particular discussion to consider fully how these distinctions might matter to the connection of history with transgender, but a female impersonator, who dresses in drag for money, might have a different relationship to commercial endeavors such as Plimoth Plantation than transsexuals, who posit their cross-dressing as "natural" and/or corrective. There are interesting arguments to explore in these analogies, especially in terms of transgender's and history's relationships to capitalism, nature, correction, and spectacle. The distinctions among different types of transgender might help to make useful distinctions among different types of historical representation.

4. For more on history as it relates to the emerging field of complex systems — in particular how history parallels "meta-historical sciences" — see David C. Krakauer's article, "The Quest for Patterns in Meta-History," which investigates the quantitative elements of historical analysis and deconstructs the division between science and art/humanities.

5. Of course, it is not simply left-wing revisionists who fall into this trap. Conservative politicians and educators succumb to a more simplistic version of this dynamic. Lynne Cheney, Ronald Reagan's NEH director (and now a former U.S. Second Lady), published an educational report in 1987 which blamed history teachers for failing to teach the "truth." Allan Bloom and E. D. Hirsch have similarly critiqued American educational systems for failing to get it right. These three critics, in opposition to critics such as Loewen, are concerned that the "facts" of history are getting lost in a politically correct movement of multi-culturalism, revisionism, and free critical thinking (Lipsitz 22–23).

6. Revisionist historians tend to find it politically irresponsible to question the relevance of "new facts" which grant autonomy and agency to non-dominant historical figures. But flipping the power differential from Parris to Tituba (for ex-

ample) does not, in fact, alter the structure of power at all. Thus, it may be more politically useful to question how it is history has assigned agency to various textual characters over time, than to ferret out a new reading of any particular person.

7. Andrew Ross' *The Celebration Chronicles* does a good job explaining the differences between a small town and a planned community made to offer an "authentic" small-town experience. Many small towns are now starting to perform the "small-townness" that has been naturally theirs for years. For example, Plymouth, New Hampshire (population about 6,000), now advertises itself as the seventh best small town in America, a title which it earned in Norman Crampton's *100 Best Small Towns in America*, and the town boasts a community improvement group called "Main Street Plymouth" dedicated to preserving the historic character of and improving the flow of tourist dollars within its Main Street business district.

8. For more on this deferral, as well as for a discussion of the particular theory that guides the *historical* tourist, see Marita Sturken's *Tourists of History*, especially pages 9–15.

9. I am indebted to Dean MacCannell's *The Tourist* for providing the theoretical foundation for much of my discussion of tourism in this chapter. For more on his argument — and the places in which my own framework diverges from his — see the introduction on MacCannell, and on "camp" and how it challenges and extends MacCannell's basic premises.

10. See Sturken, 26–31, for more on the role of repetition and referentiality as they apply to tourism and trauma.

11. One example of this occurs in Civil War reenactment communities. Reenactors have three categories for those who participate in the reconstructed war events: "farbs," hard-cores," and "authen-

tics" (Stanton 91). "Farbs" are those who just reenact for fun and who aren't particularly concerned with replicating the past (they might drink Gatorade out of a plastic bottle on a hot day). "Hard-cores" are the folks who insist that even the thread that stitches their uniforms together be spun with period processes. "Authentics," interestingly, is a catchall phrase which refers to the group in between farbs and hard-cores. This implies that "authenticity" is not about perfect simulation, but about a kind of "real" feeling that reenactors experience when everything at the scene — including themselves — matches their vision of Civil War events.

12. It's also interesting that the dirt does not come from the spot where the victims were actually hanged, since nobody, to this day, has been able to say for certain where that spot was (Foote 3). The fact that the package holds "dirt" somehow makes the product read as authentic, since we often associate the natural world and the "unpretty" with the "real." So the souvenir is actually quite intelligently produced, since it takes a completely random and cheap item — the dirt — and uses it to signify the real past with all of its ugly and "true" events. At the same time, it capitalizes on its own silliness, and sells well amongst educated visitors who want to bring home a souvenir of Salem's rampant commercialism.

13. The film is a wonderful documentary that first aired on PBS, called *Witch City*, which explores many of the topics that I discuss in Chapter Five.

Chapter 1

1. See below for a discussion on the production, collection, and publication of these transcripts.

2. For more on the nature of the existing records, see the prefatory "Notes" section in Richard B. Trask's "*The Devil*

Hath Been Raised." Trask also explains other gaps in the records besides those left by theft, fire, and mishandling. He considers the gaps left at the very moment of creation, as the documents were subjected to both the biases of their authors and the slowness of pen-and-ink transcription (xx).

3. For more on the mistakes in *The Salem Witchcraft Papers,* and how they have affected subsequent Salem scholarship, see Jane Kamensky's article, "Salem Obsessed: Or, *Plus Ça Change:* An Introduction." A new collection from Cambridge University Press of transcript papers and other primary source documents from Bernard Rosenthal, *Records of the Salem Witch-Hunt.* For more on the publication of this new collection of materials, see Margo Burns and Bernard Rosenthal's article, "Examination of the Records of the Salem Witch Trials."

4. An interesting phenomenon occurs in Boyer and Nissenbaum's 2008 article, *"Salem Possessed* in Retrospect." As they tell the story of the initial writing and publication of the seminal 1974 study, they offer photos of their original notes and scrawled drafts of maps that would, in later iterations, become the famous maps of the esteemed collection. The original book is, of course, consumed with a focus on the Salem primary sources, and to see the article supplant that focus with a focus on their own drafts of the book as a kind of archived primary source aptly demonstrates the way their own study has become, over the years, original and primary.

5. For more on antitheatricalism, see Jonas Barish's *The Antitheatrical Prejudice.*

6. Upham, for example, claims that witches used their gaze to bewitch the afflicted: "Instantly upon coming within the glance of [the witch's] eye, [the afflicted] would scream out, and fall down as in a fit. It was thought that an invisi-

ble and impalpable fluid darted from the eye of the witch, and penetrated the brain of the bewitched" (Vol. I, 412). What is intriguing about this is the way that the eyes, the windows to the interior soul, become launching pads for an externalized attack.

7. For more on the relationship of the performed to the real as it connects with Puritan antitheatricalism, see Laura Levine's *Men in Women's Clothing: Anti-Theatricality and Effeminization, 1579–1642.*

8. This passage comes from Mary Bradbury's "answer"; it appears to have been written by her (or, more likely, dictated by her), as opposed to transcribed by a court clerk or judge.

9. See, for example, Richard Godbeer's article, "Chaste and Unchaste Covenants: Witchcraft and Sex in Early Modern Culture," in which he discusses the "representation of witchcraft [that] constituted a thinly veiled attack on Puritan orthodoxy itself." He concludes that for Salem's deponents, "Satan and Congregationalism were … interchangeable" (66).

10. See, for example, Bernard Rosenthal's "Medievalism and the Salem Witch Trials," which considers the relationship among folk belief systems, magic, and witchcraft.

11. For more on how God (or Christ, in this example) functions as an "ultimate signified," see Catherine Belsey's article *"Paradise Lost* as Master-Narrative."

12. Why the "reflecting and retorting" is not recorded at all when the rest of the hearing appears to be recorded verbatim is worth considering. Perhaps Good's banter, which is characterized as "base" and "abusive" by Cheever, does some damage to the authority of the court. While Tituba's use of repetition ultimately strengthened the charges against her, Good's use of it spoils any hope of her

confessing. See below for an examination of how confession functioned as a buttress for Salem's legal and religious rules.

13. For further reading on Puritan repentance and confessional prose, see Patricia Caldwell's *The Puritan Conversion Narrative: The Beginnings of American Expression*.

14. This inverts the process in which the witch's gaze functions to externalize the internal condition of being a witch; in this case, the external characteristic of being afflicted by something outside of one's own person becomes internalized, reflecting in the end not on the witch but on the inner state of the afflicted.

15. For more on this theatrical phenomenon, see Richard Schechner's *Between Theater and Anthropology*, especially page 123 where he refers to the "non-not not" character of performance, in which actors are not fully themselves, and yet not *not* themselves at the same moment.

16. I take my definition of "ontology" primarily from the field of philosophy. Texts that have informed my definition include Kant's *Critique of Pure Reason* (especially A45/B62–A46/B63, on appearances vs. things-in-themselves); Quine's *From a Logical Point of View* (especially Chapter One, "On What There Is"); and C. J. F. Williams' *What is Existence?* (which considers the relationship of logic and language — rather than metaphysics — to the question of ontology).

17. Sarah Rivett has a useful and broader discussion of spectral evidence and its relationship to science and religion in her article "Our Salem, Our Selves." See especially pages 499–502.

Chapter 2

1. Mather was a third-generation Puritan minister who, in 1689, had published *Memorable Providences Relating to Witchcrafts and Possessions*. He was asked by the governor of the Salem colony to publish the 1692 defense of the trials, which I will be discussing here.

2. For a more complete discussion of Mather's reputation and how it has shifted between maligned and defended in Salem histories, see Richard H. Werking's article "'Reformation is Our Only Preservation': Cotton Mather and Salem Witchcraft."

3. For helping me think about the use of debate in early modern culture, I am indebted to Jesper Rosenmeier's *John Cotton's English Years, 1584–1633*, especially page 56.

4. Interestingly, Upham's own text is also described by him as "familiar, direct, and personal" as a result of the fact that it began as a series of colloquial lectures, rather than as a written text (Vol. I, vii). In this way, his own work corporealizes itself, building its levels of muscle and skin around the basic skeletal structure of the historical facts. Upham's text is as much a corpse as, say, Samuel Parris himself: both are dead/complete, both are seemingly stable and yet open to interpretation, and both function here — like ghosts — to lead the student of history into the private inner chambers of Salem's secrets.

5. See the final section of this chapter, "Pathologies of Witchcraft: A Brief Look at Psychosomatic and Biological Theories," for a brief discussion of some of the other Salem historians, including those who wrote between 1867 and 1976.

6. For a scathing critique of the famous *Salem Possessed* map that demonstrates a Salem geographically divided between accusers and accused, see Benjamin C. Ray's "The Geography of Witchcraft Accusations in 1692 Salem Village," which ultimately indicts Boyer and Nissenbaum's entire book.

7. For an expression on the part of Boyer and Nissenbaum for scholars who

oversimplify their thesis about Salem (as perhaps I am doing here), see their article "*Salem Possessed* in Retrospect," especially pages 524–533.

8. For example, her chronological approach differs from many Salem scholars, who group events according to theme or participant, and her broad approach in terms of both geography and temporality sets a wider scope for the context of the crisis than many other texts which just examine Salem Town and Salem Village in 1692.

9. For a similar argument made much earlier, see George M. Beard's 1882 publication, *The Psychology of the Salem Witchcraft Excitement of 1692 and its Practical Application to our own Time.*

10. See the front-page article announcing her hypothesis in 31 March 1976's *New York Times.* The headline reads, "Salem Witch Hunts in 1692 Linked to LSD-Like Agent."

Chapter 3

1. The first published prose fiction about Salem was *Salem, an Eastern Tale* by an unknown author. The work was published in three installments to the *New York Literary Journal and Belles-Lettres Repository* in 1820. For more on this, see G. Harrison Orians' "New England Witchcraft in Fiction."

2. George Burroughs is also a key character in Durward Grinstead's 1929 novel, *Elva,* although in that novel Burroughs is hardly the picture of heroic perfection, swept up in an adulterous affair with the protagonist, Elva Pope.

3. For a complete survey of Salem fiction to 1930, see G. Harrison Orians' "New England Witchcraft in Fiction."

4. For more on this, see Michael Davitt Bell's Introduction in the Oxford World's Classic 1991 edition of *The House of the Seven Gables.*

5. For more on the personal nature of Hawthorne's critique of Upham, see Julian Hawthorne's *Nathaniel Hawthorne and His Wife.*

6. For a different version of the discussion of the clash between romance and rationalism in *House of the Seven Gables,* see "Romance versus History: Hawthorne, Curses, and Mesmerism" in Marion Gibson's *Witchcraft Myths in American Culture* (108–112).

7. Interestingly, this quote is used as an epigram in *Witch City,* a recent documentary film about the explosion of witch-related tourism in today's Salem, Massachusetts.

8. For further reading on the significance of daguerreotype in the novel, see Michael J. Bunker Noble's short article, "Hawthorne's *The House of the Seven Gables.*"

9. For more on this moment, see Cathy N. Davidson's article, "Photographs of the Dead: Sherman, Daguerre, Hawthorne."

10. For more on the characteristics of romance novels from 1942 to 1982, see *Becoming a Woman through Romance* by Linda K. Christian-Smith. For more on the connections between romanticism and witchcraft fiction, see Philip Gould's *Covenant and Republic: Historical Romance and the Politics of Puritanism,* especially pages 199–209.

11. This is quite similar to the crystal-ball effect that occurs in Boyer and Nissenbaum's *Salem Possessed* (see Chapter Two).

12. Compare this with the association of fictionality with the whore (Abigail Williams) in Arthur Miller's *The Crucible.* See Chapter Four of this book for a discussion of the "whore" as she figures in Miller's play.

13. See Hale, Hutchinson, and volume 1 of Neal's *History of New-England,* especially pages 49–97.

14. Rosenthal writes that "there is no

evidence that Tituba and John were married, or even cohabitating, although almost every scholar assumes, without proof, that a conjugal relationship existed" (4).

15. Here begins the first of many parallels with Rose Earhart's 2000 novel *Dorcas Good: The Diary of A Salem Witch*, which rewrites the life of Dorcas Good in a way similar to Condé's rewriting of Tituba's. The real Dorcas, daughter of Sarah Good, was, like her mother, accused of witchcraft. Though she was ultimately released, transcripts reveal that mentally she was never the same after being in prison. Earhart uses Dorcas to give voice to a previously silenced group in Salem: the abused/accused children. And like Condé's, Earhart's protagonist talks with the invisible world, which becomes not a sign of her madness (as history would have us believe about Dorcas) or her status as a guilty witch (as history would have us believe about Tituba), but a sign of her humanity, her individual personality, and her will to survive in the face of oppression. The novel, presented as a dairy written by young Dorcas herself, takes the shape of a "primary source" in much the same way that Tituba's story seems to come "directly" from the mouth of Tituba herself.

16. A similarly tripled temporal moment occurs after Tituba returns to Barbados, and reflects on how Ann Putnam's confession touches off a "rehabilitation" of victims that still neglects to exonerate Tituba (Condé 150).

17. This reversal creates a foil of Nurse, whose hypocrisy is countered against Tituba's own purity. A similar effect happens in *Dorcas Good: The Diary of a Salem Witch*. Historical characters such as Nicholas Noyes are rewritten in order to demonstrate the oppression and ultimate victimization of Dorcas Good. Noyes becomes a horrendous child rapist in Earhart's novel, the better to highlight the brutality faced by the young protagonist in the text.

18. For further reading on lesbian separatism, see Dana R. Shugar's *Separatism and Women's Community*, especially chapter three ("Lesbian Separatism and Revolution through Community") and the introduction to part three ("Fantasy and the Revolution"). Shugar ultimately argues that separatist discourse, despite its many pitfalls and problems, plays a vital role in the continuation of feminism; we might argue the same for Hester's role in *I, Tituba*.

19. For more on the historical relationship of women of color to white feminism, and, in particular, the way that Tituba's opposition to feminism does not preclude dialogue with Hester, see Jeanne Garane's "History, Identity and the Constitution of the Female Subject: Maryse Condé's *Tituba*."

20. To conclude the parallels with *Dorcas Good: Diary of a Salem Witch*, we might note that Dorcas meets her end as the Gallows Hill cave collapses upon her physical body, therefore allowing her to act as a "conduit" for the ghosts of the executed witches, and to "call home" the brutish men who have abused her (Earhart 348, 370). Her victimization and ultimate death exist next to her ability to haunt her enemies and revive the martyrs of the trials.

21. Interestingly, the 2001 film version of *Acceptable Risk*, which was directed by William A. Graham and which aired on TBS Superstation, collapsed the Edward and Kim characters into one. In the film, Edward, played by Chad Lowe, is both the new owner of Elizabeth's house *and* the scientist who discovers the ergot. In some ways, the film makes more obvious many of the points I am making, since it makes explicit the yoking of science and history through Edward's character, who is intimately involved with both fields.

22. Of course, readers of *The House of the Seven Gables* are quick to note the similarities between Hawthorne's portrait of the Colonel and Cook's portrait of Elizabeth. Both portraits appear to have supernatural qualities, though no one can be sure if these qualities are truly occult or if they come to life in the minds of the characters that observe the paintings.

23. Recall, too, that the phrase "the devil incarnate" is also what Edward calls the ergot (Cook 167). The descriptor highlights the connection between the science (ergot) and the history (evidence) as well as the connection between cause (poisoning) and effect (deformity). The "which came first?" conundrum of the old chicken-and-egg riddle applies both to the poisoning-deformity aspect of the symbol (both the poison and the deformity are the devil incarnate, so originality is irrelevant) and to the ergot-evidence aspect (both the science and the history are the devil incarnate, so separation between the two is impossible).

24. The fetus is ironic in another way, too. The fact that it looks so much like the devil seems to undermine Edward's hypothesis that science can explain the witch trials and therefore reduce the "supernatural" quality of the story that surrounds Salem. The deformed fetus could prove *both* that Elizabeth was probably poisoned by mold *and* that she was possessed by the devil.

Chapter 4

1. Apparently, Giles Corey brings out in fiction writers this tendency to focus on both the political and the rhetorical issues involved in the witch hunt. In her 1893 play, *Giles Corey, Yeoman*, Mary E. Wilkins Freeman uses the Corey story to comment on the post–Civil War New England decline at the same time as she explores the philosophical boundaries between lies and truth. I do not deal with the Freeman play here because of its similarity to Longfellow's drama, but those interested might read Donald R. Anderson's article, "Giles Corey and the Pressing Past," which provides a good analysis of these twin agendas in the Freeman play.

2. This idea is fully explicated in Boyer and Nissenbaum's *Salem Possessed*, which I have discussed at length in Chapter Two. In many ways, Longfellow was the first writer who directly and explicitly linked witchcraft to discourses of social power.

3. To a new generation, *The Crucible* is famous not as a play, but as the 1996 Daniel Day-Lewis/Winona Ryder film directed by Arthur Miller's son, Robert. Bruce C. Daniels summarizes the differences between play and film this way: "The film has more explicit sex, is about half the length of the play, and collapses the preliminary hearings and subsequent trials into one set of proceedings" (55). To me, what is most important about the film is not its minor edits, but the way in which it re-popularized *The Crucible* and repackaged it for a new target audience.

4. This is a discussion that Miller expands on in his 1996 article "Why I Wrote *The Crucible*" and again in his 1999 article "*The Crucible* in History."

5. Joseph Valente describes it this way: "The gambit of enclosing within the written texts an extended critical perspective on the action represented can only be designed to foreground authorial intention so as to garner a more direct and rationally efficient rhetorical force than Miller felt was available to him strictly as a dramatist" (122).

6. For more on how Miller thematizes the vexed issue of "truth" in the play, see Stephen Marino's "Arthur Miller's 'Weight of Truth' in *The Crucible*." Marino argues, in contrast to me, that "truth" functions in the drama to set the heroes apart from the flawed society that

accuses them. I would argue that this association of heroism and truth rings ironic in the play given Miller's tendency to supplant the "true" with the symbolic, the dramatic, and the speculative.

7. The posited connection between illicit romantic affairs and witchcraft has produced other fictional and sexualized accounts of Salem. The fraught relationship between George Burroughs and afflicted girl Elva Pope in the 1929 Durward Grinstead text, *Elva*, caused Bernard Rosenthal to call the novel a "neglected Freudian tale" (*Salem Story*, 149). The little-known 1926 opera, *A Witch in Salem*, is, similarly, another ancestral text to *The Crucible*; in the opera, spurned lover Sheila Meloy, jealous over the fact that her childhood sweetheart, Arnold Talbot, is now in love with the angelic Claris Willoughby, accuses Claris of witchcraft and nearly causes her execution (Eberhart). Finally, the 1903 Marvin Dana novel *A Puritan Witch* also features a jealous female protagonist making witchcraft accusations about her rival in love.

8. This is, I would argue, strikingly similar to the way that confession to witchcrafts functioned in the trial transcripts; to confess to a lie would free the accused, and retracted or inverted confessions were common. Confession became in many ways an empty category, even if its deploying had very real repercussions.

9. Consider Act Two, Scene Two, which is often included as an appendix to the play, and which is not always performed during runs of *The Crucible*. In this scene, Abby and Proctor discuss their relationship and the witchcraft hysteria, and Abby is portrayed as obsessed by love, as a desperate child, and as mad. She seems to believe in what she is doing, and seems to have been deeply wounded by Proctor's dismissal (Miller 148–152).

10. Wendy Schissel's entertaining article, "Re(dis)covering the Witches in Arthur Miller's *The Crucible:* A Feminist Reading," elaborates on the idea of Abigail's power. While I argue that the play itself does not so clearly contain Abigail's power as it might seem, Schissel condemns Miller for his sexism, but offers a kind of "Shakespeare's sister" approach to imagining Abby's alternate story. Schissel's article imagines "Mary" Miller's story of what happened, suggesting that Arthur could have had a radical feminist sister who would have written a *Crucible* in which Abigail and Elizabeth celebrate the death of Proctor together, satisfied that both the "alleged seductress" and the "cold wife" were vindicated by the death of "a man who does not deserve either" (Schissel).

11. In contrast to this reading of the prostitute, Joseph Valente argues that "What was supposed to be a dramatic case against the witch trial turns out to be a displaced repetition of it, and through this patently self-defeating representational strategy, this rupture between mythopoetic means and avowed political ends, Miller betrays the patriarchal limits of his vision" (125). In addition, Marion Gibson, in contrast to my argument here, argues that *The Crucible* is a condemnation of feminine wiles and an elegy about the tragedy of American masculinity (64).

12. Marion Gibson playfully suggests a parallel between *Maid of Salem* and the television show, *Bewitched*. On the show, Endora, Samantha's witch of a mother, can never remember Samantha's husband's name (it is Darin). She mistakenly calls him "Durward" in what Gibson suggests is an homage to the author of one of the earlier "marrying a witch" texts (209).

13. For more on how Jennifer-as-undomesticated-witch threatens patriarchal power in the film, see "Marrying a Witch" in Marion Gibson's *Witchcraft Myths in American Culture*, especially page 197.

14. This kind of post-structural ten-

sion exists in the *Sabrina* series in the question of whether or not the show asserts or subverts feminist values. For more on this, see Sarah Projansky's and Leah R. Vande Berg's article, "Sabrina, the Teenage...? Girls, Witches, Mortals, and the Limitations of Prime-Time Feminism."

15. For a feminist reading of Samantha's plea for tolerance and acceptance, see Marion Gibson's "Marrying a Witch" in *Witchcraft Myths in American Culture*, especially page 216.

Chapter 5

1. My use of the word "tourist" is deliberate, if controversial. Many critics have suggested that the term is derogatory. Mark Okrant, for example, prefers the term "visitor," asserting that "tourist" is generally accompanied by an implied modifier such as "annoying" or "damned" (Okrant)]. I use the term precisely because it is so loaded with tension. In my use of "tourist" I wish to stress both the aspect of tourist-as-invited-guest *and* the aspect of tourist-as-appropriator. This dynamic dual-identity — both insider and outsider — parallels the relationship between the past and historical tourism that both represents that past *and* fails, over and over again, to bring it back to life. For more on the etymology of the word "tourist" and the differences between "travelers" (or "visitors") and "tourists," see page 288 of Donna R. Braden's *Leisure and Entertainment in America*.

2. Notably, it is generally accepted that the very first "living history" museum — a museum that features live performers or "interpreters" interacting with tourists — was the 1685 John Ward House in Salem. The Essex Institute began to restore the house in 1909, and "over the next few years, the organization's secretary, George Francis Dow, experi-

mented with re-creating a live atmosphere in the house. He placed objects in casual arrangements and selected three women 'dressed in homespun costumes of the time when the house was built' to show the house to visitors" (Leon 66). Thus, Salem's performative tourist industry and its tendency to absorb spontaneous interaction into a more scripted overall drama were present even before the main period of growth in Salem's tourist sector. Salem's performative tourism did not emerge out of a more traditional museum presentation style; instead, Salem's living history style seems to have generated a backlash of more reifying, stable presentation styles that react against (and perhaps ultimately strengthen) Salem's main performative thrust. See later in this chapter for more on this relationship between traditional presentation and living history. See also Jay Anderson's *Time Machines: the World of Living History* for more on the definition of "living history."

3. We voted 11–8 against Bishop ... and five of the eight votes for her innocence came from me and my students. Interestingly, we were not voting on the final question of her guilt but just on whether or not she should be held over for trial, as if the production wanted to shy away from the possibility that we might actually re-hang Bridget Bishop.

4. For more on Peale and his museum, see Gary Kulik's "Designing the Past: History Museum Exhibitions from Peale to the Present."

5. Ironically, the House of the Seven Gables site itself works to elide Salem's witch history. Though many tourists go to the site because of apocryphal tales of its spookiness or because they know the novel — and therefore know of its connection to witchcraft — the Gables tour never once mentions witchcraft. In order to avoid talk of witches, the site actually has to avoid all talk of the novel's plot, con-

sumed as Hawthorne's tale is with the question of hauntings. On a recent tour I took of the house, the only hint that witchcraft was at least present in visitors' minds (if not in the tour) was when a young boy was invited by the guide to open a small closet next to a fireplace. As he did so, a male tourist shouted, "Boo!" at which point the boy and all the rest of us gave a momentary collective shriek. As we laughed, the guide talked right over us, explaining that the closet was used to hold firewood.

6. For more on the genocide of Native Americans by European settlers, see Ward Churchill's *A Little Matter of Genocide: Holocaust and Denial in the Americas, 1492 to the Present.*

7. For more on the importance of the interior to touristic desire, see Roland Barthes' *The Eiffel Tower and Other Mythologies*, especially the chapter called "The Eiffel Tower," in which Barthes explores "what becomes of the great exploratory function of the inside when it is applied to [the tower's] empty and depthless monument which might be said to consist entirely of an exterior substance" (15).

8. Mannequins are in no short supply in Salem, and their presence suggests to me this kind of paradox between a frozen, stagnant, death-like objectification, and a dynamic, lively, subjectivity. In an article about an art exhibit that featured mannequinesque figurative sculptures, critic Johannes Birringer asserts that the false alive-ness of the figures comprises a "fantasmatics of denial"; for Birringer, the "fictions of self-expression ... and eternal youth ... function obsessively as a simultaneous denial of death and imperfection" (209). This paradigm is complicated with the Salem mannequins, since their alive-ness not only defies the fact of their waxen or plastic materials, but also the trajectory of history, which through both a linear

passage of time and a narrative progression of the story relegates the mannequins' "real" counterparts to the realm of the dead. The mannequins, then, continually reify *and* animate the characters from the past, paralleling the process by which history itself is made both scrutable and contemporary in Salem's tourist productions. In another interesting note, several tourist sites in Salem make use of the "fake mannequin." At the Pirate Museum, for example, the walk-through museum contains a multitude of mannequins positioned to look somewhat real: beheaded with fake blood spewing from the neck, in one memorable case. But then, at the end of the display, visitors walk by one mannequin sitting in a dark cell. It looks very fake, with a hackneyed plaster-esque face atop an oddly positioned body. As visitors gather to squint into the cell, the mannequin suddenly comes alive, revealing itself to be a real person disguised not so much as a pirate's victim, but as a mannequin. The irony of mannequins working to look like real people and real people working to look like mannequins complements the kind of irony that Birringer notes and the kind that emerges in Salem's complex relationship to history long past and yet very much alive. My thanks to my students Jess Dube, Bob Feeny, Nicole Bailey, Aimee LaBarre, and Sarah Sinclair for helping me talk through these connections.

9. Thanks to Bridget Marshall for pointing this out in her 1999 New England Modern Language Association conference paper "Salem's Ghosts and the Cultural Capita/ol of Witches."

10. The Witch Museum's use of entertainment and education might help to elucidate why I am not particularly concerned in this study with the differences between for-profit, non-profit, and not-for-profit attractions. In general, the profit motive does not seem to predict a

site's interaction with the education/entertainment scale; instead, profit seems to behave much like the educational goals of a site in that such goals are always wrapped up in their own self-opposing tendencies. For more on the fallacy that claims non-profits are "neutral" and free from "vested interests" that plague their for-profit counterparts, see Philip Burnham's *How the Other Half Lived: A People's Guide to American Historic Sites*, especially pages 210–11.

11. This phenomenon is common in Salem, even at the city's most "educational" sites. The House of the Seven Gables, which does not include witchcraft or the plot of Hawthorne's novel in its regular tour, hosts "Spirits of the Gables" during the Halloween season. During this presentation, a reenactment of scenes from Hawthorne's novel takes place in the rooms of the "actual" house. The same house that the rest of the time is aggressively unhaunted and uninhabited by witches suddenly comes alive with corpses and ghosts. The day after Halloween, all traces of "Spirits" is/are removed from the premises.

12. Another site working in this way is the new Lizzie Borden museum. Though the Borden murders of 1892 happened two hundred years after the witch trials in Fall River, Massachusetts, seventy miles from Salem, the museum came to Salem presumably to capitalize on Salem's reputation as a tourist epicenter for all things macabre. But despite its clearly commercial relationship to Salem and despite its gift shop — filled as it is with plastic bloody axes and postcards of the dead Borden family — the advertising for the site promises an authentic and educational look back in history. One side of a recent Borden Museum brochure promises "the true story of Lizzie Borden," and notes that visitors will "study the evidence, investigate the clues, and separate fact from

fiction." Of course, the flip side of the brochure has this grotesque state slogan splashed across it: "Mass. Murder" (Lizzie Borden Museum). The site is caught between the two poles of education and entertainment, and it is this tension that defines and enlivens the museum.

13. Actually, Boris Karloff's Witch Mansion has recently closed, but it has been replaced by other similar sites, such as the Nightmare Factory, which is a good, old-fashioned haunted house. Haunted houses like Boris Karloff and the Nightmare Factory function like revolving doors in Salem: just as one closes, a replacement opens. They don't have the sticking power of more permanent pseudo-educational sites, but the fact that the general genre of site persists means that the haunted house is alive and well in Salem's tourist market.

14. This dual nature of earnestness and parody recalls John Sears' understanding of how tourists relate to many tourist sites. He writes, "It is this dual nature — the function of tourist attractions as sacred places and as arenas of consumption — that induces many tourists to approach them with a double consciousness, with religious awe or poetic rapture on the one hand and a skeptical, sardonic attitude on the other" (213). This double consciousness allows tourists to be both critical or disappointed *and* satisfied and pleased at the same time.

15. For more on the relationship of absence to memorial architecture, see "Architectures of Grief and the Aesthetics of Absence" in Marita Sturken's *Tourists of History*.

16. The fact that Salem tourists are attracted, rather than repelled, by Salem's parodic qualities makes an interesting parallel to the reception of tourists by host cultures. For example, the doubled reaction of many Salem locals such as restaurant owners and shopkeepers — fed up

with witches and yet fully dependent on the tourist industry — is not unlike the doubled attracted/repelled feelings of Salem tourists toward the attractions that greet them in Salem. Relatedly, anthropologist Theron Nunez discusses this doubled reaction in the context of indigenous or "primitive" people and the way that they receive modern tourists into their cultures, irreparably changing their cultures, but not necessarily all for the worse (273–274).

Bibliography

Acceptable Risk. Dir. William A. Graham. With Chad Lowe. WTBS, 2001.

Adler, Judith. "Origins of Sightseeing." *Annals of Tourism Research* 16 (1989): 7–29.

Anderson, Donald R. "Giles Corey and the Pressing Past." *American Transcendental Quarterly* 14.2 (2000): 113–26. *OCLC FirstSearch*. Lamson Library, Plymouth, NH. 4 May 2002. <http://newfirstsearch.oclc.org>.

Anderson, Jay. *Time Machines: The World of Living History*. Nashville: The American Association for State and Local History, 1984.

Anderson, Perry. *In the Tracks of Historical Materialism*. London: Verso, 1983.

Architectural Guide to Houses. Brochure. Salem, MA: Peabody Essex Museum, 2002.

Bank, Rosemarie K. "Archiving Culture: Performance and American Museums in the Earlier Nineteenth Century." *Performing America: Cultural Nationalism in American Theater*. Edited by Jeffrey Mason and J. Ellen Gainon. Ann Arbor: The University of Michigan Press, 1999.

Baris, Jonas. *The Antitheatrical Prejudice*. Berkeley: University of California Press, 1985.

Barthes, Roland. "The Discourse of History." Translated by Stephen Bann. *Comparative Criticism: A Yearbook 3*. Edited by E. S. Shaffer. 7–20. Cambridge: Cambridge University Press, 1981.

_____.*The Eiffel Tower and Other Mythologies*. Translated by Richard Howard. New York: Hill and Wang, 1979.

Baudrillard, Jean. *Simulacra and Simulation*. Ann Arbor: The University of Michigan Press, 1994.

Beard, George M. *The Psychology of the Salem Witchcraft Excitement of 1692 and Its Practical Application to Our Own Time*. Stratford, CT: John E. Edwards, 1971.

Bellis, Peter J. "Mauling Governor Pyncheon." *Studies in the Novel* 26.3 (1994): 199–217. *OCLS FirstSearch*. Lamson Library, Plymouth, NH. 14 May 2002. <http://newfirstsearch.oclc.org>.

Belsey, Catherine. "*Paradise Lost* as Master-Narrative." *Paradise Lost*. Edited by William Zunder. New York: St. Martin's, 1999.

Bergman, David. *Camp Grounds: Style and Homosexuality*. Amherst: University of Massachusetts Press, 1993.

Bhabha, Homi. *The Location of Culture*. London: Routledge, 1994.

"A Bill against Conjurations, Witchcraft, and Dealing with Evil and Wicked Spirits." 135.68–69 (1692).

Birringer, Johannes. *Theatre, Theory, Post-*

modernism. Bloomington: Indiana University Press, 1991.

Bob. Personal interview. Salem, MA, Boris Karloff's Witch Mansion, 17 July 2002.

Boris Karloff's Witch Mansion. Guided tour. Salem, MA, 17 July 2002.

Bowman, Michael S. "Performing Southern History for the Tourist Gaze: Antebellum Home Tour Guide Performances." *Exceptional Spaces: Essays in Performance and History.* Edited by Della Pollack. Chapel Hill: University of North Carolina Press, 1998.

Boyer, Paul, and Stephen Nissenbaum. *Salem Possessed: The Social Origins of Witchcraft.* Cambridge, MA: Harvard University Press, 1974.

_____. *"Salem Possessed* in Retrospect." *William and Mary Quarterly* 65.3 (2008): 503–534.

_____. *The Salem Witchcraft Papers: Verbatim Transcripts of the Legal Documents of the Salem Witchcraft Outbreak of 1692.* 3 vols. New York: De Capo Press, 1977.

_____. *Salem-Village Witchcraft: A Documentary Record of Local Conflict in Colonial New England.* Boston: Northeastern University Press, 1972.

Braden, Donna R. *Leisure and Entertainment in America.* Dearborn, MI: Henry Ford Museum and Greenfield Village, 1988.

Bradford, William. *Of Plimoth Plantation, 1620–1647.* New York: Random House, 1981.

Brown, Curtis. *Star-Spangled Kitsch.* New York: Universe Books, 1975.

Burge, Kathleen. "Witch City Brews a New Image." *Boston.com.* 30 September 2004 <http://www.boston.com/news/local/articles/2004/09/30/witch_city_brews_a_new_image/>.

Burnham, Philip. *How the Other Half Lived: A People's Guide to American Historic Sites.* Boston: Faber and Faber, 1995.

Butler, Judith. *Gender Trouble: Feminism and the Subversion of Identity.* New York: Routledge, 1990.

Caldwell, Patricia. *The Puritan Conversion Narrative: The Beginnings of American Expression.* Cambridge: Cambridge University Press, 1983.

Calef, Robert. *Another Brand Pluckt out of the Burning, Or, More Wonders of the Invisible World.* Salem, MA: William Carlton, 1796.

Caporael, Linnda. "Ergotism: The Satan Loosed in Salem?" *Science* 192.4234 (2 April 1976): 21–26.

Christian-Smith, Linda K. *Becoming a Woman through Romance.* New York: Routledge, 1990.

Churchill, Ward. *A Little Matter of Genocide: Holocaust and Denial in the Americas, 1492 to the Present.* San Francisco: City Lights Books, 1997.

Cohen, Erik. "Authenticity and Commoditization in Tourism." *Annals of Tourism Research* 15.3 (1988): 371–386.

Condé, Maryse. *I, Tituba, Black Witch of Salem.* Translated by Richard Philcox. Charlottesville, VA: Caraf Books, 1992.

Cook, Robin. *Acceptable Risk.* New York: Berkley Books, 1995.

Cousins, Mark. "The Practice of Historical Investigation." *Post-structuralism and the Question of History.* Edited by Derek Attridge, Geoff Bennington and Robert Young. 126–136. Cambridge: Cambridge University Press, 1987.

Crampton, Norman. *The 100 Best Small Towns in America.* New York: Macmillan General Reference, 1995.

"The Crucible." *Sabrina, the Teenage Witch.* Perf. Melissa Joan Hart. Warner Bros., May 9, 1997.

Cry Innocent! Brochure. Salem, MA, 2008.

Culler, Jonathan. "Semiotics of Tourism." *American Journal of Semiotics* 1.1–2 (1981): 127–40.

Dana, Marvin. *A Puritan Witch: A Romance.* New York: Smart Set Publishing, 1903.

Daniels, Bruce C. "Hollywood's Hester Prynne: *The Scarlet Letter* and Puritanism in the Movies." *Canadian Review of American Studies* 29.3 (1999): 27–60.

Davidson, Cathy N. "Photographs of the Dead: Sherman, Daguerre, Hawthorne." *South Atlantic Quarterly* 89:4 (Fall 1990): 667–701.

Davis, Natalie Zemon. *Fiction in the Archives: Pardon Tales and Their Tellers in Sixteenth-Century France.* Stanford: Stanford University Press, 1987.

Deleuze, Gilles. *Difference and Repetition.* Translated by Paul Patton. New York: Columbia University Press, 1994.

Demos, John. *Entertaining Satan: Witchcraft and the Culture of Early New England.* Oxford: Oxford University Press, 1982.

Donna. Personal Interview. Salem, MA, Salem Witch Village, 17 July 2002.

Eagleton, Terry. *The Function of Criticism: From 'The Spectator' to Post-Structuralism.* London: Verso, 1984.

Earhart, Rose. *Dorcas Good: The Diary of a Salem Witch.* New York: Pendleton Books, 2000.

Eberhart, Nelle Richmond. *A Witch of Salem: Grand Opera in Two Acts (Book).* Boston: Oliver Ditson Company, 1926.

Felt, Thomas E. *Researching, Writing, and Publishing Local History.* Nashville: American Association for State and Local History, 1981.

Foote, Kenneth E. *Shadowed Ground: America's Landscapes of Violence and Tragedy.* Austin: University of Texas Press, 1997.

Garane, Jeanne. "History, Identity and the Constitution of the Female Subject: Maryse Condé's *Tituba.*" Carole Boyce Davies, ed. *Moving Beyond Boundaries, Volume 2: Black Women's Diasporas.* New York: New York University Press, 1995.

Gencarella, Stephen Olbrys. "Touring History: Guidebooks and the Commodification of the Salem Witch Trials." *The Journal of American Culture.* 30.1 (2007): 271–284.

Gibson, Marion. *Witchcraft Myths in American Culture.* New York: Routledge, 2007.

Godbeer, Richard. "Chaste and Unchaste Covenants: Witchcraft and Sex in Early Modern Culture." *Wonders of the Invisible World: 1600–1900.* Edited by Peter Benes. Boston: Boston University Press, 1995.

Gould, Philip. *Covenant and Republic: Historical Romance and the Politics of Puritanism.* Cambridge: Cambridge University Press, 1996.

Grinstead, Durward. *Elva.* New York: Covici Friede Publishers, 1929.

Hale, John. "A Modest Inquiry into the Nature of Witchcraft." *Narratives of the Witchcraft Cases.* Edited by G. L. Burr. 399–432. New York, 1914.

Handler, Richard, and William Saxton. "Dyssimulation: Reflexivity, Narrative, and the Quest for Authenticity in 'Living History.'" *Cultural Anthropology* 3 (1988): 342–360.

Hansen, Chadwick. "The Metamorphosis of Tituba, or Why American Intellectuals Can't Tell an Indian Witch from a Negro." *New England Quarterly* 47 (1974): 3–12.

_____. *Witchcraft at Salem.* New York: George Braziller, 1969.

Hawthorne, Julian. *Nathaniel Hawthorne and His Wife: A Biography.* Irvine, CA: Reprint Services Corporation, 1992.

Hawthorne, Nathaniel. *The House of the Seven Gables.* Edited by Michael Davitt Bell. Oxford: Oxford University Press, 1991.

Hockett, Homer Carey. *The Critical*

Method in Historical Research and Writing. New York: The Macmillan Company, 1955.

Hutcheon, Linda. *A Theory of Parody*. New York: Methuen, Inc., 1985.

Hutchinson, Thomas. *History of the Province of Massachusetts Bay*. Edited by Lawrence Shaw Mayo. Vol. 2. Cambridge: Harvard University Press, 1936.

Johnson, Barbara. *The Wake of Deconstruction*. Oxford: Blackwell, 1994.

Jonson, Ben. *Bartholomew Fair*. Edited by G. R. Hibbard. New York: W. W. Norton, 1977.

Kamensky, Jane. "Salem Obsessed; Or, *Plus Ça Change:* An Introduction." *William and Mary Quarterly* 65.3 (2008): 391–400.

Kant, Immanuel. *Critique of Pure Reason*. Translated by N. Kemp Smith. London: Macmillan, 1929.

Kirshenblatt-Gimblett, Barbara. *Destination Culture: Tourism, Museums, and Heritage*. Berkeley: University of California Press, 1998.

Kittredge, George Lyman. *Witchcraft in Old and New England*. Cambridge, MA: Harvard Press University, 1929.

Knox, Marion. "Seeing What the Rain Means: James Cutler Architects." *Architalx*. Edited by Christine Corcoran Cantwell. Portland, ME: Architalx, 1999.

Krakauer, David C. "The Quest for Patterns in Meta-History." *Santa Fe Institute Bulletin* (Winter 2007): 32–39.

Leon, Warren, and Margaret Piatt. "Living History Museums." *History Museums in the United States*. Edited by Warren Leon and Roy Rosenzweig. Urbana: University of Illinois Press, 1989.

Lepore, Jill. *The Name of War: King Philip's War and the Origins of American Identity*. New York: Alfred A. Knopf, 1999.

Levine, Laura. *Men in Women's Clothing: Anti-Theatricality and Effeminization, 1579–1642*. Cambridge: Cambridge University Press, 1994.

Lipsitz. *Time Passages: Collective Memory and American Popular Culture*. Minneapolis: University of Minnesota Press, 2001.

Loewen, James W. *Lies Across America: What Our Historic Sites Get Wrong*. New York: Touchstone Books, 2000.

_____. *Lies My Teacher Told Me*. New York: The New Press, 1995.

Longfellow, Henry Wadsworth. "Giles Corey of the Salem Farms." *Henry Wadsworth Longfellow: Poems and Other Writings*. Edited by J. D. McClatchy. New York: Library of America, 2000.

Lyotard, Jean-Francois. *The Postmodern Condition*. Manchester: Manchester University Press, 1984.

MacCannell, Dean. *The Tourist: A New Theory of the Leisure Class*. Berkeley: University of California Press, 1999.

Mappen, Marc. *Witches and Historians: Interpretations of Salem*. Malabar, FL: Krieger Publishing, 1996.

Marino, Stephen. "Arthur Miller's 'Weight of Truth' in *The Crucible*." *Modern Drama* 38.4 (Winter 1995): 488–495. *OCLC FirstSearch*. Lamson Library, Plymouth, NH. 22 August 2002 <http://newfirstsearch.oclc.org>.

Marshall, Bridget M. "Salem's Ghosts and the Cultural Capita/ol of Witches." Unpublished paper. Conference presentation. University of Massachusetts at Amherst, 1999.

Mather, Cotton. *The Wonders of the Invisible World: Being an Account of the Tryals of Several Witches, Lately Executed in New-England: And of several remarkable Curiosities therein Occurring*. Boston: Benjamin Harris, 1692.

McCormick, Robert H., Jr. "Return Passages: Maryse Condé Brings Tituba Back to Barbados." *Black Imagination and the Middle Passage*. Edited by

Maria Diedrich, Jr., Henry Louis Gates, and Carl Pedersen. New York: Oxford University Press, 1999.

Michaels, Leila. Personal interview. Salem, MA, Salem Witch Museum, 17 July 2002.

Miller, Arthur. *The Crucible.* New York: Penguin Books, 1981.

_____. *Echoes Down the Corridor: Collected Essays, 1944–2000.* New York: Viking, 2000.

_____. "Why I Wrote *The Crucible.*" *The New Yorker* (1996): 158–160, 162–164.

Miller, Perry. *The New England Mind: From Colony to Province.* Cambridge: Harvard University Press, 1953.

Munslow, Alan. *Deconstructing History.* London: Routledge, 1997.

Neal, Daniel. *History of New-England.* 2 vols. London, 1720.

Neal, John. *Rachel Dyer.* Amherst, NY: Prometheus Books, 1996.

Noble, Michael J. Bunker. "Hawthorne's *The House of the Seven Gables.*" *Explicator* 56.2 (1998): 72–74. *OCLC FirstSearch.* Lamson Library, Plymouth, NH. 14 May 2002 <http://newfirstsearch.oclc.org>.

Norton, Mary Beth. *In the Devil's Snare: The Salem Witchcraft Crisis of 1692.* New York: Knopf, 2002.

Nunez, Theron. "Touristic Studies in Anthropological Perspective." *Hosts and Guests: The Anthropology of Tourism.* Edited by Valene L. Smith. Philadelphia: University of Pennsylvania Press, 1989.

Official Guidebook and Map. Salem, MA: Chamber of Commerce, 2000.

Official Guidebook and Map. Salem, MA: Chamber of Commerce, 2001.

Official Guidebook and Map. Salem, MA: Office of Tourism and Cultural Affairs, 2002.

Okrant, Mark. Personal interview. Plymouth, NH, 5 August 2002.

Orians, G. Harrison. "New England Witchcraft in Fiction." *American Literature* 2.1 (1930): 54–71.

Pappas, Charles. Personal interview. Salem, MA, National Park Service Regional Visitor Center, 16 July 2002.

Pfaff, Françoise. *Conversations with Maryse Condé.* Lincoln: University of Nebraska Press, 1996.

Phelan, Peggy. "Introduction: The Ends of Performance." *The Ends of Performance.* Edited by Peggy Phelan and Jill Lane. New York: New York University Press, 1998.

Phillips Library: Overview. Peabody Essex Museum <*http://www.pem.org/museum/lib_strengths.php*>.

Pollack, Della. "Introduction: Making History Go." *Exceptional Spaces: Essays in Performance and History.* Edited by Della Pollack. Chapel Hill: University of North Carolina Press, 1998.

Projansky, Sarah, and Leah R. Vande Berg. "Sabrina, the Teenage...? Girls, Witches, Mortals, and the Limits of Prime-Time Feminism." *Fantasy Girls: Gender in the New Universe of Science Fiction and Fantasy Television.* Lanham, MD: Rowman & Littlefield Publishers, Inc., 2000.

Quine, Willard V. *From a Logical Point of View: Nine Logico-Philisophical Essays.* Cambridge: Harvard University Press, 1980.

Ray, Benjamin C. "The Geography of Witchcraft Accusations in 1692 Salem Village." *William and Mary Quarterly* 65.3 (2008): 449–478.

Rebecca Nurse Homestead: Nurse Graveyard. Rebecca Nurse Homestead. January 6, 2009 <http://www.rebeccanurse.org/RNH/main2.htm>.

Rivett, Sarah. "Our Salem, Our Selves." *William and Mary Quarterly* LXV.3 (2008): 495–502.

Root, Deborah. *Cannibal Culture: Art, Appropriation, and the Commodification of Difference.* Boulder, CO: Westview Press, 1996.

Rosenmeier, Jesper. "John Cotton's English Years, 1584–1633." Unpublished Manuscript.

Rosenthal, Bernard. "Medievalism and the Salem Witch Trials." *Medievalism in the Modern World: Essays in Honor of Leslie J. Workman.* Edited by Richard Utz and Tom Shippey. Turnhout, Belgium: Brepols, 1998.

_____. *Salem Story: Reading the Witch Trials of 1692.* Cambridge: Cambridge University Press, 1993.

_____. "Tituba's Story." *New England Quarterly* 71.2 (1998): 190–203.

_____, Margo Burns, Gretchen A. Adams, Peter Grund, Risto Hiltunen, Leena Kahlas-Tarkka, Merja Kytö, Matti Peikola, Benjamin C. Ray, Matti Rissanen, and Marilynne K. Roach, eds. *Records of the Salem Witch-Hunt.* Cambridge: Cambridge University Press, 2009.

Ross, Andrew. *The Celebration Chronicles: Life, Liberty, and the Pursuit of Property in Disney's New Town.* New York: Ballantine, 1999.

St. George, Robert Blair. *Conversing by Signs: Poetics of Implication in Colonial New England Culture.* Chapel Hill: University of North Carolina Press, 1998.

Salem Witch Museum. Brochure. Salem, MA, 2009.

Salem Witch Museum. Presentation. Salem, MA, 27 September 2008.

Salem Witch Museum. "Witches: Evolving Perceptions." Exhibit. Salem, MA, 27 September 2008.

Salem Witch Village. Guided tour. Salem, MA, 17 July 2002.

"Samantha's Thanksgiving to Remember." *Bewitched.* Dir. Richard Kinon. ABC, 23 November 1967.

Schechner, Richard. *Between Theater and Anthropology.* Philadelphia: University of Pennsylvania Press, 1985.

_____. "Restoration of Behavior." *Studies in Visual Communication.* Philadelphia: Annenberg School Press, 1981.

Schissel, Wendy. "Re(dis)covering the Witches in Arthur Miller's *The Crucible:* A Feminist Reading." *Modern Drama* 37.3 (Fall 1994): 461–473. *OCLC First-Search.* Lamson Library, Plymouth, NH. 22 August 2002 <http://newfirstsearch.oclc.org>.

Sears, John. *Sacred Places: American Tourist Attractions in the Nineteenth Century.* Amherst: University of Massachusetts Press, 1989.

Shugar, Dana R. *Separatism and Women's Community.* Lincoln: University of Nebraska Press, 1995.

Snow, Stephen Eddy. *Performing the Pilgrims: A Study of Ethnohistorical Role-Playing at Plimoth Plantation.* Jackson: University Press of Mississippi, 1993.

Sontag, Susan. *Against Interpretation.* New York: Farrar, Straus, 1966.

Stanton, Cathy. "Being the Elephant: The American Civil War Reenacted." M.A. Thesis. Norwich University, 1997.

Starkey, Marion L. *The Devil in Massachusetts.* New York: Alfred A. Knopf, 1950.

_____. *The Visionary Girls.* Boston: Little, Brown and Company, 1973.

Steiner, Christopher B. "Authenticity, Repetition, and the Aesthetics of Seriality: The Work of Tourist Art in the Age of Mechanical Reproduction." *Unpacking Culture: Art and Commodity in Colonial and Postcolonial Worlds.* Edited by Ruth B. Phillips and Christopher B. Steiner. Berkeley: University of California Press, 1999.

Sturken, Marita. *Tourists of History: Memory, Kitsch, and Consumerism from Oklahoma City to Ground Zero.* Durham: Duke University of Press, 2007.

Tourists. Personal interviews. Salem, MA, Witch History Museum, 16 July 2002.

Trask, Richard B. *"The Devil Hath Been Raised": A Documentary History of the*

Salem Village Witchcraft Outbreak of March 1692. Danvers, MA: Yeoman Press, 1992.

Trefry, Catherine. Personal interview. Salem, MA, Witch Dungeon Museum, 16 July 2002.

Upham, Charles. *Salem Witchcraft; with An Account of Salem Village, and A History of Opinions on Witchcraft and Kindred Subjects.* 2 vols. Boston: Wiggin and Lunt, 1867.

Valente, Joseph. "Rehearsing the Witch Trials: Gender Injustice in *The Crucible.*" *New Formations* 32 (Autumn/Winter 1997): 120–134.

Waldner, Liz. *Self and Simulacra.* Farmington, ME: Alice James Books, 2001.

Welcome to Danvers, Massachusetts, formerly Salem Village. Brochure. Danvers, MA: The Danvers Preservation Commission, 2002.

Welcome to Salem: America's Bewitching Seaport. Circular. Salem, MA, 2002.

Werking, Richard H. "'Reformation is Our Only Preservation': Cotton Mather and Salem Witchcraft." *William and Mary Quarterly* 29 (1972): 281–290.

Where Past is Present. Film. Salem, MA: National Park Service, 2002.

White, Hayden. "The Historical Text as Literary Artifact." *Tropics of Discourse: Essays in Cultural Criticism.* Edited by Hayden White. Baltimore: Johns Hopkins University Press, 1978.

_____. "The Value of Narrativity in the Representation of Reality." *Critical Inquiry* 7.1 (1980): 4–24.

Wilde, Oscar. *The Importance of Being Earnest and Related Writings.* Edited by Joseph Bristow. London: Routledge, 1992.

Wilford, John Noble. "Salem Witch Hunts in 1692 Linked to LSD-Like Agent." *The New York Times,* March 31, 1976, sec. 1: 1, 44.

Williams, C. J. F. *What is Existence?* Oxford: Clarendon Press, 1981.

Witch City. Dir. Joe Cultrera. Picture Business Productions and Zingerplatz Pictures Documentaries, 1991.

Witch Dungeon Museum. Brochure. Salem, MA, 2002.

Witch Dungeon Museum. Guided tour. Salem, MA, 16 April 2002.

Index

Abbott, Nehemiah, Jr. 47, 53–54
Adams, John Quincy 32
Adler, Judith 158
Alden, John 52
Anderson, Perry 7, 10
authenticity 2, 7, 13–18, 27, 183–184, 188*n*11
The Autobiography of Benjamin Franklin 33

Bank, Rosemarie K. 155
Barker, William, Sr. 30, 41, 56
Barthes, Roland 7
Baudrillard, Jean 5
Bayley, James 84, 134–135
Bellis, Peter J. 104
Bergman, David 19–20
Bewitched 26, 126, 146, 148–150, 194*n*12
Bhabha, Homi 14
Bishop, Bridget 36–37, 54, 57–58, 59, 150, 153–154, 168, 195*n*3
Bloom, Harold 185
Boris Karloff's Witch Mansion 18, 26, 175–179, 197*n*13
Bowman, Michael S. 184
Boyer, Paul 23, 24, 34–36, 80, 81–91, 95, 97–98, 189*n*4, 190*n*6, 190*n*7, 191*n*11, 193*n*2
Bradbury, Mary 39, 52–53, 189*n*8
Bradford, William 7
Brattle, Thomas 65, 68
Braybrook, Samuel 48
Bridges, Mary, Jr. 40
Bridges, Sarah 40
Bromage, Hannah 37
Brown, William, Jr. 84

Burroughs, George 40, 99, 191*n*2, 194*n*7
Butler, Judith 6

Calef, Robert 23, 24, 64–74, 75, 80–81, 91, 95, 151, 171, 175
camp 19–20, 27, 176, 188*n*9
Caporael, Linnda R. 24, 25, 91, 93–95, 97, 120
Carrier, Martha 40
Cheever, Ezekiel 46, 55, 189*n*12
Cohen, Erik 15, 26
Colonial Society of Massachusetts 2, 11–12
Colonial Williamsburg 2
Coman, Richard 54
Condé, Maryse 25, 97, 124, 192*n*15; *I, Tituba, Black Witch of Salem* 112–119, 192*n*18
confession 22, 33, 47–51, 60, 73, 110–111, 150, 190*n*12, 190*n*13, 192*n*16, 194*n*8
Cook, Robin 25, 95, 97, *Acceptable Risk* 100, 119–124, 192*n*21
Corey, Giles 26, 128–132, 167, 168, 170, 193*n*1
Corey, Martha 54–55, 128–129, 131
Corwin, Judge Jonathan 43, 47
Cousins, Mark 8
Cry Innocent 153–154
Culler, Jonathan 183

Danvers Archival Center 182
Danvers, Massachusetts 13, 18, 165, 181–184
Davis, Natalie Zemon 33–34, 60
Deleuze, Gilles 14
Demos, John 2, 11, 89, 91

207

Index

devil 37, 40, 41, 42, 49, 55–56, 60, 64–74, 170–171, 193*n*23, 193*n*24; *see also* Satan

Eagleton, Terry 7, 10
Earhart, Rose 192*n*15, 192*n*17
Easty, Mary 43–44, 47
education 1, 15, 19, 26, 27
ergot poisoning 24, 25, 91, 93–95, 120–122, 192*n*21, 193*n*23

Felt, Thomas E. 21, 29–32, 60
Frost, Archie N. 35

Gallows Hill 17, 19, 27, 79–80, 104, 179–180, 192*n*20
Gedney, Bartholomew 84
Gencarella, Stephen Olbrys 157
Gettysburg 13
Good, Dorcas 192*n*15, 192*n*17, 192*n*20
Good, Sarah 45–47, 48–49, 58, 59–60, 110, 116, 163, 189*n*12, 192*n*15
Gottlieb, Jack 94–95
Gray, Samuel 54
Grinstead, Durward 140, 191*n*2, 194*n*7

Hale, John 89, 91, 113, 191*n*13
Handler, Richard 13, 16
Hansen, Chadwick 24, 91–95, 114
Hathorne, Judge John 3, 17, 36–37, 43, 45–46, 47, 84, 101, 128, 130–132, 150
Haunted Happenings 3
Hawthorne, Nathaniel 26, 97, 124, 140, 156, 160, 191*n*5, 191*n*9, 196*n*5, 197*n*11; *House of the Seven Gables* 18, 25, 100–108, 127, 132, 191*n*4, 191*n*6, 191*n*7, 193*n*22; *The Scarlet Letter* 117–118, 127
Herrick, Joseph 59
Herrick, Mary 59
Hobbs, Abigail 31, 56, 90
Hobbs, Deliverance 52
Hockett, Homer Carey 21, 32–33, 60
House of the Seven Gables (tourist site) 17, 195*n*5, 197*n*11
Hubbard, Elizabeth 31, 45, 47, 59
Hutcheon, Linda 184–185
Hutchinson, Thomas 89, 91, 113, 191*n*13

I Married a Witch 26, 126, 140, 142–146
Indian, John 117, 192*n*14
Indian Wars 90

Jacobs, George 180–181
Jacobs, Margaret 50–51
Johnson, Barbara 7, 9, 40
Johnson, Elizabeth, Jr. 38, 55–56

King Philip's War 12
King William's War 90
Kirshenblatt-Gimblett, Barbara 18, 26
Kittredge, George Lyman 89, 91
Knapp, Elizabeth 89
Knox, Marion 179–180

Lacey, Mary, Sr. 38
Lawson, Deodat 76–77, 84
Lepore, Jill 12
Lewis, Mercy 31, 44, 53, 56
living history 2, 14, 16, 195*n*2
Loewen, James 10–11
Longfellow, Henry Wadsworth 26, 140, 193*n*1, 193*n*2; "Giles Corey of the Salem Farms" 126–132
Lyotard, Jean-François 8

MacCannell, Dean 13, 15–16, 18, 26, 184, 188*n*9
Madison, James 32–33
Maid of Salem 26, 126, 140–142, 145–146, 194*n*12
Main Street U.S.A. 12–13
Marshall, Bridget M. 3, 180–181, 196*n*9
Marxism 7
Mather, Cotton 18, 23, 24, 63–74, 75, 80–81, 89, 91, 93, 95, 109, 123, 128–130, 151, 185, 190*n*1, 190*n*2
McCormick, Robert, Jr. 117
Memorial 179–180
Miller, Arthur 27, 114–115, 127, 193*n*5; *The Crucible* 25, 26, 36, 82, 113, 126, 132–140, 171, 191*n*12, 193*n*3, 193*n*4, 193*n*6, 194*n*9, 194*n*10, 194*n*11
More Wonders of the Invisible World 64–74
multiculturalism 8
Munslow, Alan 8

Neal, John 25, 97, 191*n*13; *Rachel Dyer* 98–99, 113
New Historicism 7, 8
Nissenbaum, Stephen 23, 24, 34–36, 80, 81–91, 95, 97–98, 189*n*4, 190*n*6, 190*n*7, 191*n*11, 193*n*2

Norton, Mary Beth 90–91
Nurse, Rebecca 3, 22, 55, 59, 87, 116–117, 142, 180–182, 192*n*17
Nurse Homestead 181–182

Of Plimoth Plantation 7
Osbourne, Sarah 110, 182
Osburne, Sarah *see* Osbourne, Sarah
Oyer and Terminer, Court of 21, 34, 35, 45, 47, 49, 50, 164

Parris, Betty 11, 99
Parris, Elizabeth 182
Parris, Rev. Samuel 40, 41, 48, 85–86, 99, 111, 134, 140, 142, 182, 187*n*6, 190*n*4
Peabody Essex Museum 19, 20, 26, 27, 155, 161–162, 164, 166–167, 173–175, 184
Peale, Charles Wilson 155, 195*n*4
Perkins, William 65
Phelan, Peggy 165
Phillips Library 3, 161–165, 175, 179, 182
Plimoth Plantation 2, 5–6, 15, 19, 20, 149, 187*n*2, 187*n*3
Pollack, Della 152–153
poppets 38
post-structuralism 7–9
primary sources 1, 14, 20, 21, 27–28, 29, 34, 35, 61, 77, 91, 97–99, 150, 165, 185, 189*n*4, 192*n*15
Procter, Elizabeth *see* Proctor, Elizabeth
Proctor, Elizabeth 42–43, 59, 111, 137–139, 165–166
Proctor, John 36, 42–43, 109, 129, 135–139, 194*n*9
Prynne, Hester 48, 116–119, 192*n*18, 192*n*19
Puritans 37, 38–39, 41, 42, 47, 48, 50, 64, 101, 141, 149, 152–154, 160, 169, 171, 184
Putnam, Ann, Jr. 31, 37, 41, 44, 47, 52–53, 109, 182, 192*n*16
Putnam, Edward 54–55
Putnam, Joseph 182
Putnam, Mary Veren 87
Putnam, Thomas 85, 87, 134–135

Rooney, Mickey 10
Root, Deborah 17
Rosenthal, Bernard 21, 63, 113–114, 189*n*3, 189*n*10, 191*n*14, 194*n*7

Sabrina, the Teenage Witch 26, 126, 146–150, 195*n*14
St. George, Robert Blair 22
Salem Visitor's Center 155, 158–161, 163
Salem Wax Museum 27, 173–174, 179
Salem Witch Dungeon Museum 26, 27, 165–170, 175, 179, 183–184
Salem Witch History Museum 163–164
Salem Witch Museum 12, 19, 20, 26, 27, 169–173, 175, 196*n*10
Salem Witch Village 27, 173–175, 179, 184
Salter, Henry 41
Satan 23, 40, 42, 47, 48, 49, 56, 71, 189*n*9; *see also* devil
Saxton, William 13, 16
Schechner, Richard 9–10, 190*n*15
Schindler's List 19
Shapiro, Meyer 17
Sheldon, Susannah 58
Sibley, Samuel 59–60
simulacrum 5
Smith, Thorne 142
Snow, Stephen 5–7, 20, 187*n*3
Sontag, Susan 19–20
Spanos, Nicholas P. 94–95
spectral evidence 22, 52, 56–57, 59, 78, 190*n*17
Stacy, William 57
Starkey, Marion L. 25, 82, 97, 113–115, 124; *The Visionary Girls* 108–112
Steiner, Christopher 14, 18

Tercentenary 27, 157, 179
Tituba 11–12, 25, 45–46, 47, 48, 109–119, 124–125, 127–131, 158, 163, 165, 170, 187*n*6, 189*n*12, 192*n*14, 192*n*15, 192*n*16, 192*n*17, 192*n*19
Toothaker, Mary 42

Upham, Charles 21, 24, 25, 75–83, 91, 95, 97–98, 101, 108, 113, 171, 189*n*6, 190*n*4, 191*n*5
Usovicz, Stanley J., Jr. 155–156, 160–161

The Visionary Girls 25

Wabanakis 90
Walcot, Mary *see* Walcott, Mary
Walcott, Mary 31, 37, 53, 57, 130–132
Warren, Mary 41, 51, 54, 109, 137–138, 165–166

Index

White, Hayden 9
Wiccan religion 156, 173–174
Wilds, Sarah 52
Willard, Samuel 66
Willard, Simon 30
Williams, Abigail 11, 26, 26, 136–140,
    191n12, 194n9

Wilson, Sarah, Sr. 49
witch cake 11
The Wonders of the Invisible World 63–74
Works Progress Administration (WPA)
    35